The Revelatory Body

The Revelatory Body

Theology as Inductive Art

Luke Timothy Johnson

WILLIAM B. EERDMANS PUBLISHING COMPANY
GRAND RAPIDS, MICHIGAN / CAMBRIDGE, U.K.

Published 2015 by
Wm. B. Eerdmans Publishing Co.
2140 Oak Industrial Drive N.E., Grand Rapids, Michigan 49505 /
P.O. Box 163, Cambridge CB3 9PU U.K.

Printed in the United States of America

21 20 19 18 17 16 15   7 6 5 4 3 2 1

Library of Congress Cataloging-in-Publication Data

Johnson, Luke Timothy.
The revelatory body: theology as inductive art / Luke Timothy Johnson.
        pages   cm
ISBN 978-0-8028-0383-2 (pbk.: alk. paper)
1. Human body — Religious aspects — Christianity.
2. Theology.   3. Revelation — Christianity.
I. Title.

BT741.3.J64   2015
233'.5 — dc23

2015013109

www.eerdmans.com

To my colleagues in the Candler School of Theology

Contents

Preface   viii

Introduction: Toward an Inductive Theology   1

1. The Way Not Taken: A Disembodied Theology of the Body   21

2. Scripture and the Body   36

3. Spirit and Body   64

4. The Body at Play   86

5. The Body in Pain   107

6. The Passionate Body   130

7. The Body at Work   156

8. The Exceptional Body   180

9. The Aging Body   206

Epilogue   231

Index of Subjects   234

Index of Scripture References   237

Index of Other Ancient Sources   245

Preface

The title of this book borrows from Sandra Schneiders's excellent study of New Testament hermeneutics, *The Revelatory Text.*[1] Schneiders argues that, rather than contain revelation, the New Testament (indeed, Scripture as a whole) *participates* in the process of divine revelation. I want to argue here for the way the human body — shorthand for human experience — participates in the same process by which the Living God is made known in the world, not just long ago and far away but in our neighborhood, not simply in dramatic acts but in ordinary patterns of behavior. Attention to both the ordinary and extraordinary manifestations of the spirit in and through the body is essential, I believe, for theology to recover its nature as an inductive art rather than a deductive science, and to serve as an expression and articulation of authentic faith in the Living God.

The first four sections of the book have a more theoretical character, even though they seek to make a case for taking somatic experience seriously. The following sections present a series of sketches of how somatic activities and conditions might be approached both inductively and theologically. By no means do I suggest that the close observation of the body yields easy or entirely positive results. And I certainly do not pretend that my efforts at such close observation are in any way adequate to the task. But I do think that a willingness to risk engaging actual human situations — rather than abstract conceptualizations about those situations — is required of the theologian; thus, adequate or not, these short studies indicate a direction that I think others might also follow.

1. The full title is *The Revelatory Text: Interpreting the New Testament as Sacred Scripture,* 2nd ed. (Collegeville, MN: Michael Glazier, 1999).

My convictions concerning the revelatory power of the body undoubtedly began with my experience as a Benedictine monk between the years 1963 and 1973. Although most of every day was spent either in silence or in choir, I found myself constantly fascinated — in choir itself, in procession, at meals, at work — with how expressive body language could be: states of elation, depression, exhaustion, distraction, concentration, alienation — all could be read from the way fellow monks walked or sat or ate or used their tools at work. During those same years, I steeped myself in the writings of Jose Ortega y Gasset, Søren Kierkegaard, and, above all, Gabriel Marcel, all of whom in different ways demanded that attention be given to the particular more than the abstract. I was affected most of all by Gabriel Marcel (1889-1973), the French Roman Catholic existentialist and phenomenologist, traces of whose insights I find everywhere in my own work. Already in 1970, as a young monk with only an MA to recommend me, I introduced seminarians to the history of the liturgy with an analysis of body language and of play as proleptic of ritual.

Attention to the expressive character of the human body was at the heart of my 1976 Yale dissertation,[2] and it became thematic in several of my subsequent books.[3] But my interest gained added focus when I was invited to participate in a symposium on "The Phenomenology of the Body" at Duquesne University in 2002, where I delivered a paper entitled "The Revelatory Body: Notes Toward a Somatic Theology."[4] Stimulated by that experience, I resolved to try to fill in those sketchy notes and provide a sense of what it might mean if theology really took seriously what Scripture surely does: that the privileged arena of divine disclosure is the human body.

I must apologize beforehand for my indiscriminate use of biblical translations, if this is an issue that bothers anyone. I use almost entirely the RSV and the NRSV, even though I have some problems with both. In some very few instances, I alter the translation to better express the original language. I am acutely conscious of questions of gender, and I

2. *The Literary Function of Possessions in Luke-Acts,* SBL Dissertation Series 39 (Missoula, MT: Scholars Press, 1977).

3. See esp. L. T. Johnson, *Sharing Possessions: What Faith Demands,* rev. and enlarged ed. (Grand Rapids: Eerdmans, 2011); *Faith's Freedom: A Classic Spirituality for Contemporary Christians* (Philadelphia: Fortress, 1990); and *Religious Experience in Earliest Christianity: A Missing Dimension of New Testament Studies* (Minneapolis: Fortress, 1998).

4. See D. J. Martino, ed., *The Phenomenology of the Body* (Pittsburgh: Simon Silverman Phenomenology Center at the University of Duquesne, 2003), pp. 69-85.

have tried, when speaking of human bodies, to alternate male and female pronouns appropriately.

My thanks especially go to those who helped me with research, notably Jared Farmer and Christopher Holmes (who also gave editing help), and to the indispensable Steve Kraftchick, who patiently listened to and heard my ramblings, and helped to keep them on track. This book is dedicated to my Candler colleagues, past and present, who through their decades-long commitment to contextual education have provided many models of how theology might learn to be inductive. And, as always, my deepest gratitude to my sweetie Joy, whose gracious love never fails and always delights.

LUKE JOHNSON
August 12, 2014

Toward an Inductive Theology

Two simple convictions animate this exercise in theology. The first is that the human body is the preeminent arena for God's revelation in the world, the medium through which God's Holy Spirit is most clearly expressed. God's self-disclosure in the world is thus continuous and constant. The second conviction is that the task of theology is the discernment of God's self-disclosure in the world through the medium of the body. Therefore, theology is necessarily an inductive art rather than a deductive science.

An even simpler premise underlies these convictions: authentic faith is more than a matter of right belief; it is the response of human beings in trust and obedience to the one whom Scripture designates as the Living God, in contrast to the dead idols that are constructed by humans as projections of their own desires. The Living God of whom Scripture speaks both creates the world at every moment and challenges the ways in which human freedom tends toward the distortion of creation — and indeed of the Creator. Among the idols that authentic faith must resist are the idols of human thought concerning God. Living faith remains aware that the most subtle and sophisticated of all idolatries might actually be the one constructed by theologians who claim to know and understand God.

Theology tends toward idolatry because of the way words can seduce us into thinking that they adequately express and represent reality. Language is a great blessing, perhaps the most distinctive mark of our humanity, and it does many things well. But while language enables us to perceive and interpret our experience of the world, it does so at a cost. In the first place, language fixes what is in fact fluid and ever-changing — our experience of the world — into something that appears stable and secure. In the second place, the stability created by words can seem to be the only way

1

in which experience can be perceived and interpreted, can even claim to be an adequate replacement for the experience of the world that is always fluid, ever-changing.

Language's distorting power appears in everyday life. The word "cancer," for example, can not only become the sole lens through which a person perceives and interprets his or her experience, but can actually become hypostasized as an inimical entity apart from the complex processes of one's specific organic existence. Language can operate the same way in the case of the experience of divine presence and power in the world. Both the words of Scripture and the statements of creeds can shift subtly from participating in the process of revelation to the claim of being such revelation. In some circumstances they can actually interpose themselves in such a way as to block access to God's self-disclosure in human experience.

Language, to be sure, remains the indispensable medium for the doing of theology. Words enable us to make sense of all our experience, and they are indispensable for making sense of the experience of God in the world. In the broadest sense, language is indeed an intrinsic element in every "experience" itself. There is no such thing as a "raw" experience that does not have at least an implicitly verbal character. Symbols shape our perception of experience as it happens, just as they also shape our interpretation of such experience in hindsight. Our capacity as humans to use language to abstract from the flow of experience and to construct concepts and propositions is likewise entirely positive. Language — even abstract language — is necessary to theology as it is to all serious human discourse. But to be necessary is not the same as being sufficient: the idolatrous dimension of theological language appears when it claims to be sufficient to the interpretation of God's work in the world as well as necessary to such interpretation.

In this essay I seek to enliven theological language by challenging the sufficiency of abstract propositions for the discernment of God's work in the world. I do this by using language as a means of observing and thinking about the human experience of God or — perhaps better — of observing and thinking about human bodily experience as the self-disclosure of God's Spirit in creation. This may seem to be a slight shift, but it is actually fundamental. I hold that theology seeks to articulate and praise the presence and power of God in the world, and that this power and presence is an ever-emergent reality. In this search for God's self-disclosure, language takes its proper place as a participant in revelation rather than as the adequate expression of revelation. Actual human experience in the body —

inasmuch as we can apprehend it — is taken to be the essential arena of a never-ceasing process of divine revelation.

By shifting theology's attention to living bodies rather than ancient texts, I mean to show no disrespect to Scripture or the creeds. Instead, Scripture is restored to its original and proper role of articulating the experience of God in the lives of humans. Its time-conditioned but truthful expression of that experience remains of the greatest importance for the present-day theological task of discerning God's power and presence in the world. I will try to show that, from the beginning, Scripture functioned as a participation in the process of revelation. It was never intended to be the sole or exclusive repository of truth about the living God. To make such a claim for Scripture — not to mention for interpretations of Scripture — would be to displace the living God with language, and that is idolatrous.

If such is the case with Scripture, it is even more the case with the creeds and the doctrines developed out of the creeds. In another book I have tried to show just how important the creeds are as guides to reading Scripture, and as communal expressions of the framework of Christian conviction.[1] No matter how necessary the creeds are, however, their language is even more abstract, even more removed from the actual experience of God, than is the language of Scripture. To make the creeds the starting point for theology is to edge even closer to the idolatrous use of language. Theology must always begin and always find renewal, not with words found in texts, but with the experience of actual human bodies.

Shifting the focus of theology from texts and propositions to the examination of concrete human experience seems at first to be fraught with ambiguity and peril. Words, after all, seem to provide an anchor, and they seem to provide at least the appearance of certainty; by contrast, human experiences are unpredictable, often irrational, and appear capable of leading almost anywhere. The dangers are so obvious that, for many, the shift to experience appears to be irresponsible.

The first danger is that the language of Scripture and the creeds might not only be declared insufficient, it might be abandoned altogether. But I have already stated my conviction that the language of Scripture and the creeds is absolutely necessary for Christian theology to be Christian. Nothing could be more scriptural, for example, than the conviction that the one God is the Living God who creates the world anew at every moment. This

---

1. L. T. Johnson, *The Creed: What Christians Believe and Why It Matters* (New York: Random House, 2004).

premise does not derive from philosophy or from the observation of human experience, but from the witness of Scripture. Furthermore, nothing could be more in conformity with the creeds than the conviction that the human body is the privileged arena of God's self-disclosure. The Apostles' Creed states not only that the Holy Spirit has spoken through the prophets, but that God's Son was born, suffered, and died in his human body.

The second danger expands on the first: it views human experience as dangerously erratic, all too susceptible to delusion and sin. Human experience needs to be disciplined and transformed by the words of Scripture and the teachings of the church. To privilege experience as a source for theology is, in effect, to reject the formative importance of the tradition. At its worst, a commitment to experience becomes a new Gnosticism, in which private and individual "revelations" displace the common heritage of the church. There is certainly some element of truth to this position; in a number of essays, in fact, I have spoken against just such a "new Gnosticism" that reduces Christianity to individual spirituality.[2] In other writings I have worked hard to define exactly what I mean by "the experience of God" in the world.[3] I fully recognize that this is a difficult topic. But I also insist that abandoning the serious effort to engage human experience theologically runs the even greater danger of ignoring what God might be up to in our world, and of preferring a theology that we can control to a God whom we cannot control.

The third danger is a variation of the first two: attention to the ever-shifting, always unstable realm of human bodily existence means abandoning the scientific character of theology, which traditionally has been able to claim status as *scientia* (science) precisely because it is based on a secure body of knowledge located in Scripture and creed, from which further corollaries might be developed through deductive reasoning. Indeed, theology so conceived can even claim to have a "systematic" character. But taking ongoing human experience of and in the body as a source of God's continuing revelation in the world disrupts any claim to systematic knowledge, simply because the data concerning God's work in the world never

2. See L. T. Johnson, "The New Gnosticism: An Old Threat to the Church," *Commonweal* 131 (2004): 28-31; my review of E. Pagels, *Beyond Belief: The Secret Gospel of Thomas*, *Commonweal* 130 (2003): 24-26; and my review of Pagels, *Revelations: Visions, Prophecy and Politics in the Book of Revelation*, *Commonweal* 139 (2012): 36-38.

3. See L. T. Johnson, *Religious Experience in Early Christianity: A Missing Dimension in New Testament Studies* (Minneapolis: Fortress, 1998) and esp. Johnson, *Faith's Freedom: A Classic Spirituality for Contemporary Christians* (Minneapolis: Fortress, 1990).

ceases to press upon us, never stops challenging our pretense of possessing full and adequate knowledge on the basis of ancient texts and professions.

There is also, to be sure, an element of political self-interest in the third objection. If theology is a deductive science based in Scripture and creed, then it is primarily an academic exercise controlled by experts in ancient language, philosophical idiom, and the history of ideas. Experts in these areas have an assumed authority over the content, meaning, and application of God's revelation. Theology begins in language and ends in action, with power over the movement in the hands, not of pastoral practitioners, but of scholarly theorists. If the process were to be reversed, that is, if theology were to begin with the discernment of God's word in the complex world of human bodily experience, and then move toward theory, more power would then be exercised by those who are most immediately in contact with the divine self-disclosure in the context of concrete human situations. The ability to perceive, bear witness to, and articulate the signs of divine activity in human bodily experience resembles art more than science. Thus the point of this essay, namely, that theology should move more toward being an inductive art than a deductive science. A consequence of this shift, should it happen, would be to challenge the assumed superiority of the classic disciplines within theological education and give more honor to those who serve as researchers of God's work in the messiness of human experience.

Please note my careful phrasing: I speak of moving "more toward." The three dangers I have identified naturally loom larger if the turn toward experience is taken to be absolute rather than relative, a replacement of Scripture and creeds rather than an enlivening of them, an overturning of all theological precedent rather than the restoration of a badly needed balance. My project in this essay is not to overthrow all precedent or to replace Scripture and creeds; rather, it is very much an effort to restore a balance. A turn to human experience, I argue, actually opens Scripture to what it was intended to address in the first place; likewise, an attention to the ever-active self-disclosure of God in the world actually supports the statements of the creeds.

Moreover, it is important to assert that there is at least as much danger to the theological enterprise — not to mention living faith in the Living God — when ongoing human experience in the world is *not* engaged theologically, when Scripture is taken as the adequate container of revelation, or when the creeds are regarded as sufficient for articulating what God is up to in the world. The danger is precisely that of idolatry, of making "the work of human hands" absolute rather than relative, and thereby running the risk of missing the call of God to humans in these present circumstances. If there is the danger of running amok in the messiness of bodily experience and the ambiguity of claims to the work of the Spirit in human lives, there is certainly much more danger in proceeding as though God were not at work in bodily experience and the Holy Spirit were not active in human lives here and now. When theologians' eyes turn resolutely away from the experience of the body and the work of the Spirit in the here and now, and turn instead to ancient texts as though they contained all that God wanted humans to learn, then, as Paul says in 2 Corinthians 3:6, "the letter kills."

In contrast, Paul declares in that same passage that "the Spirit gives life." This leads to a final possible misunderstanding of my project, namely, to regard it as a kind of materialistic reduction, as a glorification of the body as such without regard to the Spirit. There are, in fact, any number of "theologies of the body" that argue an anti-Manichaean theme: they state that the body is not bad but good; in particular, the sexual body is not bad but good. They insist that a Christian theology privileging the Spirit has led to distorted perceptions and practices with regard to bodies. A major task of theology, they insist, is to assert the goodness of the body — indeed, of all material things — as God's good creation.[4] While I do not entirely disagree with that argument, it is not mine. My argument as a theologian is above all about the Spirit, since, as Scripture says, "God is Spirit" (John 4:24). The body is of interest, above all, as the arena in which God's self-disclosure as Spirit takes place in the world. The point here is not "spirit" alone or "body" alone but the living human body as the medium of the spirit's expression. I am fully aware of the ambiguity in my language: Do I mean the human spirit expressing itself through a body, or do I mean the divine Spirit who is God expressing itself through a body?

---

4. See, among many others, M. T. Prokes, *Toward a Theology of the Body* (Grand Rapids: Eerdmans, 1996); J. B. Nelson, *Body Theology* (Louisville: Westminster John Knox, 1992); Nelson, *Embodiment: An Approach to Sexuality and Christian Theology* (Minneapolis: Augsburg, 1978); C. E. Gudorf, *Body, Sex, and Pleasure: Reconstructing Christian Sexual Ethics* (Cleveland: Pilgrim, 1994); C. M. Martini, *On the Body: A Contemporary Theology of the Body,* trans. R. M. Gianmanco Frongia (New York: Crossroad, 2001). Academics have chimed in as well: T. K. Beal and D. M. Gunn, *Reading Bibles, Writing Bodies: Identity and the Book* (London: Routledge, 1996); M. D. Kamitsuka, ed., *The Embrace of Eros: Bodies, Desires, and Sexuality in the Church* (Minneapolis: Fortress, 2010); M. W. Shoop, *Let the Bones Dance: Embodiment and the Body of Christ* (Louisville: Westminster John Knox, 2010).

I actually mean both, which is why this is both an important and difficult subject of analysis.

But it is the living human body — individually and communally — that I take to be the arena or medium of the disclosure of the divine Spirit, the primary place where the Living God's work in creation finds expression, and thus the constantly shifting site that demands the theologian's constant attention. Body apart from spirit does not have the same theological interest. A dead human body, a corpse, can reveal all kinds of things to the trained observer; an autopsy can trace the past of the former human's existence in exquisite detail through the examination of dead organs and limbs. The dead body can give up the cause of its death; but lacking spirit, such a corpse cannot give the reasons why it lived.[5] The pathologist and the criminologist should have the most intense interest in the body from which the human spirit has fled and which has become food for other living things. The theologian likewise should have the most intense interest in the ways the living human body gives expression to spirit and thereby is a medium through which the Spirit of God is revealed.

The greater part of this book develops the conviction that human experience in the body is the preeminent arena for God's self-revelation in the world, and it tries to demonstrate how, by paying attention to such bodily experience, theology might become an inductive art. Especially for those not steeped in the history of Christian theology, however, it may be helpful to provide a quick sketch of the process by which Christian thought about God turned quickly and decisively from the discernment of the Spirit in lives of believers to the interpretation of authoritative texts by religious professionals.

From Spirit to Letter

I will say much more later in the argument concerning the role of Scripture in the process of revelation, but for the moment I want only to say that the writings of the Old and New Testaments were composed in the first place as witnesses to the experience of God in the world.[6] The psalmist does not deliver lessons about the divine, but laments and celebrates the experience

---

5. As brilliantly imagined by Jim Crace in *Being Dead* (New York: Viking, 1999).

6. See L. T. Johnson and William S. Kurz, *The Future of Catholic Biblical Scholarship: A Constructive Conversation* (Grand Rapids: Eerdmans, 2002), pp. 119-42.

of the perceived absence or presence of God in the psalmist's life. The prophet does not speak of eternal truths from a detached distance, but speaks of present realities from within highly specific — and often deeply personal — circumstances. Paul the apostle does not instruct his readers on the basis of philosophical premises; rather, he seeks to think through the implications of the powerful experience of the Holy Spirit among them. And as Paul claims to speak in tongues through the power of the Holy Spirit, and to have been snatched into paradise, "whether in the body or apart from the body I do not know, God knows" (2 Cor. 12:3), so does John the seer on the island of Patmos write of his visions of the heavenly courts and of the dwelling place of God among humans.[7]

It is impossible to comprehend the existence of Israel apart from its claims to have an experience of God that was distinct to itself. It is impossible to explain the birth and growth of early Christianity apart from the claims of Christ-believers to have been touched by the power of God through a crucified and exalted messiah. It is impossible to understand the Old Testament or the New Testament if we disregard the experience of God's presence and power in the world out of which those compositions arose and about which they speak. If the texts of Scripture "reveal," they do so above all by witnessing to and expressing powerful convictions and experiences concerning the power of God active in the world.

This understanding of Scripture, however, proved difficult to maintain. The ideological battles within Christianity during the second century — battles that demanded and stimulated the process of self-definition within the still-youthful religion — changed the status of the New Testament compositions, and at the same time nudged orthodox Christianity toward a concentration on texts, and the right interpretation of those texts, more than on the ongoing experience of God. The challenges represented by Marcionism and Montanism and Gnosticism involved the character of the Christian reality and required a more decisive statement of the Rule of Faith. They also involved the place and authority of Christianity's earliest writings, and demanded a more explicit move toward the canonization of these writings, so that they now had, with the Old Testament, the authority of Scripture.[8]

7. For a splendid demonstration of how Paul's experience fit within the context of early Christian claims to religious experience, see J. B. Wallace, *Snatched into Paradise (2 Cor. 12:1-10): Paul's Heavenly Journey in the Context of Early Christian Experience* (Berlin: de Gruyter, 2011).

8. For a sketch of the process of canonization, see L. T. Johnson, *The Writings of the New*

The challenges of Gnosticism, and of "the New Prophecy" in particular, involved appeals to new religious experience as authoritative. Visions, revelations, prophecies given by the Holy Spirit — all these were claimed as support for the understanding of Christianity advanced by the teachers of the second century, whom the orthodox party regarded as innovative and revolutionary. In their own eyes, however, those now viewed by others as heretical seemed to be in direct continuity with the writings of the New Testament.[9] The rejection of their heresy also meant a concentration on those elements of Scripture that spoke of the truth about Christ and a minimizing of those elements that spoke of the growth in truth that would be given by the Holy Spirit. In similar fashion, the apologists who sought to present Christianity as a rational faith tended to minimize or even reject the experience of miracles that was so central to the apocryphal gospels and acts of apostles that proliferated in the second and third centuries.[10] Within orthodoxy, establishing "right teaching" meant using the writings of the New Testament as support for the Rule of Faith. The ongoing experience of the Holy Spirit among contemporary Christians tended to be ignored when not denied or condemned as the work of the devil. Scripture was regarded as medicine applied to errant human experience as a corrector and remedy; human experience was not thought of as illuminating or extending the meaning of Scripture.

Theology took on an even more verbal and logical character during the centuries of doctrinal conflict between the fourth and sixth centuries CE, generated in turn by Arianism, Nestorianism, and Monophysitism.[11] While the writings of the Old and New Testament were used from every side of the debates as the source of proof-texts for establishing one position or another, the "truth of the gospel" came to be thought of more in

---

Testament: An Interpretation, 3rd ed. (Minneapolis: Fortress, 2010), pp. 525-41; for a fuller treatment, see L. M. McDonald, *The Biblical Canon: Its Origin, Transmission, and Authority* (Peabody, MA: Hendrickson, 2007).

9. See L. T. Johnson, *Among the Gentiles: Greco-Roman Religion and Christianity,* Anchor Bible Library (New Haven: Yale University Press, 2009), pp. 172-93, 214-33.

10. Johnson, *Among the Gentiles,* pp. 194-213, 234-54.

11. See the standard surveys by J. N. D. Kelly, *Early Christian Doctrine* (San Francisco: Harper and Row, 1960); G. L. Prestige, *God in Patristic Thought* (London: SPCK, 1912); F. M. Young, *From Nicaea to Chalcedon: A Guide to the Literature and Its Background* (London: SPCK, 1983); A. Grillmeier, *Christ in the Christian Tradition: From the Apostolic Age to Chalcedon (451),* trans. J. Bowden (Atlanta: John Knox, 1975); L. Ayres, *Nicaea and Its Legacy: An Approach to Fourth Century Trinitarian Theology* (Oxford: Oxford University Press, 2004).

propositional than in experiential terms. A legitimate argument can be made that the orthodox party was fighting for the "truth of the Christian experience," but only in the sense of the experience of salvation through Christ, understood now through ontological categories.[12] It can also be affirmed that the orthodox position concerning the divinity of the Holy Spirit was based at least in part on the Spirit's work in the church (see Gregory of Nazianzus, *Oration* 31, 26). However, the evidence for such work was not derived from attention to actual human experiences of divine power among the Christians in Cappadocia, but from the testimonies provided by the New Testament.

The development toward propositional theology and the use of Scripture as the repository of revelation reached maturity in the scholastic theology of the medieval universities.[13] Peter Lombard's *Four Books of Sentences* (1155-1158) — a collection of doctrinal propositions from the Trinity to the sacraments derived from creeds and councils, each supported by a selection of biblical passages that supported each statement — became the necessary starting point for all theological reflection in the schools. The first stages of scholastic theology were, to be sure, enlivened by the challenge of Aristotelian philosophy, not least in its insistence on all knowledge beginning in the senses, and by the vigorous use of dialectic. But as it settled into its place as a body of knowledge required for preachers and teachers, rather than as a distinctive way of thinking, scholastic theology could claim to be a *scientia,* whose proofs were the propositions found in Scripture.[14]

One might legitimately ask whether my sketch is not only overly simple but also fundamentally unfair. What about all the rich interpretations of Scripture found in patristic and medieval sermons? What about the theological implications of the liturgical practices of the church and the catecheses based on them? What about the poetry and hymnody of Nazianzus and Ambrose and Thomas? What about the *apophthegmata* of the desert fathers and mothers with their keen insight into the ascetic life? What about the monastic rules and discourses, especially the *Institutes*

12. See G. P. Prestige, *Fathers and Heretics: Six Studies in Dogmatic Faith* (London: SPCK, 1963).

13. See G. R. Evans, ed., *The Medieval Theologians: An Introduction to Theology in the Medieval Period* (Oxford: Oxford University Press, 2001); I. P. Wei, *Intellectual Culture in Medieval Paris: Theologians and the University (1100-1330)* (Cambridge, UK: Cambridge University Press, 2012).

14. For an overview, see U. G. Leinsle, *Introduction to Scholastic Theology,* trans. M. J. Miller (Washington, DC: Catholic University of America Press, 2010).

and *Conferences* of Cassian, with their profound dissection of virtue and vice and their psychologically acute analysis of progress and failure in the spiritual life? Above all, what about the many theologians who practiced and wrote of the path of contemplation, from Origen through Evagrius of Pontus and Gregory of Nyssa, to *The Cloud of Unknowing* and Julian of Norwich's *Revelations*? Isn't all this great flood of piety and composition also part of the history of theology?[15]

Surely it is, or ought to be. The influence of the liturgical and mystical tradition on doctrinal theology should not be minimized, whether we consider the way *hesychasm,* with its close attention to the body's breathing, builds on and contributes to the understanding of *theiosis* in the Orthodox tradition, or the way the *Mystical Theology* of Pseudo-Dionysius helps shape the theological vision of Thomas Aquinas — or, for that matter, the way the Eucharist made real convictions concerning both the incarnate and mystical body of Christ. Indeed, mysticism is the primary way in which actual human experience continued to play a role within Christian theology in the patristic and medieval periods. In Saint Bonaventure, mysticism is theological and theology is mystical.[16] In both the Reformation and Counter Reformation, however, this living exchange weakened and sometimes disappeared. Christian mystics continued to practice contemplation and to write about their visions; but their writings tended to fall into a separate category of edifying literature called "devotional."

Moreover, as important as their contributions were, worship and mystical practice represent only a small portion of the somatic experience from which theology might have learned. After the struggles of the second century, claims to other kinds of spirit-generated experiences, such as speaking in tongues or prophecy, were regarded with the distrust that was increasingly directed by ecclesiastical authorities toward anything associated with "enthusiasm."[17] And the wider spectrum of human experiences in the body that might be considered pertinent to theology — experiences

---

15. For a sense of how I see such literature playing an essential role in the interpretation of Scripture, and therefore of theology, see my *The Future of Catholic Biblical Scholarship*, pp. 35-118; and my *Brother of Jesus, Friend of God: Studies in the Letter of James* (Grand Rapids: Eerdmans, 2004), pp. 61-83; see also my "Dry Bones — Why Religion Needs Mysticism," *Commonweal* 137 (2010): 11-14.

16. Bonaventure, *The Journey of the Mind to God,* ed. S. F. Brown, trans. P. Boehner (Indianapolis: Hackett Publishing Company, 1993).

17. R. A. Knox, *Enthusiasm: A Chapter in the History of Religion, with Special Reference to the XVII and XVIII Centuries* (New York: Oxford University Press, 1961).

of work and play, of sexuality and of pain — was neglected almost entirely. Theology sought the safety of doctrinal formulas and the scriptural texts that supported them. Theology secured its position as a science by closing itself off from anything that God might actually be doing outside the pre-scribed channels of grace within the church, that is, in the wider world, or even in the neighborhood of the theologian. Theology could thereby take its place with classics and philosophy as an entirely academic exercise, since what could be said about the divine was adequately expressed in ancient texts, and theologians had nothing to learn from the activity of the Living God. Thus "systematic theology" — a wonderfully oxymoronic des-ignation — can legitimately be called idolatrous both because it presumes to comprehend God with its constructions, and because it effectively ne-glects the possibility of God's acting in new ways in the world.[18]

From Letter to Spirit

The theologians of the twentieth and early twenty-first centuries have not scorned human experience as lacking pertinence to theology. Indeed, ever since Friedrich Schleiermacher (1768-1834), many theologians have char-acteristically "turned to the subject": that is, rather than begin with the ex-plication of classical doctrine, they begin with the human subject, seeking to link what is said in Scripture with the human condition in the world.[19] The major exception to such a turn to the subject is Karl Barth (1886-1968), who emphatically rejects an appeal to human experience, even human religious experience, as itself a manifestation of human idolatry, and insists that theology — "church dogmatics" — must be based root and stem in the witness of Scripture.[20] He deliberately opposes "the Word of God" to the

18. Compare the treatment of topics in J. M. Frame, *Systematic Theology: An Introduc-tion to Christian Beliefs* (Philadelphia: Presbyterian and Reformed, 2013); C. Hodge, *Sys-tematic Theology*, 3 vols. (Peabody, MA: Hendrickson Publishers, 1999 [1981]); F. Schüssler Fiorenza, *Systematic Theology: Roman Catholic Perspectives*, Theology and the Sciences series (Minneapolis: Fortress, 2011).

19. For Schleiermacher, see above all his *Religion: Speeches to Its Cultured Despisers*, ed. R. Crouter, Cambridge Texts in the History of Philosophy (Cambridge, UK: Cambridge University Press, 1996 [1799]); see also Schleiermacher, *The Christian Faith* (Apocryphile Press, 2011 [1821-22]).

20. For a sense of Barth's position, see his *The Epistle to the Romans* (New York: Oxford University Press, 1968 [1918]); see also Barth, *Dogmatics in Outline* (New York: Harper Pe-rennial, 1959 [1949]); see also his massive *Church Dogmatics* (1932 forward).

"word of man." A brilliant and creative interpretation of Scripture, Barth's dialectical theology provides a critical restraint to forms of liberalism in the late nineteenth and early twentieth centuries that were in danger of baptizing human culture and equating social progress with the rule of God.

Among Barth's many followers, who inherited neither the master's brilliance nor his creativity, any mention of human experience as theologically significant, perhaps even revelatory, evokes the dreaded specter of Schleiermacher and triggers revulsion.[21] Indeed, the Schleiermachian understanding of "religious experience" lies behind efforts to marginalize what is termed the "experiential-expressivist model" from doctrinal discussions.[22] But language about human experience — and even about human religious experience — need not in the least be defined in Schleiermacher's terms. In other words, the dismissal of Schleiermacher's psychological and individualistic understanding of religious experience does not automatically disqualify other ways of speaking about human experience and about God's work in and through human experience.[23]

Indeed, many other Protestant theologians, including Rudolf Bultmann,[24] Paul Tillich,[25] Wolfhart Pannenberg,[26] and Jürgen Moltmann,[27] while not subscribing to Schleiermacher, and while not abandoning the

21. In an issue of the journal *Nova et Vetera* devoted to responses to my book *The Future of Catholic Biblical Scholarship,* both David Yeago and Richard Hays criticize my argument that experience should be a feature in interpreting Scripture because, they say, it represents a return to Schleiermacher — which it does not. See my response: "Conversation, Conversion, and Construction," *Nova et Vetera* 4 (2006): 172-85; see also Hays's ambivalent view of the "experience" angle of the Wesleyan Quadrilateral in Richard Hays, *The Moral Vision of the New Testament: A Contemporary Introduction to New Testament Ethics* (San Francisco: HarperSanFrancisco, 1996), pp. 209-11.

22. See G. Lindbeck, *The Nature of Doctrine: Religion and Theology in a Post-Liberal Age* (Philadelphia: Westminster John Knox, 2009 [1984]).

23. See the careful discussions in Johnson, *Among the Gentiles,* pp. 17-21; see also Johnson, *Religious Experience in Earliest Christianity,* pp. 39-68.

24. Fundamental to Bultmann's argument in 1941 concerning demythologizing the New Testament is the (supposedly nonmythic) contemporary experience of the world; see Bultmann, *New Testament and Mythology and Other Basic Writings,* selected and edited by S. M. Ogden (Minneapolis: Fortress, 1984).

25. See esp. Tillich, *The Courage to Be* (New Haven: Yale University Press, 2000); and *Systematic Theology,* vol. 1 (Chicago: University of Chicago Press, 1973).

26. See W. Pannenberg, *Anthropology in Theological Perspective* (London: T & T Clark, 1999).

27. See J. Moltmann, *Experiences in Theology* (Minneapolis: Fortress, 2000); see also Moltmann, *God in Creation* (Minneapolis: Fortress, 1993).

primacy of Scripture, have argued that human experience in some form has an essential role to play in theology. Attention to human experience is also found in important twentieth-century Roman Catholic theologians, including Karl Rahner,[28] Hans Urs von Balthasar,[29] Bernard Lonergan,[30] David Tracy,[31] and — in some ways most dramatically — Pierre Teilhard de Chardin.[32]

With the exception of Teilhard de Chardin, however, in whose work Scripture just about disappears, and even human "experience" is secondary to his vision of humans evolving toward the "Omega Point," the recognition of the experiential in these major theologians seldom gets beyond the merely formal. Or, perhaps more accurately, it seldom moves from highly general statements to the analysis of the particular and actual experiences. Thus, Tillich and Bultmann, each in his own fashion, seek to define a contemporary existential situation or cultural correlative for the gospel, but these constructions have little contact with lived experience. In Pannenberg and Moltmann, the acknowledgment of experience tends to be subsumed by conceptions of the historical. Among Roman Catholic theologians, human experience likewise tends to get swallowed by philosophical (Rahner, Tracy) or psychological/epistemological (Lonergan) or cultural (von Balthasar) categories, and remains more of an abstract notion than the basis of close and specific analysis.

In short, we do not find in these theologians either a sustained interest in particular and embodied human experience, or an indication that such particular and embodied human experience can disclose the presence and power of the Living God in the world today. I do not think that I am alone when I confess that, in reading these eminent theologians, even those from whom, like Rahner, I have learned so much, I sometimes have had the

---

28. Rahner perfectly exemplifies a "turn to the subject" that begins with the human experience of transcendence; e.g., see Rahner, *Spirit in the World,* trans. W. Dyck (New York: Continuum, 1994); *On the Theology of Death,* trans. C. H. Henkey (Freiberg: Herder, 1965).

29. Von Balthasar's work was intimately connected to the mystical teachings of his companion, Adrienne von Speyer; for examples of attention to experience, see *Heart of the World* (San Francisco: Ignatius Press, 1980), and *The Christian and Anxiety* (San Francisco: Ignatius Press, 2000). For the fascinating influence of his companion's experience on his thought, see K. Kilby, *Balthasar: A (Very) Critical Introduction* (Grand Rapids: Eerdmans, 2012).

30. See Lonergan, *Method in Theology,* 2nd ed. (Toronto: University of Toronto Press, 1990).

31. See Tracy, *Blessed Rage for Order* (Chicago: University of Chicago Press, 1996).

32. See Teilhard de Chardin, *The Divine Milieu* (New York: Harper, 2001); *The Phenomenon of Man* (New York: Harper, 2008); and *The Future of Man* (New York: Image, 2004).

sense that theology remains a discipline concerned above all with texts and propositions based in the past, rather than the discernment of the work of the Living God in the present.[33] Perhaps others have sensed, as I have, that the introduction of a specific and particular human experience into this academic conversation would be something of an embarrassment.

A longing for a theology less preoccupied with academic discourse and more passionately engaged with human beings in their actual social and political settings, above all in the concrete experience of oppression and suffering, I think, generated such a powerful positive response to liberation theology when it first appeared in the second half of the twentieth century. Whether writing out of the context of poverty and economic oppression in Latin America,[34] or out of the context of racial injustice in the United States,[35] or out of the context of gender discrimination against women,[36] or, above all, the context of women of color,[37] theologians who adopted a liberation perspective explicitly invoked the Living God of ancient Israel who had led the people out of bondage, and would lead the marginal populations of today into a more just and equitable society. The recent emergence of queer theology, obviously and explicitly rooted in the experience of gay, lesbian, and transgendered persons, must also negotiate a long history of suppression and persecution.[38]

Exhibiting a passion for social justice and embracing a biblical rather than a philosophical understanding of God's righteousness — expressed above all in God's "preferential option for the poor" — such forms of liber-

---

33. My debt to Rahner is most obvious in my discussion of body and spirit; in many ways I continue to find him the most satisfying — even if often most maddeningly obscure — of the theologians who begin with a turn to the subject.

34. E.g., G. Gutiérrez, *A Theology of Liberation: History, Politics, and Salvation* (Maryknoll, NY: Orbis Press, 1988); L. Boff and C. Boff, *Introducing Liberation Theology* (Maryknoll, NY: Orbis Press, 1987).

35. James H. Cone, *A Theology of Black Liberation* (Maryknoll, NY: Orbis Press, 1970).

36. R. R. Reuther, *Sexism and God-Talk: Toward a Feminist Theology* (Boston: Beacon Press, 1993); M. Daly, *Beyond God the Father: Toward a Philosophy of Women's Liberation* (Boston: Beacon Press, 1993); E. Johnson, *She Who Is: The Mystery of God in Feminist Theological Discourse* (New York: Crossroad, 2002).

37. D. Williams, *Sisters in the Wilderness: The Challenge of Womanist God-Talk* (Maryknoll, NY: Orbis, 2013); B. Hooks, *Ain't I a Woman: Black Women and Feminism* (New York: South End Press, 1999).

38. E.g., P. S. Cheng, *Radical Love: Introduction to Queer Theology* (New York: Seabury, 2011); G. Laughlin, ed., *Queer Theology: Rethinking the Western Body* (Oxford: Wiley-Blackwell, 2007).

ation theology seemed at first to be far removed from the dogmatic parsing of systematic theologians and far more in touch with the experience of actual human beings: now the bodies of the wretchedly poor, the bodies of the systemically rejected, the bodies of the abused women become the starting point for theology. God's work in liberating human action (praxis) is the cutting edge of God's ongoing revelation. At its best, liberation theology provides a refreshing awareness of the God who works to renew the earth — above all by changing those sinful human social arrangements that resist his will — and a new sense of how discipleship demands a participation in God's work for justice.

As domesticated within schools of theology, however, the inherent limitations of liberation theology also began to appear. Proponents could argue, with some justification, that its highly selective use of Scripture was not more extreme than that practiced by systematic theologians, or that its problematic preference for a Christology based on "the historical Jesus" was not more reductionist than that of other theologians arguing for a "Christology from below."[39] More problematic was the way liberation theology's melding of process thought and Marxist political theory tended to supplant specific and particular human experience with a rigid grid of ideological analysis: the categories of gender and race and class tend to replace the analysis of actual and varied human experiences.[40] Only those experiences that fit within the accepted theoretical framework counted; the experiences that escaped ideological generalization counted for little. Liberation theology today appears to be nearly as abstract and academic as the forms of theology it sought to displace. It does not focus its attention, any more than they do, on the specific contours of bodily experience to discern the ways in which God's Spirit is disclosed.

My Approach

The present exercise builds on, and seeks to refine and extend, the approach I took in two earlier books. In *Decision Making in the Church: A Biblical Model*, I worked at establishing a theological framework for an induc-

39. As, e.g., E. Schillebeeckx, *Jesus: An Experiment in Christology* (New York: Crossroad, 1981), or R. Haight, *Jesus, Symbol of God* (Maryknoll, NY: Orbis, 2013).

40. The influence of P. Freire's *Pedagogy of the Oppressed*, trans. M. Ramos (New York: Continuum, 1986 [1970]), is profound and pervasive.

tive theology.[41] I argued that the church as community of faith was called to discern the work of God in the world and "decide for God" in response to such discernment. Building on the narrative argument developed by Acts 10–15, in which the evangelist Luke shows the earliest church responding to the movement of the Holy Spirit in the Gentile mission, I tried to show how God's work could be articulated first of all by the stories concerning the experience of God by individuals, and that when such narratives combined and grew to become a pressing social reality, they rose to the level of ecclesial discernment.

I take it as axiomatic that the church is able to perceive (discern) in such stories the work of the Holy Spirit — or its absence — because its perceptions are shaped by the symbols of Scripture. But since God is able to do new things in the world, even such unexpected things as sending a crucified Messiah, or turning a rabid persecutor into an apostle, or including within God's people those disdained as idolators, the church also finds that its "reading" of experience also involves a "rereading" of the symbols of Scripture. The first edition of my book offered only a few brief examples of how the dialectic between Scripture and experience might work, and it left open the question of the criteria by which experience might be assessed as demanding the positive response of the church. A second edition of that book included an analysis of Paul's letters that yielded a scriptural formal and material criterion for discernment.[42] The formal criterion requires that narrated experience build up (edify) the church; the material criterion demands that the narrated experience build the church in holiness. But I went no further in suggesting how either individuals or communities could actually perceive these in specific human experiences.

A second book, *Faith's Freedom: A Classic Spirituality for Contemporary Christians,* attempts to suggest a way of "reading" human experience that corresponds to the framework for reading Scripture offered by *Scripture and Discernment.*[43] Beginning with certain "critical

---

41. L. T. Johnson, *Decision Making in the Church: A Biblical Model* (Philadelphia: Fortress Press, 1982).

42. *Scripture and Discernment: Decision-Making in the Church* (Nashville: Abingdon, 1996). The analysis of the criteria can also be found in "Edification as a Formal Criterion for Discernment in the Church," *Sewanee Review* 39, no. 4 (1996): 362-72, and "Holiness as a Material Criterion for Discernment in the Church," *Sewanee Review* 39, no. 4 (1996): 373-84.

43. L. T. Johnson, *Faith's Freedom* (Minneapolis: Fortress Press, 1990).

theological concepts" offered by the Nicene Creed — God as creator, judge, savior, sanctifier — I seek to test the adequacy of these concepts for the analysis of lived human experience within the symbolic world of Scripture. After locating the ways in which the human project of freedom is constrained by physical, psychological, social, and hermeneutical factors, and arguing that the experience of the Living God finds a space for freedom within those constraints, I posit a fundamental drama involving God and humans. The drama is one in which God, as the one who creates at every moment, always initiates the action, and humans respond to the ever-acting God. The drama has four fundamental moments: idolatry, grace, sin, and faith. Within this flexible framework, I then seek to provide some sense of how that drama is displayed through diverse human experiences involving power, possessions, sexuality, anger, and freedom.

Even though *Faith's Freedom* came closer to the actual practice of discernment in the experience of everyday individuals — asking, for example, how, in specific circumstances, one could consider a decision as one of openness to God's activity or as one of closure to the Spirit, and providing a down-to-earth understanding of grace as gift — it still skated along the edges of the mystery of human embodiedness. My sense of the ambiguous character of the human body as disclosing spirit certainly comes through most clearly in that book's analysis of power and possessions.[44] But I now think it important to push beyond *Faith's Freedom* in two important ways. First, I want to develop more fully than I have before the theological implications of creation and the new creation (the resurrection/exaltation of Christ) for the discernment of the body as the medium of the spirit's self-expression. Second, I want to push harder on the analysis of specific human situations in which the body is precisely that which requires interpretation, and to carry out this analysis more widely and perhaps more neutrally, without immediate reference to the framework of "idolatry/faith" that I used in *Faith's Freedom* (though I by no means disavow that framework).

The first task involves a rereading of Scripture guided by the single question of how the living God is said to disclose God's power and presence in the world. This task, though itself daunting, is relatively straight-

44. I carry out an explicit analysis of body language even more thoroughly in my *Sharing Possessions: What Faith Demands,* 2nd enlarged ed. (Grand Rapids: Eerdmans, 2010).

forward, since texts stand still and allow themselves to be interrogated more or less directly. If we have a good question to put to the texts, we have some confidence that the texts will be responsive. The means of putting the questions and hearing the answers are familiar to all who read carefully and critically.

The second task promises to offer much more adventure. I want to ask how we can see what needs to be seen in somatic experience. How does body display or conceal spirit? How can we begin to read bodies in motion as the basis for "narratives of faith" in the first place? How is the word that God wants us to discern to be heard in the actual circumstances of worldly existence? The challenge here is learning how to see and how to hear, learning specifically how to observe in a detailed and accurate way, and how to report on what we observe in a way that is faithful to the particularities of the body in its experience.

Poets and novelists and the essayists of everyday life teach us the most of how to engage in such close observation of the body. Contemporary novelists such as Anne Tyler, Louise Erdrich, Marilynne Robinson, Margaret Atwood, Iris Murdoch, Margaret Drabble, and Ruth Rendell enable us to observe somatic and spiritual states with an almost painful attention to detail. I like to think of such careful attention and reportage as a form of phenomenology. I may even use that word from time to time. I don't mean by it the kind of rigorous conceptual discipline of a Maurice Merleau-Ponty,[45] but the down-to-earth, close-to-the bone sort of observation that I have found so instructive in the novelists I have mentioned, as well as writers such as Johan Huizinga[46] and Peter Berger,[47] G. K. Chesterton[48]

45. E.g., *Phenomenology of Perception,* trans. C. Smith (New York: Humanities Press, 1962); *Sense and Non-Sense,* trans. H. Dreyfus and P. A. Dreyfus (Evanston: Northwestern University Press, 1964). An example of a phenomenological approach that is closer to what I want to achieve is D. Leder, *The Absent Body* (Chicago: University of Chicago Press, 1990).

46. Huizinga, *Homo Ludens: A Study of the Play Element in Culture* (New York: Roy Publishers, 1950).

47. See Berger, *The Social Construction of Reality: A Treatise in the Sociology of Knowledge* (Garden City, NY: Doubleday, 1967); *The Sacred Canopy: Elements of a Sociological Theory of Religion* (Garden City, NY: Doubleday, 1967); *A Rumor of Angels: Modern Society and the Rediscovery of the Supernatural* (Garden City, NY: Doubleday, 1970).

48. I have in mind not only works such as *Orthodoxy* and *Heretics,* but especially his marvelous shorter essays in which he made so many brilliant observations on everyday life. See D. Ahlquist, ed., *In Defense of Sanity: The Best Essays of G. K. Chesterton* (San Francisco: Ignatius Press, 2011).

and Gabriel Marcel,[49] Jose Ortega y Gasset,[50] and Robert Farrar Capon.[51] I will certainly fall short of such writers in my ability to evoke the "rumors of angels," the intimations of transcendence in ordinary human experiences, but I am dedicated to trying, convinced that unless we school ourselves with such careful attention, theology will remain a matter of texts rather than a matter of life, an academic enterprise rather than an inductive art.

49. E.g., Gabriel Marcel, *Being and Having: An Existentialist Diary* (Gloucester, MA: Peter Smith, 1976); *The Mystery of Being*, 2 vols., trans. G. S. Fraser (South Bend, IN: St. Augustine's Press, 2001).

50. Like Marcel, Ortega y Gasset mixes existentialism and phenomenology with a profound interest in the arts; see, e.g., *What Is Philosophy?* (1929), *The Revolt of the Masses* (1930), and *Ideas on the Novel* (1924).

51. E.g., Capon, *An Offering of Uncles: The Priesthood of Adam and the Shape of the World* (New York: Crossroad, 1982); *Bed and Board: Plain Talk about Marriage* (New York: Simon and Schuster, 1965). I should also mention here the rigorous attention to her own lived experience as theologically laden in the work of my former colleague R. Bondi, *Memories of God: Theological Reflections on a Life* (Nashville: Abingdon, 1995), and *Houses: A Family Memoir of Grace* (Nashville: Abingdon, 2000).

CHAPTER ONE

The Way Not Taken:
A Disembodied Theology of the Body

Among the many books available that in one way or another call themselves theologies of the body, perhaps the most notable is the collection of conferences delivered at papal audiences by the late (and now Saint) John Paul II, published as *Theology of the Body: Human Love in the Divine Plan.*[1] Appearing with such a title, under the name of the (then) sitting leader of Christianity's largest denomination, the book was bound to attract attention, and it did, especially among conservative Roman Catholics, who have greeted *all* papal teaching on sexuality with extravagant praise. Archbishop Charles J. Chaput, OFM Cap., for example, has declared that Pope Paul VI was a prophet because, in the encyclical *Humanae Vitae,* he was correct in forbidding artificial birth control. Janet Smith believes that Catholics who disagree with the papacy's condemnation of contraceptives have not appreciated or understood the full richness of papal teaching on sexuality, above all in the work of John Paul II.[2] Similarly, Jennifer Popiel declares that, "unlike many women, I find the church's doctrinal statements on contraception and reproduction to be clear and compelling," and she argues that natural family planning is fully compatible with feminism, since "only when we control our bodies will we truly control our lives."[3]

In a lengthy blog response to an earlier version of this present chapter,[4]

---

1. John Paul II, *Theology of the Body: Human Love in the Divine Plan* (New York: Pauline Books and Media, 1997).

2. In "Contraception: A Symposium," *First Things* (December 1998).

3. "Necessary Connections? Catholicism, Feminism, and Contraception," *America* (November 27, 1999).

4. L. T. Johnson, "A Disembodied 'Theology of the Body': John Paul II on Love, Sex, and Pleasure," *Commonweal* 128 (2001): 11-17.

Christopher West, another papal apologist, declares that "the theology of the body has already begun the sexual counter-revolution . . . . [I]t's a revolution that Luke Timothy Johnson doesn't understand, isn't ready for, or doesn't desire."[5] The implication of West's crisp statement is that if I really understood the pope, I would be intellectually compelled to agree with him, and if I understood the pope's position and still did not agree, my resistance would be due to moral rather than intellectual inadequacy.

The preeminent papal apologist, however, is George Weigel. In his biography of John Paul II,[6] Weigel takes particular pains to trace the pope's systematic response to what he terms the "pastoral and catechetical failure" of Paul VI's encyclical *Humanae Vitae* (1968), infamous for its rejection of every form of artificial birth control.[7] John Paul II's 130 fifteen-minute conferences (delivered between 1979 and 1984) were gathered together under four headings: "The Original Unity of Man and Woman," "Blessed Are the Pure of Heart," "The Theology of Marriage and Celibacy," and "Reflections on *Humanae Vitae*." As Weigel himself observes, the arrangement of the collection reveals its intention as a theological rationalization for Paul VI's encyclical on birth control.

Weigel is rhapsodic concerning what he considers John Paul II's resounding success. The collection of sermons, he says, is a "theological time bomb" that may take a hundred years fully to appreciate. It "may prove to be the decisive moment in exorcizing the Manichaean demon and its depreciation of human sexuality from Catholic moral theology," precisely because the pope takes "embodiedness" so seriously. The book has "ramifications for all of theology," and is a "critical moment not only in Catholic theology, but in the history of modern thought." High praise, indeed; no wonder Weigel is surprised that so few priests preach from the book, and only a "microscopic" portion of the Catholic people even seem aware of this great accomplishment. He attributes the neglect to the density of the Pope's thought, the fascination of the media with incidentals, and the controversial character of the pontiff. Weigel con-

5. "Response to TL [sic] Johnson's Critique of JP II's Theology of the Body" at Theology of the Body.net: The Online Resource for John Paul II's "Theology of the Body." Among West's several published works dedicated to explicating and propagating the pope's teaching, see *Theology of the Body for Beginners: A Basic Introduction to Pope John Paul II's Sexual Revolution* (West Chester, PA: Ascension Press, 2010).

6. *Witness to Hope: The Biography of John Paul II* (New York: Harper, 2005)

7. *Humanae Vitae: Encyclical Letter of His Holiness Paul VI* (San Francisco: Ignatius Press, 2002).

cludes that it will take time to appreciate the pope and his magnificent achievement.

Weigel is certainly on target with regard to the polarizing character of the late pope and the media's chronic inability to transcend the trivial. He is accurate as well (if perhaps overly charitable) in calling the 130 talks "dense." They are, in fact, exceptionally difficult to read and almost mind-numbingly repetitious. What must they have been like to hear? But are they, nevertheless, as theologically important as Weigel proposes? Do they represent the future direction of thinking theologically about the body? I don't think they do. Indeed, I regard the pope's effort as exemplifying precisely the wrong kind of approach to the mystery of human embodiedness.

I do not challenge the proposition that in some respects John Paul II's teaching on sexuality could be called "prophetic," above all in his resistance to what he termed the "culture of death" (exemplified by millions of abortions) in contemporary society, and his critique of the pervasive sexualization of identity in the West. But his effort in this book falls far short of adequate theological thinking on the subject of the human body as the arena of God's self-disclosure. The pope's book is inadequate, not in the obvious way that all theology is inadequate to speak of God (and should therefore exhibit intellectual modesty), but in the sense that it simply does not engage what ought most to be engaged in a theology of the body. Because of its theological weakness, the pope's teaching does not really respond to the anxieties of those who, seeking a Christian understanding of the body and of human sexuality, look for practical guidance for their lives as sexually active adults.

If John Paul II had made only passing remarks on his chosen subject in a single homily, then a full-fledged critical response would be unfair. But everything suggests that he intended these collected conferences to be read as a "theology of the body" in the fullest sense of the term "theology." The pope uses academic terms such as "phenomenology" and "hermeneutics"; he refers to contemporary thinkers; he provides copious notes; and in the very commitment to the subject over a period of five years in 130 conferences, he indicates that he wants his thought to be given the most serious consideration. Weigel's dismay at the lack of such attention certainly suggests that he has had the same expectation. It is appropriate, then, to treat John Paul II's words as those of a theologian and to test them for their intellectual adequacy, especially since his approach is in some ways characteristic of others who are seeking a "theology" of the body.

The Problem of Focus

Perhaps the title of this collection of talks was not chosen by John Paul II himself, but it legitimately derives from his frequent reference to a "theology of the body" and his concentration on "human love in the divine plan." Surely, though, adequate theological reflection on the body must encompass far more than human love, even if that were comprehensively treated. Sex is simply not the only mysterious aspect of the body, or the exclusive expression of human love! The pope cites Paul's statement in 1 Corinthians 6:18 with approval: "Flee fornication. Every sin a person commits is apart from the body. But the one who fornicates sins in his own body." But Paul's rhetoric in this case cannot be taken as sober description of reality. Do not the sins of gluttony and drunkenness and sloth have as much to do with the body as fornication, and do not all forms of avarice also involve dispositions of the body?

To be sure, a responsible theological phenomenology of the body as primordial mystery or symbol of human freedom and bondage must include every aspect of sexuality. But it must also embrace all the other ways in which human embodiedness both enables and limits human freedom (and the freedom of the Spirit) through the body, as in the use of material possessions, engagement with the environment, artistic creativity, and suffering — both sinful and sanctifying. The pope's title provides the first clue to the way in which a grander — or to use his word, "vast" — conceptual framework serves to camouflage a distressingly narrow view of his chosen topic.

As for "human love in the divine plan," the conferences provide few glimpses of human love as actually experienced. The topic of human love in all its dimensions has been wonderfully explored by the world's literature, but none of its grandeur or giddiness appears in these talks, which remain at a level of abstraction far removed from novels and newspapers that carry stories of love among people who look and act like us. John Paul II claims to be practicing "phenomenology," but from the evidence of these homilies, he seems to have paid little attention to actual human experience. Instead, he dwells on the nuances of words in biblical narratives and propositions, while fantasizing an ethereal and all-encompassing mode of mutual self-donation between man and woman that lacks any of the messy, clumsy, awkward, charming, casual, and yes, silly aspects of love in the flesh. Carnality, it is good to remember, is at least as much a matter of humor as of solemnity. In the pope's formulations, though, human sexuality is observed by telescope from a distant planet. Solemn pronouncements are made on the basis of scriptural exegesis rather than living experience. The effect is something like that of a sunset painted by the unsighted.

The Use of Scripture

An objection might be made like this: Isn't it proper to base theology in Scripture, and isn't John Paul II correct to devote himself so sedulously to the analysis of biblical texts rather than the slippery and shoddy stuff of experience? Much more must be said on this subject later, but for now it can be noted that the Catholic tradition takes seriously the continuing work of God's Holy Spirit in the world. If we believe — and this is a cru- cial point — that revelation is not exclusively biblical but occurs in the continuing experience of God in the structures of human freedom, then at least an occasional glance at human experience as actually lived might be appropriate even for the magisterium.[8]

The pope's way of reading Scripture, however, also falls below the level of serious theological engagement. John Paul II certainly shows care with the passages he considers, and he does not misrepresent in a major way the texts he discusses, though he leaves the clear impression that Mat- thew's "Blessed are the pure of heart" (Matt. 5:8) refers to chastity, when he knows full well that the beatitude does not have so restricted a sense. More questionable is the way John Paul II selects and extrapolates from specific texts without sufficient grounding or explanation. An adequate theological engagement with Scripture concerning sexuality would require, I submit, both an assessment of everything said in the Old and New Tes- taments touching on the subject — both the good and the bad — and then a judicious inquiry into how these diverse testimonies might or might not be taken normatively. One simply cannot move from a flat and uncritical reading of the text to normative claim. But this is what John Paul II does.

Given that the pope has reduced "human love" to "human sexuality," it is striking that his discourses center on only a handful of (admittedly) important passages, with a mere nod in the direction of other rich texts that might have rewarded much more attention, such as the Song of Songs

---

8. See the Constitution on Divine Revelation of the Second Vatican Council, *Dei Ver- bum*, 2.8.

(three conferences) and the Book of Tobit (one conference). Other important texts are given scant or no attention. A far richer understanding of the apostle Paul would have resulted, for example, from a more sustained and robust reading of 1 Corinthians 7, which truly does reveal the mutuality and reciprocity — as well as the complexity — of married love. And if the pope had engaged some of the Bible's "texts of terror" on sexuality (such as Judges 19 or Ezekiel 16), he would have done the service of showing how the scriptural witness is indeed complex and ambiguous, and the relationships between men and women susceptible to the terrible as much as to the tender.[9]

John Paul II's flat, surface reading of texts consistently fails to deal with the difficulties presented by the passages he has selected to discuss. For example, he manages to use Matthew 19:3-9 (on the question of the indissolubility of marriage) without ever adverting to the clause introduced by Matthew in both 5:32 and 19:9, which allows divorce on the grounds of *porneia* (sexual immorality). By not mentioning those texts, he is not required to deal with what that exceptive clause might suggest about the gap between the ideal "in the beginning" invoked by Jesus (and the pope) and the hard realities of actual marriages faced by the Matthean (and every subsequent) church. The refusal to recognize this textual difficulty — and what it suggests about the struggles of the earliest believers with Jesus' radical demand for fidelity in marriage — amounts to a kind of interpretive shell game, above all when the sleight of hand is carried out by the church's highest authority in the presence of eager and credulous pilgrims (and readers).

For all of John Paul II's celebrated philosophical sophistication, he seems unaware of the dangers of deriving ontological conclusions from ancient narrative texts. He inveighs against the "hermeneutics of suspicion," but the remedy for that problem is not a completely uncritical reading that moves directly from the ancient narrative to conclusions about the essence of the human condition. He spends much time reflecting on the Yahwist Creation account in Genesis 2, because that is the passage cited by Jesus in his dispute with the Pharisees over divorce (Matt. 19:5). The passage's narrative texture, not to mention its human feel, also allows for the kind of "phenomenological" deduction that the pope so clearly enjoys. But as the pope surely understands, this version of the creation must be joined

9. See P. Trible, *Texts of Terror: Literary-Feminist Readings of Biblical Narratives* (Minneapolis: Fortress, 1984).

to that in Genesis 1, in which God creates humans in God's image as male and female. If this version were to be engaged with equal vigor, certain conclusions drawn by John Paul II would need to be qualified.

He wants the term "man," for example, to mean both male and female. But the Genesis 2 version pushes him to virtually equate "man" with "male," with the unhappy result that males experience the original solitude that the pope wants to make constitutively human, as well as the domination over creation that is expressed in the naming of the animals. In this scenario, females appear in the story not as "original" and "equal" sharers in humanity but as "helpers" who are complementary to the already rather complete humanity found in males. Small wonder that in none of his further reflections on sexuality do women appear as moral agents. Men can have lust in their hearts, but women cannot. Men can struggle with concupiscence, but women apparently do not. Men can exploit their wives sexually, but women never exploit their husbands sexually.

Such an exclusive focus on male and female in the biblical account also leaves out all the interesting ways in which human sexuality refuses to be contained within these standard gender designations, not only biologically but also psychologically and spiritually. What appears in the guise of description subtly serves as prescription: human love and sexuality can occur in only one approved form. Every other way of being either sexual or loving is left out altogether. No matter how useful the scriptural categories of male and female are, however — as useful in general as the categories day and night — they cannot be taken as prescriptive for all humans at the empirical level, any more than "day" and "night" adequately account for all the shades of difference in light denoted by "dawn" and "dusk."

Is it not important at least to acknowledge — if we are actually trying to be "phenomenological" — that a significant portion of humans (even if we take a ludicrously low proportion, tens of millions of humans) are homosexual? Should we not take into account that 1-3 percent of humans come into the world with a range of organic and hormonal sexual arrangements that are summarized by the term "intersexual"? Are all of these left outside "human love in God's plan" if they do not appear in the biblical account? Would not a more adequate phenomenology of human sexuality, concerned more with persons, after all, than with statistics, take very seriously these participants in the human family who are surely also called by God to be loving, and in different ways to foster the work and joy of creation?

Even within this normative framework, however, the pope's treatment is narrow. Out of all the things that might be taken up and discussed within married love and the vocation of parenting, John Paul II's conferences finally come down to a concentration on "the transmission of life." In these conferences the "theology of the body" has been reduced to sexuality, and that complex dimension of human embodiedness is reduced, in turn, to the act of intercourse, and the act of intercourse is of interest only with regard to its "openness" to reproduction. By the time he reaches his explicit discussion of *Humanae Vitae*, it is difficult to avoid the conclusion that every earlier textual selection and phenomenological reflection has been directed to a defense of his predecessor's encyclical. There is, however, almost nothing in that defense, when it comes, that is given actual support by the conferences preceding it.

What the Pope Leaves Out

The pope's effort to place knotty and disputed questions concerning procreation within a more comprehensive theology of the body is, in and of itself, legitimate — even if slightly guilty of false advertising. But even on their own terms, the statements of John Paul II and his apologists leave out some truly important things.

Most important, I think, is their lack of intellectual modesty, not only with regard to the "facts" of revelation but also concerning the "facts" of human embodiedness. In everything having to do with the body, we are in the realm of what Gabriel Marcel calls "mystery."[10] Although the practice of medicine sometimes pretends that this is the case, the body does not simply present a series of problems that we can solve by detached analysis. Rather, the body presents us with mystery in two significant ways. First, we don't understand everything about the body, particularly our own bodies; the means by which we reveal ourselves to others and unite lovingly (or otherwise) with others is not unambiguous. The body simultaneously makes itself available to thought and conceals itself from our minds. Second, we cannot detach ourselves from our bodies — better, from our "selves" as bodies — as though they were simply what we "have" rather than what preeminently we "are."

We are inextricably implicated in our bodies and cannot distance ourselves from the body without self-distortion. It follows that our bodies are

10. G. Marcel, *Being and Having*, trans. K. Farrer (Philadelphia: Westminster, 1949), p. 117.

28

not only to be schooled by our minds and wills; they also instruct and discipline us, often in humbling ways. Should not a genuine "theology of the body" begin with a genuine phenomenology of the body, with a posture of receptive attention to and learning from our own and others' bodies? Human bodies are part of the image of God and are the means through which absolutely everything we can learn about God must come to us.

I find the constant emphasis on "controlling the body" exactly contrary to such humility in the face of mystery, whether such language derives from technocrats seeking to engineer reproductive processes or naturalists seeking the same results through continence. I am not suggesting that lack of continence (i.e., intemperance) is necessarily desirable. But neither is "self-control" the entire point of sexual love. Celibacy is not the ideal expression of marriage! Excessive worry about controlling the (sexual) body echoes the very Manichaean anxieties that John Paul II's discourses purport to overcome. If the main point about the sexual body is that it be controlled, we have scarcely moved to a positive valorization of the sexual body as a medium of divine activity.

More than that, language about "control" in sexual matters almost inevitably raises a political question: Whose body is being controlled by whom? It is appropriate to remember that Dante's *Inferno* assigned a deeper place in hell to the cold and the cruel masters of control than he did to the carnal and the lustful. Furthermore, from the evidence of recent history, it can be argued that more evil has been visited on humanity by various Hitlers and Stalins of sexless self-control than by the (quickly exhausted) epicures of the erotic. Recognition of the ways in which we suffer rather than steer our bodies is a beginning of wisdom.

Similarly, valuing the body beyond its willingness to be controlled should include some appreciation for the goodness of sexual pleasure — and, for that matter, any bodily pleasure. The lack of any such appreciation in the pope's discussions is striking, if not altogether surprising: approving of pleasure has never been popular among controllers. But pleasure is God's gift. A sadly neglected text pertinent to this subject is 1 Timothy 6:17, where Paul says that God supplies us all things richly for our enjoyment. In papal teaching, sexual passion and pleasure appear primarily as an obstacle to authentic love. But many of us have experienced sexual passion and pleasure as both humbling and liberating, a means through which our bodies know better and more quickly than our minds, choose better and faster than our reluctant wills, even get us to where God apparently wants us in a way our calculating minds never could.

Along the same lines, the pope might have found a good word to say about the sweetness of sexual love — also, I think, God's gift. Amid all the noble talk about self-donation and mutuality, we should occasionally add, "Plus, it feels good!" Come to think of it, why not, when speaking about sexual love, devote some meditation to the astonishing triumph of sexual fidelity in marriage? True faithfulness is the result of a delicate and attentive creativity between partners, not merely the automatic product of an individual's "self-control." In short, a more adequate theology of the sexual body would at least acknowledge the positive ways in which the body gifts us by "controlling" us.

As with pleasure, so also with pain. A theology of the body should recognize the ways in which human sexual existence is difficult. Honesty about ourselves requires recognition of how arduous and ambiguous a process it is for any of us to become mature sexually; how unstable and shifting are our patterns of sexual identity; how unpredictable and vagrant are our desires and cravings; how unexpected and hurtful are our times of revulsion and rejection. It demands appreciation for how little support there is for covenanted love in our world; how threatened sexual integrity is by the pansexualism of our culture; how much the stresses of life together — and apart — bear upon our capacity to express sexual love. John Paul II and his apologists seem to think that concupiscence is our biggest challenge. How many of us would welcome a dose of concupiscence — when the grinding realities of sickness and need have drained the body of all its sap and sweetness, just as a reminder of the joys of sentience!

I would welcome the honest recognition that, for many who are married, the pleasure and comfort of sexual love are most needed precisely when least available, not because of fertility rhythms, but because of sickness and anxiety and separation and loss. An adequate theology of the sexual body should address not only an imagined "original solitude" that is supposedly cured by marriage but also the very real "continuing solitude" of those — both married and single — whose vocation is not to celibacy, yet whose erotic desires find, for these and many other reasons, no legitimate or sanctified expression — and, in these papal conferences, neither recognition nor concern.

The pope fails to examine these and many other aspects of the body and of "human love in the divine plan." Instead, his theology of the body is reduced to sexuality, and sexuality to the "transmission of life." The descent to biologism is unavoidable. What is needed is a more generous appreciation of the way sexual energy pervades our interpersonal relationships and creativity — including the life of prayer! — and a fuller understanding of covenantal love as life-giving and life-sustaining in multiple forms of parenting, community-building, and world enhancement.

Revisiting *Humanae Vitae*

As even George Weigel acknowledges, John Paul II's "theology of the body" was actually a long and not entirely ingenuous defense of Paul VI's encyclical forbidding the use of artificial birth control. Paradoxically, it has actually served to remind anyone with historical memory of how truly flawed that earlier papal instrument was — and of how badly it is in need of a more thorough revisiting than John Paul's rehabilitative effort. Weigel terms *Humanae Vitae* a "pastoral and catechetical failure," as though the encyclical's deficiencies were merely those of tone or effective communication. But the encyclical suffers from substantive rather than stylistic defects. John Paul II's reflections on the Bible, indeed, can most plausibly be read as a massive effort to ground *Humanae Vitae* on a base broader and firmer than natural law, an implicit recognition of the argumentative inadequacy of Paul VI's encyclical. As I have already tried to show, the pope's biblical engagement itself appears less convincing because of its patent ideological interest in defending an earlier papal statement.

It would be a weary business to mount a full-scale reconsideration of Paul VI's encyclical. But since John Paul II himself takes it up and defends its logic, and since papal apologists insist that the Vatican's position on birth control is flawless, I think it's necessary to expose certain fundamental defects in its argument. When I speak of "artificial birth control," I will be referring solely to the use of a condom, diaphragm, or other mechanical device. This is because I have real reservations about chemical/hormonal interventions (such as "the pill"), not because of their legitimacy as conception-prevention but because of their possible effect on women's long-term health. I touch on five basic issues.

First, Paul VI's encyclical represents a regression in moral reasoning. It features a completely act-centered morality, and it ignores the important maturation in Catholic moral thinking leading up to and following Vatican II, which emphasizes a person's fundamental dispositions as more defining of moral character than isolated acts.[11] Specific acts are, to be

---

11. See, for example, L. Monden, SJ, *Sin, Liberty, and Law* (New York: Sheed and Ward, 1965).

sure, morally significant. But individual acts must always be placed within the context of a person's character as revealed in consistent patterns of response to God and world. The difference in perspective is critical. Both the encyclical and John Paul II insist that it is not enough for a married couple to be open to new life through their sexual activity; rather, *every act of intercourse* must also be open to procreation. They argue that the use of a contraceptive in any single act in effect nullifies any disposition of openness to conception.

This position is simply nonsensical. Do I cancel my personal and long-standing commitment to breathing by holding my breath for a time, or by undergoing anaesthesia when having surgery? Such individual acts of the stoppage of breathing do not nullify my dedication to breathing; they may, in fact, strengthen it. Understanding the overall pattern of moral dispositions is essential for the assessment of any individual act. A woman who kills an abusive husband in self-defense (or in defense of her children) does not thereby have the moral disposition of a "murderer." She has killed, but her moral commitment was to life. The papal focus on each act of sexual intercourse rather than on the persistent moral commitments of married couples profoundly distorts human reality, the kind of real-life experience that we all instinctively recognize as true.

Second, the arguments of Paul VI and John Paul II sacrifice logic to a rhetorical brinksmanship. When Paul VI, for example, equates birth control and abortion, he not only defies science, he also provokes the opposite result than the one he intended. He wants to elevate the seriousness of birth control by making it equivalent to abortion; but he actually helps trivialize the horror of abortion by categorizing it as a form of contraception. In a similar fashion, John Paul II recognizes, from one side of his mouth, two ends of sexual love, namely unitive intimacy and procreation. But from the other side of the mouth, he declares that if, in an act of intercourse, procreation is blocked, not only that end has been cancelled, but the end of unitive intimacy has as well. He has thereby, despite his protestations to the contrary, simply reduced the two ends to one. This can be demonstrated by applying his logic in reverse: Would we insist that an act of sexual intercourse that did not manifest unitive intimacy also cancel the procreative end of the act? The papal position could actually be read as approving as moral an act of intercourse within marriage that was coerced, even violently, so long as a contraceptive was not used.

Third, the position of the popes and their apologists continues to reveal the pervasive sexism that is ever more obvious within official Catholicism.[12] I noted earlier how John Paul II's reading of Scripture tended to reduce the moral agency of women within the marriage covenant and sexual relationships. The tendency becomes glaringly obvious in his argument that artificial contraception is wrong because it tends to "instrumentalize" women for men's pleasure by making the woman a passive object of passion rather than a partner in mutuality. Yet the pope's argument makes more experiential sense in reverse. Few things sound more "objectifying" than the statements of the Natural Family Planners, whose focus remains tightly fixed on biological processes rather than on emotional and spiritual communication through the body. The view that "openness to life" is preserved with moral integrity by abstaining from intercourse during fertile periods (arguably times of greatest female pleasure in making love) and is not served — and becomes morally reprehensible — by the mutual agreement to use a condom or diaphragm, would be laughable if it did not have such harmful consequences for so many married couples who have taken it seriously. And what could be more objectifying of women than speaking of birth control as though it were something that arose only from male concupiscence? How about women's moral agency in the realm of sexual behavior? All of us living in the world of real sexual bodies know that women have plenty of reasons of their own to be relieved of anxieties about pregnancy for a time and to be freed for sexual enjoyment purely for the sake of intimacy and even of celebration.

Fourth, the absolute prohibition of artificial birth control becomes increasingly scandalous in the face of massive medical realities. One might want to make the case that distributing condoms to teenagers as part of sex education is a mistake. But that case is based on misgivings concerning sex education in schools generally, combined with the pervasive atmosphere of sexual permissiveness among the young. But what about couples who can no longer have sexual relations because one of them has innocently been infected with HIV, when not using a condom means exposing one's partner to a potentially fatal virus? When does "openness to life" in every sexual act become a cover for "death-dealing"? Given the fact that, in Africa, AIDS affects tens of millions of men, women, and children (very many of them Christians), is the refusal to allow condom usage — leaving aside for the moment other medical interventions and changes in sexual mores — coming dangerously close to assisting in genocide? These are matters that demand the most careful consideration by the church — and the deepest compassion.

12. L. T. Johnson, "Sex, Women, and the Church," *Commonweal* 130 (2003): 11-17.

It is difficult to avoid the sense that the failed logic marshaled in the defense of "openness to life" is having just the opposite result. If the political enslavement of millions of Asians and Europeans led the papacy to combat the Soviet system in the name of truth and compassion, and if the enslavement and murder of millions of Jews led the papacy (at last) to renounce the anti-Semitism of the Christian tradition in the name of truth and compassion, should not the same commitment to truth and compassion lead at the very least to a reexamination of logic, when millions of Africans are enslaved and killed by a sexual pandemic?

Fifth and finally, shouldn't *Humanae Vitae* be revisited rather than simply defended for the same reasons that it was a "pastoral and catechetical" failure the first time around? It failed to convince most of its readers, not least because they knew that Paul VI issued his condemnation of artificial birth control against the recommendation of his own birth-control commission. His encyclical became, in Weigel's terms, a "new Galileo crisis," not simply because it pitted papal authority against science, but because the papal position was wrong both formally and substantively. It generated an unprecedented — and still unresolved — crisis for papal authority precisely because it was authority exercised not only apart from, but even in opposition to, the process of discernment. Sad to say, John Paul II's theology of the body, despite all its attention to (parts of) Scripture, reveals the same deep lack of interest in the ways the experience of married people, and especially women, might inform theology and the decision-making process of the church. If papal teaching showed signs of attentiveness to such experience, and a willingness to learn from God's work in the world as well as God's word in the tradition, its pronouncements would find greater receptivity. A theology of the body should at least have feet that touch the ground.

Another Direction

Since God is the Living One who continuously presses upon us at every moment of creation, calling us to obedience and inviting us to a painful yet joyous quest of wisdom, theology must learn to be an inductive art rather than a deductive science. Our reading of Scripture must indeed shape our perceptions of the world, but our understanding of Scripture must, in turn, be reshaped by our experience of God in our mortal bodies, in the fabric of our human freedom and in the cosmic play of God's freedom. Theology that takes the self-disclosure of God in human experience — in the bodies of actual women and men — with the same seriousness as it does God's revelation in Scripture does not turn its back on tradition, but recognizes that tradition must constantly be renewed by the powerful leading of the Holy Spirit if it is not to become a form of idolatry, a falsification of the Living God.

Theology so understood is, to be sure, a delicate and demanding conversation that, like sexual love itself, requires patience as well as passion. If we are ever to reach a better theological understanding of human love and sexuality, then we must, in all humility, be willing to learn from the bodies and the stories of those whose response to God and God's world involves sexual love — at least as much as we listen to the opinions of those who have removed themselves by choice from this dimension of bodily activity. That, at least, would be a good starting point. But if "theology of the body" is to be about more than sexuality — an elaborate way of saying that, within tightly defined limits, sex is good — then a more fundamental inquiry into Scripture and experience is required.

CHAPTER TWO

Scripture and the Body

Making Scripture the starting point for theological reflection, as John Paul II does in his *Theology of the Body*, is a natural instinct for Christians who are heirs to the Reformation, and one learned more recently by Catholic theologians. The instinct is sound for a number of reasons. First, the theologian can engage the wide variety of discourses found in Scripture, a range of expressions for the truth far richer and more complex than those offered by the doctrinal propositions of the creeds. Second, Scripture, in its various voices, bears testimony to the diverse works of the living God in the world with unparalleled directness and vividness. Third, Scripture is the necessary — the indispensable — source of knowledge for the specific ways in which God has gifted humans through the story of Israel and the ministry, death, and resurrection of Jesus Christ. Fourth, the symbols through which the Scripture interprets the story of Israel and the mystery of Christ provide the necessary and enduring symbolic framework for any subsequent interpretation of God's presence and power in the world that is specifically Christian. Humans continue to experience the presence and power of God, but they would not be able to recognize them as being of the Holy Spirit without the symbols made available to them by Scripture.

The problem with making Scripture the starting point for theology lies less with Scripture itself and more with how it is used. As I noted in my criticism of John Paul II, his reading of Scripture did not respect the complexity of the scriptural witness: he privileged the second creation account in Genesis rather than the first, for example, without providing either a sense of how these accounts differ or why he preferred one over the other. Even more significant, the pope drew anthropological — even ontological — conclusions from the creation narrative of Genesis 2, constructing an understanding of human nature "according to creation," but paid little attention to the witness of Paul about the effects of the resurrection that amount to a "new creation" (2 Cor. 5:17; Gal. 6:15).

In his discussion of the resurrection, Paul draws a sharp contrast between the "first Adam" and the "last Adam" who, through his exaltation to the right hand of God, became "life-giving spirit" (1 Cor. 15:45-49). The humanity represented by the first Adam is being re-created according to the image of the new Adam, Christ (Rom. 5:12-21; see also Eph. 4:24, Col. 3:10); consequently, just as humans have borne the image of the first Adam, so shall they bear the image of the last Adam (1 Cor. 15:49). Paul himself does not show how all this can be, and he struggles with the implications of the new creation when it collides with the first, not least in matters of gender (as his tortured discussion in 1 Cor. 11:3-16 indicates). The scriptural witness, in short, is complex rather than simple, raises as many questions as it provides answers for. But the pope does not even acknowledge the tensions created by these passages in Paul. Like many other theologians, he does not admit that his ability to find clear answers in the Bible depends a great deal on being carefully selective in what he reads.

John Paul II's practice in reading Scripture falls into another familiar and unfortunate pattern, whereby he offers the texts of Scripture as support for theological positions without the texts themselves being interrogated in their historical and literary contexts. I do not suggest that a complete historical and literary analysis is required before any passage of Scripture can enter into a theological discussion; but neither can the difficulty and complexity of scriptural passages be ignored. The pope is not alone in acting as though Scripture offers a set of clear answers; in fact, for those who read carefully, it presents an array of tangled questions. The texts of the Old and New Testament are not easy to understand. The deepest insights offered by Scripture are often discovered through the arduous process of working through the difficulties they present. When passages of Scripture are never actually read but merely cited, Scripture is not fully honored.

Such tendencies arise from the failure to take seriously enough the dialectical character of Scripture and experience — at two levels. First, Scripture is read as a finished product rather than as witness to a dynamic process of interpretation carried out by believers within Israel and the early church. The impetus to write was given by the experience of God in the world, and the writings of the Old and New Testament give testimony, first of all, not to a set of static and systematic truths about reality but to the time-conditioned efforts of humans across the centuries to express the meaning of what God was up to in their lives. Because such interpretations of experience were carried out by diverse persons in diverse circumstances, and in response to different experiences — conquest is not the same as exile, suffering not the same as exaltation — the witness of Scripture is necessarily complex and heterogeneous. When the dynamic process of Scripture's coming into being is ignored, the true character of Scripture is missed.

But the dialectic with the experience of God in the present is also neglected when the texts of Scripture are arranged into a set of propositions to form a doctrine, and then that doctrine is elaborated into a set of prescriptions for human behavior without giving any attention to the ways in which God is presently at work among God's people; when that happens, a potentially idolatrous use of Scripture is at work. Scripture is made not merely necessary but also sufficient for theology, and this it cannot be, for the function of the interpretations offered by Scripture is to enable the continuing perception and interpretation of God's activity here and now. Scripture has been reduced to a storehouse of propositions from which deductions can be made, rather than a collection of witnesses that also enable believers to witness to God's work and glorify God's presence among them.

This chapter, then, seeks to restore Scripture to its proper role in revelation, and thus in theology. I begin by considering more fully what I have termed the dialectic of Scripture and experience, leading to the conclusion that Scripture is best understood, not as containing revelation, but as participating in revelation. Then I argue that, when read as a whole, Scripture does not point to itself as the locus of revelation, but points readers instead to the human body as the preeminent place of God's self-disclosure. Finally, I show how complex the witness of Scripture itself is concerning the body via a close consideration of Paul's language in 1 Corinthians, language that invites consideration not simply of the words he uses but the realities to which his words point.

Scripture and Experience

The canonization of Scripture — a process that began with the first circulation of New Testament compositions and reached its effective completion by the third century — proved to be both blessing and bane to theology. It was a blessing because the authoritative list of compositions from the Jewish scriptures and the early Christian movement helped define Christianity both with respect to the writings of Judaism and to the various heretical writings that challenged the primacy of the apostolic tradition. The establishment of the canon was critical to the shaping of a catholic sense of the church, since Christians, turning away from the vagaries offered by newly forged compositions, became readers not only of Johannine or Pauline writings, but of both together and in conversation; not only of Matthew's version of the gospel, but of Mark's and Luke's and John's as well.[1]

The creation of "the Bible" as a single book was the creation of a vast intertextual world extending from the account of the first creation in Genesis to the climax of the new creation in Revelation, and it enabled Christian thinkers to imagine the world imagined by all these writings in a more comprehensive and coherent way.[2] A truly "Christian" theology thus became possible on the basis of a stable collection of books that could mediate the same textual identity through every future generation of the church. This is an inestimably great blessing, and one never to be renounced.

The bane of canonization, however, is no less real than the blessing. When the canon of Scripture was not simply a list of discrete compositions to be read in the assembly, but now an anthology gathered into a single volume with a fixed "canonical order" of compositions set within covers, perceptions of the canon inevitably changed as well. The Bible appears as a holy book set apart from other codices because of its special liturgical and catechetical functions. It is holy not only by function but by nature: Scripture is universally understood to be inspired by God. The divine inspiration of all the writings of the Old and New Testaments not only provides the ultimate warrant for the authority of Scripture, but naturally tends to the perception that all of Scripture has but a single, divine author. It is "God's Word." The more the Bible is perceived as the word of God through divine inspiration, the less significant the identity, historical situation, and experiences of the human authors become. The writings appear less the result of an interpretive process by humans in the past than a divinely guided recitation of divine actions.[3]

---

1. See L. T. Johnson, *The Writings of the New Testament: An Interpretation,* 3rd ed. (Minneapolis: Fortress, 2010), pp. 525-42.

2. See N. Frye, *The Great Code: The Bible and Literature* (San Diego: Harcourt Brace Jovanovich, 1983); see also L. T. Johnson, "Imagining the World That Scripture Imagines," in L. T. Johnson and W. S. Kurz, *The Future of Catholic Biblical Scholarship* (Grand Rapids: Eerdmans, 2002), pp. 119-42.

3. See L. T. Johnson, "Rejoining a Long Conversation," in Johnson and Kurz, *The Future of Catholic Biblical Scholarship,* pp. 35-64.

Human Experience and the Composition of Scripture

The way to remedy this static — and in some ways alienating — under-standing of revelation-in-Scripture is not by way of denying divine inspi-ration or by rejecting canonization. It lies rather in restoring a sense of the canon as a collection of discrete compositions rather than as chapters of a book that have been arranged by editors into a single volume, and in recovering an appreciation for the human process of composing those discrete writings through which God's Holy Spirit speaks. The best way forward is to observe how the texts of Scripture arose in the first place out of experiences of God in the body, and gave expression to such experiences of God. We can see the process at work first in the compositions of the Old Testament.

The process is less evident in the narratives about Israel's past, or in the laws, or in the Wisdom writings. The evidence of experience is not lacking in such historical narratives: think of Abraham's vision in Genesis 15:12-16 or Moses' ascent into the presence of the Lord in Exodus 24:9-11. But in these narratives the personal experiences of God have been thoroughly integrated into larger storytelling purposes. The Laws and the Wisdom lit-erature, in turn, are plainly prescriptive: whatever experiences and behav-iors stimulated their production, their entire point is to shape experience and behavior. It is above all in the Old Testament poetic literature — the Psalms and the Prophets — that we see how the texts of Scripture arise from and express human experience in the body.

Some of Israel's psalms are straightforwardly didactic (see Pss. 1, 19, 119), while others, like the narrative books, recount the works of God for Israel in the past in the expectation of experiencing such visitation again in the future (see Pss. 78, 95, 96, 103, 104, 105, 106), while still others display a connection with the royal court (see Pss. 2, 24, 30, 45, 110) and the worship in the temple (see Pss. 121-135). In such psalms, the element of personal experience is muted or conveyed through the experience of the entire people. In many other psalms, however, the first-person ("I") emerges as the singer, bringing to expression a remarkable range of deeply personal experiences. These are not crude outpourings of feeling. The psalms clearly follow the patterns of set literary genres for thanksgiving and petition and lament. But to say that experience has been given literary shape is simply another way of acknowledging that it is experience that is being shaped.

In fact, the "I" of these psalms is a powerful and vibrant presence. Readers through the centuries have been able to identify themselves with the singer of these psalms precisely because he speaks so truly about a God-intoxicated life: when he makes lament or complaint, it is because enemies or circumstances have somehow separated him from a sense of the Lord's presence (see Pss. 6:6; 10:1; 13:1-2; 22:1-18; 32:3-4; 38:1-22; 55:1-7; 69:1-36; 88:1-18; 120:1-7; 130:1-4; 142:1-7; 143:1-12); when he makes petition, it is because he seeks from God what only God can give (see Pss. 6:2; 12:1; 16:1-2; 17:1-2; 22:19; 25:16; 26:1, 9-10; 28:1-2; 39:12-13; 43:1-5; 51:1-5; 54:1-7; 61:1-2; 71:1-21); when he expresses hope or trust (17:15; 25:1-2; 27:1-3, 13; 39:7-11; 52:8-9; 56:10-11; 62:1-12; 131:3), or thanksgiving (7:17; 9:1; 13:6; 18:49-50; 22:22-24; 57:7-11; 59:16-17; 69:30-33; 71:22-24; 138:1-8), it is because the Lord has already shown salvation to him in his life (3:5-7; 4:1, 8; 6:8-9; 9:13; 16:8; 18:6-19, 32-46; 23:1-4; 28:6-7; 30:1-3, 11-12; 31:21-22; 34:4; 40:1-3; 66:13-20; 116:1-19). The psalmist gives expression to his joy (16:5-6, 9; 33:1-3) and wonder (8:3-4; 27:4) and bursts into praise of the Lord (30:1-3; 100:1-5; 111:1; 117:1-2; 145:1-21). Above all, the psalmist provides vivid glimpses of a life dedicated to seeking the Lord and in turn being sought by him (27:8; 63:1-8; 69:9; 71:6; 73:23-28; 77:3-6; 84:1-2; 119:20; 121:1-2; 130:5-6; 137:5-6; 139:1-18). The psalms are composed and sung for a variety of reasons and in a variety of forms, but certainly the need to give expression to the experience of life before God — both positive and negative — is an obvious reason for their composition that extends across all the forms.

The prophetic books provide particularly impressive evidence that the experience of God generated the oracles that eventually were gathered and written in the names of individual prophets. Like the Psalms, the prophetic writings are literarily shaped, at least at the level of the individual oracles; they are not artless outpourings but rhetorical instruments. The prophets themselves, moreover, were figures active in the public life of Israel: they offered counsel, encouragement, and condemnation of the social and political practices in the time of the monarchy and restoration. Their visions and oracles represented "readings" at public events and dispositions in light of what they "read" as God's vision for humans in covenant with the Lord.

What distinguishes the classical prophets above all, however, is that they spoke not out of a designated office or official position, nor even out of their own volition, but out of the impulse given by an experience of a call by God (Isa. 6:1-13; Jer. 1:4-10; Ezek. 1:4–3:4; Hosea 1:2–3:5). As Amos memorably responded to an opponent who regarded him as one temple prophet among others, "I am no prophet, nor a prophet's son; but I am

41

a herdsman and dresser of sycamore trees, and the Lord took me from following the flock, and the Lord said to me, 'Go, prophesy to my people Israel'" (Amos 7:14-15). Even when using a set formula, the prophets insist that their vision for Israel comes not from their own cunning but from a word provided by the Lord (see Obad. 1:1; Mic. 1:1; Nah. 1:1; Hab. 1:1; Zeph. 1:1; Hag. 1:1-3; Zech. 1:1, 7). In a number of the prophetic texts, as well, the personal experience of the prophet appears to form both the stimulus and the symbolic basis for the word that is spoken to the people (see Isa. 8:1-4, 16-17; 38:1–39:8; Hosea 1:2–3:5; Jer. 7:1-20; 12:1-4; 13:1-11; 15:10-21; 16:1-9; 17:14-18; 18:1-23; 20:1-18; 25:15-29; Ezek. 4:1-7; 5:1-12; 8:1–9:11; 12:1-21; 24:15-27). The combination of the experience of the prophet and the prophet's perception of what the Living God is doing now and will do in the future both to reward and to punish through his visitation of the people, makes the prophetic texts of the Old Testament a powerful witness to the ongoing work of God in human bodies. And it is out of such witness that the writings of the Old Testament were composed and collected.

The role of experience in generating the compositions of the New Testament is even more obvious. In the New Testament, the precise kind of experiences and convictions that shaped the writings can be confidently identified through comparison to other first-century Jewish compositions. As in other Jewish writings, the symbolic world of Torah — the writings of Scripture — is vigorously engaged. But just as the experience of Diaspora and exposure to Greek philosophy gave the interpretations of Scripture carried out by Philo of Alexandria a philosophical bent, and just as the experience of alienation from other Palestinian Jews gave the interpretations of the Scripture carried out by the Dead Sea community a sectarian turn, so do the writings of the New Testament reveal how the texts of Torah were reshaped because of the foundational experiences of this religious movement and — to a lesser extent — the continuing experiences of believers within Christian communities. If the New Testament can legitimately be called a form of Jewish literature of the first century — being composed by Jews who are committed to Judaism — it is a Jewish literature in which the symbols of Torah have been fundamentally altered because of the experience of the crucified and raised Messiah Jesus, and the experience of God's Holy Spirit among Jesus' followers.[4]

The narrative writings of the New Testament, the four Gospels and the

4. For this argument, see Johnson, *The Writings of the New Testament: An Interpretation*, pp. 95-135.

Acts of the Apostles, are like the historical books of the Old Testament in the way that they report "signs and wonders" in the ministry of Jesus and in the beginnings of the Christian movement, and in the way they use the texts of Torah, sometimes as proofs, sometimes as literary antecedents, in these narrative accounts. But of greater interest are the passion accounts of the four Gospels, which are the literary residue of a complex process of interpretation extending from the cognitive dissonance posed by the impossibility (according to Torah) of a crucified messiah who is proclaimed as living Lord — with the cross being the "stumbling block" to both Jews and Gentiles for believing such a proclamation (1 Cor. 1:18-25) — to the portrayal of Jesus' suffering and death as one in fulfillment of Torah. If that cognitive dissonance had not been experienced by believers, then there would have been no need to engage in a rereading of Scripture, and no need to compose narratives that showed Jesus to be not the contradiction but the fulfillment of Scripture.

But the role of experience is more directly attested in the writings that more closely correspond to the Psalms and the Prophets in the Old Testament, namely, the book of Revelation and the Epistles. As in the Old Testament poetic compositions that arise out of religious experience and testify to the presence of God in the here and now of the pious Jew, so do these New Testament writings arise out of and seek to interpret the powerful experiences connected to presence of the Holy Spirit among those believing in a crucified and exalted messiah whom they call "Lord" (1 Cor. 12:3; Phil. 2:11; Rom. 10:9; Acts 2:36).

Although Revelation employs the standard elements of apocalyptic literature, it also distends the genre in important ways: the vision of the seer is not of a hero of the distant past, so that the composition is pseudonymous, but is claimed to be experienced by the contemporary John, "who shares with you in Jesus the tribulation and the kingdom and the patient endurance" (Rev. 1:9). The composition contains letters from the risen Lord to the seven churches of Asia, engaging the issues of conflict and corruption in the respective communities (2:1–3:22); the visions incorporate the experiences of those who are marginalized and oppressed by the dominant society and even martyred by the empire (17:1–18:24). Most of all, the cosmic conflict being worked out among the actions of humans (a common motif of apocalyptic literature) is altered by the sovereign power of God exercised through the "lamb who was slain," yet who stands by the throne of God, Jesus the Lord (5:1-14).

Paul's letters are instruments of persuasion, rhetorically crafted to turn his readers to share certain convictions and behaviors consonant with "the mind of Christ" (1 Cor. 2:16). By no means are his letters — or those of Peter, James, John, Jude, and the anonymous author of Hebrews — artless displays of emotion; they are carefully constructed arguments. Paul's letters nevertheless provide the clearest New Testament evidence that specific experiences in the body lay behind and stimulated composition. Nowhere is this clearer than in Paul's Corinthian correspondence. These letters give us an unparalleled glimpse into the actual lives of the first urban Christians: their rivalries and conflicts (1 Cor. 1:11-13; 2 Cor. 10:1–11:33), their disagreements concerning what to eat (1 Cor. 8:1-13; 10:14-33), how to dress (1 Cor. 11:3-16), how to worship (1 Cor. 11:17-33), and how to be sexual creatures (1 Cor. 7:1-40); disagreements about the disposition of possessions (2 Cor. 8:8-21; 11:7-11), disagreements so profound as to threaten the stability of the community (1 Cor. 6:1-8; 2 Cor. 11:1-6). Interpreting the Corinthian letters is impossible without a serious attempt to grasp the nature of the all-too-human experiences they address.

But Paul addresses the community's problems out of a premise that is equally experiential. He not only speaks of himself as working powerful deeds (2 Cor. 12:12), having visions (1 Cor. 9:1; 15:8; 2 Cor. 12:1-5), hearing God's word (2 Cor. 12:9), speaking in tongues and prophesying (1 Cor. 14:18), he takes it as axiomatic that such experiences are shared by his readers as well (1 Cor. 1:5; 11:3-16; 12:4-11; 14:26-33). More than this: Paul speaks of his Corinthian readers as powerfully under the influence of the Holy Spirit that has been poured out on them through the exaltation of Jesus as Lord, the crucified Messiah who has now become "life-giving Spirit" (1 Cor. 15:45). The community as a whole has "been given to drink" this Spirit and as a result has become "the body of Christ" (1 Cor. 12:12-13). This Holy Spirit both energizes and elevates the individual bodies of the Corinthian believers, whose challenge is to direct those powerful energies in ways that build up the community as Christ's body (1 Cor. 2:6-16; 8:1-2; 10:31–11:1; 13:1-13; 14:18-19). In the case of the Corinthian community and correspondence, indeed, it can be said that unless such a powerful experiential energy field was at work, the specific problems of how to live within it would not have arisen or needed to be addressed.[5]

The very existence of the writings we call the New Testament is inexplicable apart from the premise that "something happened" in the lives

---

5. For the argument here, see L. T. Johnson, *Religious Experience in Earliest Christianity: A Missing Element in New Testament Studies* (Minneapolis: Fortress, 1998), esp. pp. 1-37.

of first-century Mediterranean Jews and Gentiles that forced them to dramatically reconfigure the symbols they had inherited. The New Testament stands as primary support for the proposition that Scripture arises out of the experience of God in the world and the need to interpret that experience. The Old and New Testaments do not construct a philosophy of life built on rational premises; they testify to the presence of the Living God in human existence that challenges all rational premises. Only when the canonical writings are freed from their bindings as book and can be engaged in all their diversity of historical setting, genre, perspective, and experience of life can "Scripture" be liberated to play its appropriate role, not as the container of revelation but as a participant in the process of revelation.

Scripture and the Interpretation of Human Experience

The clear testimony of Scripture in both the Old and New Testament is that "the One with whom we have to do" (Heb. 4:13) is a Living God whose work in the world among humans never ceases and often surprises. To deny that God continues to be powerfully present and active in the lives of humans today is to make a liar of Scripture itself. No Christian today would actually want to deny God's continuing presence and power. The issue is whether such divine activity in the present can be considered revelatory.

On this point, those who want Scripture to be not only necessary but also sufficient for theology would argue that Scripture serves as a nonnormed norm for claims to divine activity among humans today, that human experience can be affirmed only if it confirms what Scripture has said, only if it conforms to what we already know about God from Scripture. This posture does not deny that God is at work, but refuses to acknowledge that God can work in the present in a way that challenges our understanding of Scripture. God's activity in the world today is constrained not only by what God has done in the past but even more stringently by our present interpretation of how Scripture spoke of what God did in the past. God's "fidelity" is consequently understood as consistency and even predictability. Taken to an extreme, this position not only makes a liar of Scripture but makes God captive to human understanding, which is another way of speaking about idolatry.

A position more faithful to the witness of Scripture itself recognizes the absolute necessity of reading Scripture as a norm for revelation, but also asserts the equal necessity of reading human experience, in the conviction that the normative status of Scripture is itself relative to the work of the Living God in the world. Scripture as a whole and in all its parts constructs a vision of reality and invites readers to imagine the world that it imagines. The world of Scripture is one that is created anew at every moment by the Living God and that is answerable to God at every moment; it is a world in which God acts intimately and graciously within creation, above all within the freedom of those created according to the image of God; it is a world in which God acts in new and surprising ways, sending a prophet who reverses the standards of status-conscious societies, raising a crucified messiah from the dead, summoning a persecutor to be an apostle, embracing the godless Gentiles as part of God's holy people. Reading Scripture in the assembly, learning it through the sacraments, hearing it proclaimed through preaching, studying it together and meditating on its words — all these modes of shaping the minds and hearts (and practices) of believers are indispensable for them to perceive the world and their experience within it as God's world and work. This formative function of Scripture can scarcely be overstated.[6]

But if Scripture forms the minds of the faithful to perceive the work of God in the world, then Scripture's formative function falls short if attention is never turned to actual human experience in the world, and attention is given exclusively to the word spoken in Scripture rather than also to the word that is being spoken in and through human experience. If only the texts of Scripture are subject to exegesis and the experiences and stories of the human beings of which Scripture speaks are never subject to exegesis, then Scripture's capacity to reveal God's world has been truncated. The second necessary moment in the dialectic of revelation, then, is precisely the discernment of what God might be up to in the tangle of human freedom here and now. The question "what is God up to?" must always be an open one, for Scripture itself invites us to see the Living God as not only always active but capable of acting in ways that are new to human perception.

Sometimes the perception of God's activity through the lens of Scripture appears as "new" only in the sense that it is active and living. Much of human experience does not challenge the symbolic world of Scripture but confirms it: God works for the salvation and sanctification of people in ways that are immediately recognizable as being according to the mind

---

6. See L. T. Johnson, "The Bible's Authority for and in the Church," in *Engaging Biblical Authority,* ed. W. P. Brown (Philadelphia: Westminster John Knox, 2007), pp. 62-72.

of Christ. Similarly, some human dispositions and behaviors are perceived at once as contrary to the spirit of holiness and as the expression of human rebellion and sin. Such moments, both positive and negative, both sanctifying and sinful, can rightly be called "revelatory" because the work of God in the bodies of humans makes manifest in the world the Spirit of God (and the resistance to that Spirit) of which Scripture speaks. Humans do not learn something "new" about Scripture or even about God in such revelatory moments, except that the work of God is ever new and renewing.

There are other times, however, when human experience in the world does not so neatly conform to the present human understanding of what Scripture says, when the fit between the world imagined by Scripture and the world experienced in the body is not in the least obvious. In such cases, careful attention to experience is critical, for faith demands an openness to the possibility that God may indeed be up to something truly new, that God's fidelity to God's self is not the same as our human assumption that God must act in an obvious fashion according to scriptural precedent.

The New Testament, in particular, provides us with examples of how God's new action in the world challenged prior understandings of Scripture. First-century Jewish expectation of a Messiah varied, but nowhere did it have a place for a Messiah who would be executed as one "cursed by God" (Deut. 21:23; Gal. 3:13). Yet God seems to have provided just such a Messiah in Jesus. The prophets had envisioned the nations as coming to Zion, and Gentile proselytes were welcome to join the Jewish nation; yet nowhere in Scripture was there any precedent for Gentiles being accepted into the people without being circumcised and observing the law of Moses. Yet the Holy Spirit seemed to be inviting just such Gentiles into the nascent Christian movement.

One of the great gifts of the New Testament — one of the ways it is "revelatory" for Christians today — is that it also shows us in the very process of composition, as well as by narrative description, how "believers" who are open to the new things God is doing — God's "new creation" in Christ — begin with those experiences and reinterpret Scripture in light of them. The experience of a crucified yet exalted Messiah reveals new meanings in the Prophets and the Psalms that enable Christians to see that, at a deeper level than they had formerly understood, this new manifestation of God in a crucified Messiah was not contrary to but "according to Scripture" (1 Cor. 15:3-4).

The experience of Gentiles being filled with the Holy Spirit (manifested by speaking in tongues and prophesying, Acts 10:44-48) led the apostles to understand that the prophecy of Joel about the Spirit being poured out "on all flesh" in the last days (Acts 2:14-21) really did point to the inclusion of the Gentiles (Acts 11:18) and enabled James to interpret the prophet Amos in a way no other Jewish interpreter would ever have thought of doing, namely as predicting just such an embrace of the nations, declaring not that "this thing agrees with the prophets," but that "the prophets agree with this thing" (Acts 15:12-21). It is the new experience that opens up new perceptions of God's possibilities and the possible meanings of Scripture as well.[7] By such reinterpretations, believers were not in the least disloyal to Scripture; they only were loyal first of all to the Living God.

Especially in the Gospel of John, the New Testament also provides examples of those who refuse to perceive God's present work in the world because they have committed themselves to their own previous understanding of what Scripture would allow God to do; the most poignant case is that of the Pharisees, who refuse to acknowledge that Jesus healed the man born blind because such an experience did not fit what they "knew" from Moses, and whom Jesus therefore condemned (John 9:24-41). Here is a clear case in which Scripture itself shows us the peril of denying "God's work being revealed" in the healing of a human body (9:3) because of presuppositions concerning the possibility of God's working in a man "steeped in sin" (9:34).[8]

Throughout the history of Christianity, however much theologians might wish it otherwise, experience has continued to challenge prior understandings of Scripture. But because experience has rarely if ever been explicitly recognized as a legitimate and even necessary component in theology, recognition of its role has often come too late and, as a consequence, caused much unnecessary suffering. From the time Constantine made the cross of Christ a banner for battle, through the Crusades, to the savage wars of religion in Europe, for example, Christians have found the basis for a Holy War in Scripture; but the tragic lessons of war from the seventeenth to the twentieth centuries have wiped out all romantic illusions concerning the practice of war, and have rendered the supposed scriptural warrants for Holy War unpersuasive.[9]

---

7. For the argument, see L. T. Johnson, *Scripture and Discernment: Decision Making in the Church* (Nashville: Abingdon, 1996).

8. L. T. Johnson, "Homosexuality and the Church: Scripture and Experience," *Commonweal* 134 (2007): 14-17.

9. See H. A. Heath et al., eds., *Holy War in the Bible: Christian Morality and an Old Testament Problem* (Downers Grove, IL: InterVarsity, 2014).

For an equally long period of the church's existence, Christians justified their hostile and sometimes murderous behavior toward Jews on the basis of the New Testament's characterization of them; only the moral revulsion at the experience of the Holocaust in the twentieth century has made most Christians seek a way of neutralizing that dangerous legacy.[10] At least since the sixteenth century, Christians used biblical notions concerning election and mission and dominion over the earth to legitimate practices that supported colonialism, crushed indigenous cultures, and exploited the resources of the earth. Only the realization of the massive injury done to persons, cultures, and the earth itself has stimulated a re-reading of those scriptural justifications. The symbol of election is now read more in terms of service to the world rather than separation from the world; likewise, mission is understood not in terms of expanding the reach of European culture but in terms of witness to the good news; and the command to exercise dominion is interpreted as faithful stewardship rather than as exploitation.[11] The biblical symbols are not abandoned; indeed, they can be asserted with great vigor. But their meaning has changed in the light of hard experience.

Christians held slaves for many centuries and could argue persuasively that the majority of evidence in Scripture allowed such a practice. In the pre–Civil War South, in fact, debates between slaveholders and abolitionists often cited Scripture, and at the exegetical level, the slaveholders could claim victory: it is impossible to find an unequivocal condemnation of slavery in the Bible, and possible to find many texts that can be used in support of human bondage. Yet among Christians today — especially among those whose families were never enslaved — those many texts of Scripture are scarcely seen, and are certainly not regarded as normative.[12]

It was not exegesis of Scripture that created such a change of perception. It was the massive and tragic experience of slavery brought home to human consciousness, bringing with it the recognition of slaves not as

10. See L. T. Johnson, "The New Testament's Anti-Jewish Slander and the Conventions of Ancient Polemic," *Journal of Biblical Literature* 108 (1989): 419-41; see also Johnson, "Christians and Jews: Starting Over," *Commonweal* 130 (2003): 15-19; R. B. Hays, *The Moral Vision of the New Testament* (San Francisco: HarperSanFrancisco, 1996), pp. 407-43.

11. L. T. Johnson, "Caring for the Earth: Why Environmentalism Needs Theology," *Commonweal* 132 (2005): 16-20.

12. See H. Avalos, *Slavery, Abolitionism and the Ethics of Biblical Scholarship* (Sheffield: Sheffield Phoenix Press, 2011).

property but as persons, and with that belated recognition, the realization that no matter what Scripture says, owning persons cannot be compatible with the mind of Christ. Texts that formerly held only a marginal place, such as Galatians 3:28 — in Christ there is neither slave nor free — now are taken to be normative for Christian identity, while the texts that tell slaves to be obedient to their masters are put into a secondary and non-normative status.

In similar fashion, the worldwide experience of women and men in recent centuries has led to a radical critique of the patriarchal structures and systems of society — structures and systems, once more, that had found support in the patriarchal and sometimes even sexist texts of Scripture. An appreciation not only of the full humanity of women but of their full equality to males in every important aspect of being human has led to the emancipation — always partial, to be sure — of women from being defined solely in terms of biological roles or according to male expectations.[13] Such experience-driven realizations and reforms, in turn, have led believers to reconsider the patriarchal bias of Scripture, to recover texts of Scripture that point to the liberation of females, and to work for the reform of sexist perceptions and practices within churches.[14] Sadly, those who most loudly trumpet the sufficiency of Scripture often prove also to be the most resistant to such desperately needed reforms.

Rereading and reinterpreting Scripture in the light of human experience that at first appears to be dissonant with Scripture — finding texts that formerly were not seen, discovering new dimensions of commonly read passages, relativizing those texts that do not accord with God's new work — is not a form of disloyalty to Scripture. To the contrary, it is loyalty of the highest sort, for it is driven by the conviction that Scripture truly is God-inspired, truly does speak God's word to humans, when it is passionately and patiently engaged by those listening for God's word as well in human experience. But neither are these new readings and understandings of Scripture ultimate; they also are subject to revision in light of what God's Holy Spirit is doing among human bodies in the world.

---

13. See S. Ruth, *Issues in Feminism: An Introduction,* 5th ed. (Houston: Mayfield Publishing, 2000); B. Hooks, *Feminist Theory: From Margin to Center* (Cambridge, MA: SouthEnd Press, 2000).

14. For example, R. S. Chopp, *The Power to Speak: Feminism, Language, God* (Eugene, OR: Wipf and Stock, 2002); *Saving Work: Feminist Practices of Theological Education* (Philadelphia: Westminster John Knox, 1995).

Scripture Points to the Body as Revelatory

The Christian Bible is distinctive among the world's religious literatures for two reasons. The first is that the compositions of the Old and New Testaments draw scarcely any attention to themselves as revelatory. When compared to the Upanishads, the Hermetic Literature, or the Qur'an, for example, Scripture does not point to its texts as the Word of God or as the source of divine self-disclosure. The second is that Scripture consistently points to humans as the medium of revelation. This is not a matter simply of Scripture explicitly acknowledging its human authorship, or of expressing human experience within the compositions themselves. It is a matter, from beginning to end, of locating the arena of divine activity squarely in the bodily experience of its characters.[15]

Body as Symbol: Body Language

Despite the diversity found in the texts of Scripture, they everywhere agree that humans are symbolic creatures whose dispositions are expressed in the language of the body. As we read the narratives of the Old Testament, we see over and over how the characters place their bodies in statement, assertion, question, protest, or plea, and how a posture, a garment, a stick, or a sword, can extend self-expression through the body. When Adam and Eve heard the sound of the Lord God walking in the cool of the evening, they hid in the trees: "I heard the sound of thee in the garden, and I was afraid, because I was naked; and I hid myself" (Gen. 3:8-10). Before the three men who appeared before his tent, Abraham bowed to the earth (Gen. 18:2), and had his servant swear an oath by putting his hand "under Abraham's thigh" (Gen. 24:9).

To signify which of his sons would be the greater, Jacob crossed his right and left hands when laying them on the heads of Manasseh and Ephraim (Gen. 48:14). Moses stretched out his hand over the sea so the people could cross through (Exod. 14:21), held out his arm during the battle with Amalek (Exod. 17:11), and struck the rock with his rod (Num. 20:11). Joshua commanded the men of Israel to put their feet upon the

---

15. For the argument in this section, see L. T. Johnson, "Revelatory Body: Notes Toward a Somatic Theology," in *The Phenomenology of the Body,* ed. D. J. Martino (Pittsburgh: Simon Silverman Phenomenology Center at the University of Duquesne, 2003), pp. 69-85.

necks of the five kings they had captured, saying, "thus the Lord will do to all your enemies against whom you fight" (Josh. 10:24-25). In each of these instances — and there are many more — the bodily stance or gesture expresses something of larger significance. Similarly, the Levite whose concubine was raped and murdered by the men of Gibeah cut her body into twelve pieces and sent them among the tribes as a call to vengeance (Judg 19:29). Samuel tore the robe of Saul, declaring, "The Lord has torn the kingdom of Israel from you this day" (1 Sam. 15:27-28). Ahijah tore his own garments into twelve pieces and gave ten to Jeroboam — to signify the division of the kingdom (1 Kings 11:30-31).

As mentioned earlier, the prophets also used body language to express their message to Israel. Jeremiah buried a soiled waistband by the bank of the Euphrates, and when he dug it up spoiled, declared, "Thus says the Lord, 'Even so will I spoil the pride of Judah and the great pride of Jerusalem'" (Jer. 13:1-9). When the city of Jerusalem was under siege by the Chaldeans, Jeremiah bought a field in Anathoth and announced solemnly, "Thus says the Lord of Hosts, the God of Israel: 'Houses and fields and vineyards shall again be bought in this land'" (Jer. 32:6-15). The prophet Ezekiel lay on his side bound with cords before a model of a besieged Jerusalem; he ate the food of fasting; he cut his hair in batches, burning some, striking some with the sword, and scattering some to the wind; he thus expressed with his body the disaster befalling the city (Ezek. 4:1–5:12). Ezekiel also clapped his hands and stamped his foot, crying, "Alas! because of all the evil abominations of the House of Israel" (Ezek. 6:11). Ezekiel presented his body to the people as an expression of God's word: "I am a sign for you" (Ezek. 12:11). So also had the prophet Hosea spoken God's word with his body when he took a harlot to be his wife, "for the land commits great harlotry by forsaking the Lord" (Hosea 1:2).

Such body language is equally attested in the New Testament: Jesus touched the ears and tongue of the deaf-mute man (Mark 7:33); he touched the eyes of the blind man with spittle (Mark 8:22-26). He made the leper clean through a touch (Mark 1:41); he laid his hands on many who had diseases and unclean spirits (Luke 4:40; 6:18). He raised the dead man by touching him (Luke 7:14) and straightened the bent women with a touch (Luke 13:13). He ate with tax collectors and sinners (Luke 5:30), held little children in his arms (Mark 10:16), multiplied loaves and fish for the multitude (Mark 8:1-9), and at his last meal with his disciples, "took bread, and blessed, and broke it, and gave it to them and said, 'Take, this is my body'" (Mark 14:22). This Jesus spoke of raising a destroyed temple in three days, speaking, as the evangelist notes, "of the temple of his body" (John 2:19-21). All these bodily gestures express that God's rule is present (Luke 11:20), that God is visiting his people (7:16), and, in John's terms, that the Word was made flesh (John 1:14).

Creation, Covenant, Christ, Church

Scripture's use of body language urges us to think more constructively about what Scripture suggests about human bodies generally in connection with knowing the world and knowing God — that is, what it has to say about human bodies as medium of revelation — by considering in turn creation, covenant, incarnation, and church. My brief reflections on these topics could be expanded, and some will be, as my argument unfolds. For the moment, my goal is to establish the position of Scripture toward the body.

The first place to look for the understanding of *creation* in Scripture is not the beginning of Genesis, but throughout the Psalms and Prophets. In the Psalms above all, God's creation of the world is new every day (see Pss. 29:2-11; 65:9-13; 104:1-35; 139:1-18) and the premise for God's acting to save individuals and the people in the present (see Pss. 18:7-15; 33:6-9; 74:12-17; 77:16-20; 78:1-31; 107:33-43; 113:7-9). Creation is not an event of the past, the first in a series of events making up history, but the ever-present bringing into being of all that is — at every moment. Theologically, then, "the world" is everything that is now being brought into being by an unseen power, rather than a static, self-contained, or even self-evolving system that simply happened to be generated in the remote past. If creation is thus understood existentially, that is, in terms of the "coming-into-being-ness" of being, rather than essentially, that is, in terms of "what there is," then the world is properly conceived as the sensible expression of God's Spirit. If God is the power implicit in the world's explicit coming-into-being, the power implicit in the world's power to come-into-being — and if this is the case at every moment — then everything that exists potentially reveals God and has, at the very least, the capacity to disclose in its very coming-into-being a power that already "is" and that is "bringing it into being."

The Psalms speak of all creation as giving praise to God without a word and simply through its existence (Ps. 19:1-4), yet humans in particular give expression to the mute praise of other creatures: "Thou whose glory above the heavens is chanted by the mouths of babes and infants" (Ps.

8:1-2). And when we look at the creation account in Genesis, we find that the human body in particular has the capacity to make what is implicit in creation explicit. Note how delicately Genesis links the Spirit of God that hovers over the chaos (1:2) and the breath of God that is breathed into the dust of the earth and made the living being man (Gen. 2:7). It is to human creatures uniquely that Scripture assigns the designation of God's image: "And God said, 'Let us make man in our image, after our likeness; and let them have dominion over the fish of the sea and over the birds of the air, and over cattle, and over all the earth, and over every creeping thing that creeps upon the earth.' So God created men in his own image, in the image of God he created him; male and female he created them" (Gen. 1:26-27).

Theologians pondering these lines have tended to be preoccupied with identifying exactly what in humanity constitutes God's image. Attention characteristically has been directed to the intelligence and will. Partly, I think, this is due to the desire to avoid a crass anthropomorphism that would picture God in material terms. Partly, concentration on the spiritual dimension of humans has derived from a desire to relate humans to God rather than to the rest of creation. Thus, it is asked what human capacities enable a distinctive — presumably unique — relationship with a God who is spirit. Seldom if ever is the "image of God" connected to the human body; yet, it is clearly as a bodily creature that God declares humans in God's own image, for the distinction "male/female" is incomprehensible apart from the body. We note moreover that God's intention in creating humans in his image is that they should govern creation, and such governance is a function of embodiment as much as it is intelligence and will. Finally, the term "image of God" occurs again in Genesis 9:6, in connection with manslaughter: "Whoever sheds the blood of man, by man shall his blood be shed, for God made man in his own image." Manslaughter is not the killing of a mind, but a body. Genesis gives us no reason to make a divide between human spirit and body, or attribute image only to spirit. It was by God's breath that clay became body.

We might ask what inferences we might draw about the human body as created in God's image, turning our attention not to the way humans are related spiritually to God — though the biblical accounts massively support the proposition that everything learned from and about God by humans comes through their bodies — but rather how God is related to the rest of creation (including other humans) through the human body as "God's image and likeness." As the one commissioned with governance over other creatures, the embodied human at the very least represents God to other creatures. As bearer of the divine image, it follows, humans are likewise able to, and called to, reveal God to other creatures. Humans also represent creatures before God, being, as the Letter of James says, a kind of "first-fruits of creation" (James 1:18). Most of all, humans enable other creatures to make explicit their relatedness to the creator. Through their intelligent bodies, humans are able to discern the power and presence of God that are implicit in all that is coming-into-being, and able to articulate (in words and act) that power and presence, thus making them explicit.

Everything in this revelatory sequence depends on embodied spirit. Precisely as those who are thus able to articulate "the truth about the world," that is to disclose and make articulate the inarticulate power that is within all that is coming-to-be, humans bear God's image in the world somatically. To murder a human being is to kill that specific capacity of God to disclose God within creation. Such is the insight of the Talmudic statement that to kill a human being is to destroy a world.[16] As human beings engage each other somatically, moreover, they are, in an even more heightened and explicit way, enabled to have God's power and presence revealed in and through each other.

These convictions concerning the body undergird the biblical conceptions of *prophecy* and *covenant*. The prophet is one who "speaks for God" in the world through the prophet's body. The prophet sees and hears within the context of ordinary embodied existence — the cultural, political, and religious behavior of ancient Israel — deeper dimensions and implications than are discerned by others. The prophet draws inferences from what he sees and hears (and perhaps smells and touches and tastes) that form a "word of God" for Israel. In other words, the prophet makes explicit the implicit working of God's power and presence in the free play of bodies in the empirical world. The prophet then somatically "reveals" that word of God to Israel through speech and through symbolic actions (embodied gestures).

Israel, in turn, is expected to "hear and obey" this revelation of God's word through human somatic expression, so that when the prophet is heeded, God is thereby obeyed. Nowhere is it suggested that the prophets of Israel had more than ordinary mortal bodies. The letter of James stands within this tradition when he declares of Elijah that he was "of the same passions as us" (James 5:17). The prophetic tradition therefore strongly supports and extends the premise that human bodies can be revelatory of God.

16. *M.Sanh.* 4.5.

The link between prophecy and *covenant,* in turn, is direct and strong. Genesis calls Abraham a *nabi',* that is, a seer (Gen. 20:7). And Deuteronomy calls Moses a *nabi',* that is, a prophet (Deut. 18:15-22). Abraham and Moses experience the revelation of God through bodily encounters. (I referred above to Abraham's trance and Moses' ascent into the cloud.) The covenants that Abraham and Moses "cut" by means of circumcision, laws on stone, or the sacrifice of animals, are somatic expressions of the binding obligations established by the hearing and seeing of God's word in the world. The "keeping" of the covenant by the people, in turn, is through the equally somatic bearing of circumcision, the observance of laws, and the practice of ritual. Such "body language" reveals both to themselves and to others the power of God to create a people out of nothing in the same way God calls a world into being out of nothing, and organizes the life of a people in the same way God orders the moon and the stars: Israel as a "body" manifests — makes explicit — the presence and power of God in the world. Israel's faithful keeping of covenant is thus understood to be a "light of revelation to the nations."

Observations on the somatic character of revelation in the Old Testament do not surprise. Patristic writers in particular emphasized the "fleshly" nature of the earlier covenant when they argued for the superiority of the new "spiritual" covenant in Christ, finding support for this distinction in the New Testament itself (John 1:17-18; 3:6; 2 Cor. 3:1-18; Col. 2:11-12; Heb. 8:1-13).[17] But, in fact, the New Testament is no less emphatic in pointing to the human body as the medium of God's revelation. Indeed, the entire point of *incarnation* is that the human body of Jesus was capable of bearing the revealing power and presence of God *(sōmatikos).* The words of John's prologue are classic: "The Word became flesh and dwelt among us and we saw his glory [*doxa* = God's presence and power], the glory as of the Only-Begotten of the Father, full of grace and truth" (John 1:14). In the Fourth Gospel, Jesus' bodily gestures are designated as "signs" *(sēmeia)* that express the presence of the one who is implicitly present and powerful within all that is coming-into-being, by creatively transforming the material of creation. Thus, after Jesus changes water into wine, John notes, "This, the first of his signs, Jesus did at Cana in Galilee, and manifested his glory; and his disciples believed in him" (John 2:11). And in Jesus' final prayer to his Father, he makes clear that the *doxa* man-

---

17. See, for example, Origen, *Commentary on Romans* 8:7; Jerome, *Commentary on Galatians* 3:2; Augustine, *Commentary on Galatians* 3:2.

ifested by his signs is the *doxa* of the Father (17:1-26). In his body, Jesus makes explicit in the world the implicit presence of the God whom no one has ever seen (John 1:18).[18]

The first christological heresy, called Docetism — holding that Jesus' body was only an appearance rather than a real, physical, body — was repudiated as early as the First Letter of John (1 John 4:1-3). Christianity's most lingering christological controversy was between those who thought that the Word dwelt *only* in material flesh (the so-called *logos/sarx* position associated with Alexandria), and those who thought that the Word was incarnate in a full human person (the *logos/anthrōpos* position associated with Antioch).[19] For both these patristic positions, however, no doubt was expressed concerning the reality of Christ's *sōma* itself nor any doubt that his *sōma* was the medium of God's revelation. The classic mediating position of the Council of Chalcedon (451 CE) is anticipated by the Letter to the Hebrews: "He had to be made like his brothers in every respect, so that he might become a merciful and faithful high priest in the service to God, to make expiation for the sins of the people. For because he himself has suffered and been tempted, he is able to help those who are tempted" (Heb. 2:17-18). In short, the incarnation raises to the most explicit level possible the conviction implicit in creation, prophecy, and covenant: the human body not only can reveal God, it is the privileged medium of divine self-disclosure. It is not by accident that Paul speaks of Christ as "the image of the unseen God, the first-born of all creation" (Col. 1:15), and that "in him the fullness of God dwells bodily" (Col. 2:9); and that those baptized in Christ are to "put on the new nature, which is being renewed in knowledge after the image of its creator" (Col. 3:10).

Finally, the New Testament's language about *church* suggests that the spirit of the exalted Lord Jesus continues to find embodiment in the assembly that Paul provocatively — and not simply metaphorically — calls the *sōma tou Christou* ("body of Christ," 1 Cor. 12:27). Analysis of First Corinthians as a whole makes clear that Paul was not simply using a common political analogy; rather, he understood the relationship between the spirit of Christ and the community in quite a "realistic" way, with real implications for how members of the church entered into somatic engagements with

18. On this aspect of the Gospel of John, see R. E. Brown, *The Gospel according to John*, Anchor Bible (Garden City, NY: Doubleday, 1966), 1:cv-cxxvii.

19. For the terms, see A. Grillmeier, *Christ in the Christian Tradition: From the Apostolic Age to Chalcedon (451)*, trans. J. Bowden (Atlanta: John Knox, 1975).

others.[20] Some of these complications I will examine in the next section. But across his Epistles, Paul consistently connects the body that is the church to the Spirit of the risen Christ. In Colossians 2:19, for example, Paul speaks of the community as "holding fast to the head, from whom the whole body, nourished and knit together through its joints and ligaments, grows with a growth that is from God." In Ephesians, Paul argues that Jews and Gentiles are "members of the same body, and partakers of the promise in Christ Jesus through the gospel," which makes this body that is the church the place where God's plan for humanity is revealed: "[T]o make all men see what is the plan of the mystery hidden for ages in God who created all things; that through the church the manifold wisdom of God might now be made known to the principalities and powers in the heavenly places" (Eph. 3:9-10).

Paul is not alone in regarding the church, in some very real sense, as the extension of Christ's somatic presence. John's Gospel pictures the disciples as branches on the living vine that is Jesus; his mission to the world and his rejection by the world will also be their mission and experience of rejection: "Whoever receives one I send receives me, and whoever receives me receives the one who sent me" (John 13:20; see 15:1-25). The Spirit who will come to them as paraclete will strengthen them in this representative function (15:26–16:15). Similarly, Luke's portrayal of Jesus' witnesses in the Acts of the Apostles displays them as the prophetic successors of Jesus: the Holy Spirit that he pours out is embodied in them, so that in their "signs and wonders" the risen Jesus is made present through the Holy Spirit (Acts 2:17-21; 5:1-42).[21]

Matthew likewise has the risen Jesus declare that he will be with his followers "always until the close of the ages" (Matt. 28:20), and that "where two or three are gathered in my name, there I will be in their midst" (Matt. 18:20). As with the corporate body of the community, so with the bodies of individual humans: Paul says that anyone who offends a brother or sister "sins against Christ" (1 Cor. 8:12). The Gospels take pains to identify the risen Christ, especially with the bodies of children (Mark 9:33-37; 10:13-

20. For fuller analysis, see L. T. Johnson, "Life-Giving Spirit: The Ontological Implications of Resurrection in 'Corinthians,'" *Stone Campbell Journal* 15 (2012), and "The Body in Question: The Social Complications of Resurrection in 1 Corinthians," in *Unity and Diversity in the New Testament: Studies in the Synoptics and Paul,* Festschrift for Frank Matera (Atlanta: Society of Biblical Literature, 2012).

21. See L. T. Johnson, *Prophetic Jesus, Prophetic Church: The Challenge of Luke-Acts to Contemporary Christians* (Grand Rapids: Eerdmans, 2011).

16), the "stranger" (Matt. 25:34-40), and those in material need: "When you have done it to the least of these little ones, you have done it to me" (Matt. 25:45). Scripture's language about the church is consistent with its language about the body in creation, prophecy, covenant, and incarnation: the spirit of the unseen God can be disclosed through the human body.[22]

To summarize: The testimony of Scripture points away from itself as a sole or sufficient source of revelation about God. The texts of Scripture rather report and point to the revelation of God that takes place in the world outside texts in the world, preeminently through the bodies of human beings (see Rom. 3:21!). That said, Scripture also makes clear, above all in the New Testament, that precisely what is meant by body is not entirely clear, in light of the revelation of God in the exalted body of Jesus Christ.

Scripture Complicates the Body

In the previous chapter, I criticized Pope John Paul II for a reading of 1 Corinthians 6:18 that did not take into account its complexity. The entire passage (1 Cor. 6:12-20) provides a stunning example of passages in Scripture that, while pointing us to the body, also tease and even torment the careful reader. Paul says a series of quite astonishing things. Here is my very literal translation:

> I am allowed to do everything. But not everything helps. I am allowed to do everything. But I will not have anything [or perhaps "anyone"] exert authority over me. Food is for the belly, and the belly is for food. God will destroy both one and the other. But the body [*to sōma*] is not for fornication [*porneia* = sexual immorality], but for the Lord. And the Lord is for the body. God has both raised the Lord and will raise us through his power. Don't you [plural] know that your [plural] bodies [plural] are members of the Messiah? Will I therefore make the members of the Messiah members of a prostitute [*pornē*]? By no means! Or don't you know that the one clinging to a prostitute is one body? For it says, "The two shall be one flesh" [Gen. 2:24]. But the one clinging to the Lord is one spirit [*pneuma*]. Flee fornication. Whatever sin a person commits is outside the body (singular). But the one who commits fornication sins

22. For a detailed exposition, see L. T. Johnson, *Living Jesus: Learning the Heart of the Gospel* (San Francisco: HarperSanFrancisco, 1999).

against his own body [*eis to idion sōma*]. Don't you [plural] know that your [plural] body [singular] is the temple of the Holy Spirit within/among you [plural], which you [plural] have from God? You [plural] do not belong to yourselves. You [plural] have been purchased with a price. Therefore glorify God [that is, recognize God's presence] in your [plural] body [singular].

The only thing really clear in this passage is that Paul wants his Corinthians readers to avoid *porneia,* a term that can include all forms of sexual immorality, but is here conveniently translated as "fornication," especially since Paul uses sexual intercourse ("clinging," *kollōmenos*) with a female prostitute *(pornē)* as his example. Beyond that, however, Paul's argument draws us into a realm of premises that we are not sure we, as present-day readers, either share or understand: for example, about individual and collective bodies, the boundaries between them, and the relationships the singular or collective body can make and manifest. Above all, we are uncertain what to make of the premise that human bodies — both individual and corporate — are, in light of Jesus' resurrection as Lord, somehow bound to, or "clinging to" *(kollōmenos)* the Lord's Spirit in such a way that the connections these empirical bodies make with other empirical bodies have implications both individually and collectively.

Simply the way Paul shifts between the singular and the plural both in nouns and possessive pronouns — a fact obscured by many translations — makes the passage challenging. When Paul speaks of sins taking place "outside the body," for example, it is not clear whether he means the individual's empirical body or the corporate body whose members are "members of the Messiah." Similarly, when he states that the one who commits fornication sins "against his own body" *(eis to idion sōma),* it is more likely that "his own" or "proper" body means the corporate body of the community, in which the Holy Spirit dwells, than it does "his own" individual empirical body.

Because of the way the Bible is separated into chapters and verses, and because of the way we allow ourselves to think of biblical "passages" as totally defined by those arbitrary editorial decisions — not unlike the way we make assumptions about bodies — it is seldom noted that the lines I have just cited continue directly in the following (1 Cor. 7:1-4):

And concerning the things about which you wrote, it is noble for a man not to touch a woman. But because of acts of fornication, let each man have his own woman, and let each woman have her own man. The man should pay his obligation to his woman, and likewise the woman to her man. The woman does not exert authority over her own body, but the man exerts authority; likewise, the man does not exert authority over his own body, but the woman exerts authority.

Once more, the lines make one thing very clear: Paul wants sexual activity to take place within the covenanted relationship between man and woman rather than within the context of promiscuity. The issue is not sexual activity as such: Paul's language throughout shows a robust appreciation for an active and mutual sexual engagement between man and woman. Later, indeed, he suggests that it is just through such sexual engagement that man and woman can "sanctify" each other (1 Cor. 7:14). Paul's issue is the boundary within which sexual activity is to take place.

Having made that observation, we should acknowledge that it is puzzling that Paul here uses the same word for "exert authority over" *(exousiasthai)* in a positive sense that he uses negatively in 1 Corinthians 6:12, where he declares that he would not have anything (or anyone) "exert authority" over him. But here he places the right to exert authority over each other's empirical body respectively — alike with the man as with the woman. What does Paul imply about the relationship of spirit to body, or of body to body, in his language about "exerting authority over"? And how does such sexual authority over the body of another, or submission to such authority by another — to whom one "clings" sexually — connect to the authority of the Lord, to whom one "clings" in the Spirit? Paul does not make any of this clear.[23]

If this entire section of First Corinthians devoted to the sexual body were not provocative enough in its combination of clear (moral) directive and obscure (theological) premise, we can enter even further into puzzlement through two other passages in the same letter where Paul uses explicit and even outrageous language about body. Closely related to 6:12-

---

23. Paul's complex and confusing language about the body is a constant challenge to those seeking a Pauline anthropology or theology. Among many others, see J. A. T. Robinson, *The Body: A Study in Pauline Theology* (Chicago: Regnery, 1952); R. Bultmann, *Theology of the New Testament*, 2 vols., trans. K. Grobel (London: SCM Press, 1959); J. D. G. Dunn, *The Theology of Paul the Apostle* (Grand Rapids: Eerdmans, 2006); J. H. Neyrey, *Paul, in Other Words: A Cultural Reading of His Letters* (Louisville: Westminster John Knox, 1990); D. B. Martin, *The Corinthian Body* (New Haven: Yale University Press, 1995).

20 is the passage in 1 Corinthians 12, where Paul again speaks of the body of Christ:

> For just as the body is one but has many members, but all the members of the body, though they are many, are one body, thus also the Messiah. For likewise in one spirit we have all been immersed into one body, Jews and Gentiles, slaves and free, and we have all been made to drink one spirit. (1 Cor. 12:12-13)

We see at once that Paul here provides the basis for his position in 6:12-20 that each member of the community is a "member of the Messiah," and members of the community "cling to the Lord and are one spirit [with him]." We also perceive that Paul once more assumes a permeability of boundaries between the individual and the collective body that seems strange to us, and he assumes that, as part of their shared experience as members of the collective body, being "immersed [baptized] in one body [sōma]" and "being made to drink one spirit [pneuma]" have changed their individual and communal body. What is literal here, and what is metaphor? Certainly, Paul is not indulging in a bromide about everybody pulling together "in the same spirit," that is, with a shared vision. But how literally does he think of spiritual potion and immersion and body-merge?

A final passage concerning the complex character of the body in light of the "new creation" brought about by Christ occurs in Paul's discussion of the resurrection in 1 Corinthians 15. Having declared that as all died in Adam, so in the Messiah all will be brought to life, each in its order (15:21-34), Paul responds to a query: "How are the dead raised? With what sort of body do they come?" He begins with an abrupt exclamation: "You fool!" (15:36), suggesting either that the answer should be obvious or that it is utterly unknowable. But then he follows that exclamation with an extended (but to us bewildering) discourse on bodies in their mortal condition and bodies transformed by immortality, leading at last to his point in 15:42-45:

> Thus also the resurrection of dead people: It [the body] is sowed in corruption. It is raised in incorruption. It is sowed in shame. It is raised in glory. It is sowed in weakness. It is raised in power. It is sowed a psychic body [sōma psychikon]. It is raised a spiritual body [sōma pneumatikon]. If there is a psychic body, there is also a spiritual. And it is written so: "The first man Adam became a living being" (Gen. 2:7). But the last Adam became life-giving Spirit [pneuma zōopoioun].

Paul is talking, we remember, about the future bodies of those who rise to new life. But he connects their future as "spiritual bodies" to the "life-giving Spirit" of the exalted Jesus: where he is now, they are to go. But the interpenetration of spirit and body is not only future. Even in the present, their mortal bodies are being transformed through the Spirit. Thus Paul declares in 1 Corinthians 15:49: "Just as we have borne the image of the man of dust, we will also bear the image of the man of heaven." And memorably in 2 Corinthians 3:17-18:

> Now the Lord is Spirit, and where the Spirit of the Lord is, there is freedom. And all of us, with unveiled faces, seeing the glory of the Lord as though reflected in a mirror, are being transformed into the same image from one degree of glory to another; for this comes from the Lord, the Spirit.

It is a useful exercise to read 1 Corinthians from end to beginning, for Paul's expressions in chapters 15 and 12 appear to provide the rationale for his otherwise deeply puzzling statements in chapters 6 and 7. But even as we recognize that there is a logic to be found in statements such as these — namely, that a present share in the Holy Spirit begins to transform our bodies both individually and collectively in a manner proleptic of future glory — we must also acknowledge that the logic is not one that immediately persuades. The reason is that Paul's assumptions about body and spirit and the experiences of bodies with spirit are not necessarily ones we share. In order to test the truthfulness of his statements, we must necessarily think not only about the *meaning* of his various declarations, but also about how they correspond to the actual experience of bodies in the world. The process of revelation, according to Scripture itself, demands both the reading of texts and the reading of bodies in motion. But such reading of the body is by no means obvious or easy.

CHAPTER THREE

Spirit and Body

When rightly read, I have argued, Scripture demands a consideration of the human body as the privileged place for the revelation of God's Spirit in the world. Scripture participates in the process of God's self-disclosure, first, by providing the necessary lens to perceive the world as capable of revealing God, and second, through being reread in light of what God is doing in the world. And the new thing that God continually does in God's constant creation and re-creation of the world is made manifest and explicit among the bodies of human beings. But before I begin a closer examination of the body's revelatory capacity, it is necessary to think more fully about the two terms, "body" and "spirit," that I have been using already without much definition or analysis. Simply to clear some conceptual ground, I begin with four preliminary qualifications.

First, God's self-disclosure in creation cannot be restricted to human bodies alone. The logic of understanding creation as a continuous bringing-into-being of what was not demands that, at the level of existence, everything that is necessary points to the implicit power and presence that sustains it in its being. Mountains and mollusks, snakes and snapdragons, sea lions and swordfish, monkeys and mice, all point to a necessary cause underlying their all-too-obvious contingency — and they do so with a remarkable degree of egalitarianism. Simply as existing, mice evoke a creator as much as do men. The distinction between men and mice as witnesses to God's creative power lies not in degrees of existence, but in degrees of perception and articulation. The human body is privileged among all the world's beings to perceive and express what remains among the others mostly inarticulate: that they do not derive from themselves but from another, that they exist to do God's will. This special capacity of humans, in turn, points to their special vocation: among all creatures, they are required to be attentive to all other creatures, in order to learn what God might be doing in all God's creation. If the specific argument of this book is the need for theology to read human bodies as much as Scripture, it is in great part because (perceiving and thinking) human bodies provide access to God's visitation in all of creation.

Second, the human body is an ambiguous reality, as the analysis of a small section of Paul in the preceding chapter indicates. Insofar as the body is created by God, it is certainly good. But a "theology of the body" that focuses only on the positive aspects of embodied existence — in a laudable effort to escape the dreadful dualism of the Gnostic and Manichaean virus that so long infected Christianity — remains superficial. The body, both in its material self and as an instrument of human freedom, is often opaque and even resistant. The body can obscure as well as disclose the spirit. While in this book I will emphasize the ways in which bodies in motion can tell us something of the motions of God in the world, I by no means seek to diminish the long traditions of moral reflection that have examined the ways in which the body, not least when driven by violent "passions," can be a profoundly problematic arena for divine revelation.

Third, the human body is of interest above all because of its ability to express spirit. A corpse is not a human body, but something else altogether. A corpse can indeed be host to a lively swirl of activity for other forms of life, but it is no longer the locus of human life and activity. Whatever we mean by Spirit — and pinning this down is itself astonishingly difficult — viewing a corpse shows what the lack of spirit means. "The body without the spirit," the Letter of James famously declared, "is dead" (James 2:26). Only the living body serves to disclose spirit. But just as we want to avoid considering the body in isolation from spirit, so do we want to avoid privileging spirit to the detriment of the body; thus, the awkward expression "embodied spirit." The history of viewing the body as a disposable and not entirely worthy package for spirit — a history that extends at least from Plato, through forms of Gnosticism, to Descartes — is a long one.[1] The efforts to overcome the heritage of dualism have also been many and often futile. I am not certain that my effort will prove any more successful than others have.

---

1. For the Greco-Roman antecedents for religion as transcending the world, whose basic premise is that the soul must be rescued from the imprisonment of the body, and for its manifestations in early Christianity, see L. T. Johnson, *Among the Gentiles: Greco-Roman Religion and Christianity* (New Haven: Yale University Press, 2009).

Fourth, matters become still more complex when we search not only for the "human spirit" that bodies express, but also for the ways in which the embodied spirit of humans can express God's Holy Spirit. Our subject, after all, is not anthropology or psychology, but theology. Making sharp distinctions between spirit (with a small letter) and Spirit (with a capital letter) is notoriously difficult — even for biblical translators. Whose spirit, exactly, does Paul see at work in this particular passage? If that is the case in translating ancient texts, it is even more the case when discerning the complex patterns of human activity as revelatory of God's presence and power. No absolute and clear division between human spirit and God as spirit will ever be possible. How could it be if spirit as a nonmaterial reality is by definition indivisible? A certain amount of muddling through is inevitable in this sort of effort. On one side, then, we shall have to avoid intimations of pantheism (wherein spirit means always and only God), and on the other side, we must get past mere psychological reduction (wherein spirit means only an organic epiphenomenon). In effect, the analysis must be more like art and less like science, must necessarily consist more of suggestion than of hard conclusion.

The need for such delicate discernment reminds us that in thinking and speaking about body and spirit, we are in the realm of what Gabriel Marcel calls mystery. Marcel distinguishes the mysterious from the problematic. The problematic is what stands outside humans and what they can (and should) analyze dispassionately and with detachment.[2] The mysterious is that in which humans are themselves inextricably involved and from which they cannot detach themselves without distortion. The realm of the mysterious demands a kind of response that is distinct from problem-solving, a kind of response that is attentive and responsive, and resists easy reduction.[3] Humans seeking to discern the intricate bond between body and spirit are inextricably in the realms of the mysterious. We are, in fact, embodied spirit: we cannot detach ourselves from our own bodies in order to make a dispassionate analysis. Or better: we *can* reduce even our own body to the level of an object — a problem to be solved — for the sake of disposition or analysis, but when we do, we do violence to our authentic being-in-the-world. We must rather stay with and within the mystery of our own being and the being of other humans in a manner that is attentive

2. G. Marcel, *Being and Having,* trans. K. Farrer (Philadelphia: Westminster, 1949), p. 117.
3. G. Marcel, *The Mystery of Being,* vol. 1: *Reflection and Mystery,* trans. G. S. Fraser (London: Havrill Press, 1951), p. 213.

and responsive, learning what we can, respecting what we cannot, refusing to claim more than we legitimately can claim about our knowledge. At least part of wisdom is the recognition of limits.

But even if the whole point is not to separate out "body" and "spirit" conceptually as though they were separable in fact, we are forced by our limitations to devote some attention to each as a distinct topic. We do so in the spirit of the Scholastic adage *distinguer pour unir,* making distinctions in order to achieve a fuller and richer appreciation of the (in reality) indivisible whole.[4]

The Reality of Spirit

That the term "spirit" designates something real and important is an almost universal premise among most humans in most societies from ancient times until the recent past. There have been, to be sure, those who have rejected the premise. In Western thought, Epicurus and his followers were infamous for their materialistic understanding of the world, attributing all events to the accidental collisions between bits of matter (atoms). Epicurus is willing to speak of the soul, but as a material reality.[5] Such thoroughgoing materialism was, however, rarely to be found. Most of the literary evidence from antiquity — with "antiquity" here extending all the way up to "modernity" — testifies to the conviction that "spirit" is both a cosmological and anthropological reality: it is something found in the larger world, and it is a dimension of human psychology.

In ancient Greek usage — largely taken over by Latin's use of *Spiritus* — the verbal noun *pneuma* always carried the basic sense of an energy or power that could be interior (as with breath) or manifested outwardly (as in wind). As Cicero notes, power flows from spirit, is mediated by it, and disappears with it (*Divine Offices* I, 19, 37). A living person can be said to have the "spirit of life" (*pneuma biou;* see Aeschylus, *Persians* 507), and one who has died "yields up the spirit" (Euripides, *Hecuba* 57). The spirit, then, can be regarded as an element in the makeup of the human body (Epictetus, *Discourse* III, 13, 14ff.). But it can also be distinguished from

4. See J. Maritain, *Distinguish to Unite: The Degrees of Knowledge,* trans. G. B. Phelan (New York: Charles Scribner's Sons, 1959).

5. See Diogenes Laertius, *Lives of Eminent Philosophers,* trans. Robert Drew Hicks, 2 vols., Loeb Classical Library (Cambridge, MA: Harvard University Press, 1931-38), 10. 63-68.

the body as the immortal element in humans that has a destiny of its own (see Euripides, *Suppliants* 532ff.).

As "soul" *(psychē),* this spiritual dimension of humans is regarded, especially in Platonic traditions, as the enlivening element in human life even as it is confined by the limits of the body: the "soul" is the aspect of humans that is immortal (see Plato, *Phaedo* 67 C-D). In psychological terms, the *pneuma* within humans is distinguishable from the mind *(nous).* While *nous* is passive and contemplative, spirit is more dynamic and transitive, capable of reaching and touching others. This capacity is found, above all, in cases where a divine *pneuma* touches and transforms — or even replaces — the human *psychē,* as in experiences of inspiration and prophecy (see Plutarch, *On the Obsolescence of Oracles* 40 [Mor. 432D] and Strabo, *Geography* 9, 3, 5). Thus, cosmologically speaking, *pneuma* can refer to aspects of divine activity, or even (as in Stoicism) to a cosmic universal expression of the divine (see Aetius, *Placita* 1.6).

Scripture is not in the least idiosyncratic (or unique), then, when it speaks of the Spirit — *ruach, pneuma*) — of God as active in the creation of the world (Gen. 1:2) and of humans (2:7), or has God speak of the spirit that is within humans (Gen. 6:3). The Old Testament speaks most emphatically of spirit as the medium through which God moves humans to act (see Judg. 3:10; 6:34; 11:29; 13:25; 1 Sam. 10:6; 16:13) and speak for the Lord in prophecy (see Num. 11:16-25; 27:18; 1 Kings 18:12; 2 Kings 2:9, 15). In passages such as these, spirit is not imagined as an object among other objects, but is compared to things that are real and powerful, but invisible except through their effects: the spirit can be compared to the wind or a sound (see John 3:8; Acts 2:1-4; 1 Cor. 14:6-12); angels can be thought of as "ministering spirits" *(leitourgika pneumata,* Heb. 1:14; see LXX Ps. 103:4). The presence of life in humans can be accounted for by the presence of *pneuma* (Job 7:7), which comes from God (Job 33:4) and returns to God (Qoh. 12:7), just as the spirit within humans is capable of responding to God (LXX Ps. 50:10-17; 76:3, 6). God's spirit can strengthen the weakness of the human spirit (LXX 143:4, 7, 10). Humans cannot flee from the presence of God's spirit (LXX Ps. 138:7).

Biblical and Hellenistic perceptions of spirit *(pneuma)* converge in the LXX composition called the Wisdom of Solomon. Declaring that "wisdom, the fashioner of all things, taught me," the author lauds *Sophia* this way:

> For in her there is a spirit *(pneuma)* that is intelligent, holy, unique, manifold, subtle, mobile, clear, unpolluted, distinct, invulnerable, lov-

ing the good, keen, irresistible, beneficent, humane, steadfast, sure, free from anxiety, all-powerful, overseeing all, and penetrating through all spirits that are intelligent and pure and most subtle. For wisdom is more mobile than any motion; because of her pureness she pervades and penetrates all things. For she is a breath of the power of God, and a pure emanation of the glory of the almighty; therefore nothing defiled gains entrance into her. For she is a reflection of eternal light, a spotless mirror of the working of God, and an image of his goodness. Though she is but one, she can do all things, and while remaining in herself, she renews all things; in every generation she passes into holy souls and makes them friends of God and prophets. (Wis. 7:22-27, RSV)

Especially noteworthy in this passage is the conviction that spirit can serve as the medium of transmission between God and humans; indeed, it can enter into many persons and establish them as friends of God.

The New Testament is even more prolific in the use of language about spirit. In the Gospels and in Acts, *pneuma* appears as a dimension of the human person (Matt. 5:3; 22:43; 26:41; Mark 14:38; Luke 1:80; 2:27; 8:55; 13:11; 23:46; John 19:30; Acts 7:59; 16:18), as a way of characterizing cosmic entities (Matt. 10:1; 12:43; Luke 4:33; 7:21; John 3:6-8; Acts 8:7) and with reference to God (Matt. 12:28; 28:19; Luke 1:15, 35, 41; 3:22; 4:1; John 1:33; 20:22; Acts 2:4; 5:3; 7:55; 21:11). In other New Testament writings as well, *pneuma* can refer to an aspect of human interiority (Rom. 1:9; 1 Cor. 2:11, 7:34; 2 Cor. 2:13; Col. 2:5; 1 Thess. 5:23; Heb. 4:12; James 4:5; 1 Pet. 3:4; Jude 19); or to cosmic beings (1 Tim. 4:1; Heb. 1:7; 1 John 4:1; Rev. 3:1; 4:2; 16:14); or to God (1 Cor. 6:11; 1 Thess. 4:8; Heb. 2:4; 3:7; 1 Pet. 4:14; 2 Pet. 1:21; Rev. 11:11). In Paul's writings, above all, we find language that links the human spirit with the spirit of God, through the resurrection of Jesus, who became, Paul declares, "life-giving Spirit" (1 Cor. 15:45): Humans are led by the Holy Spirit (Rom. 8:14; Gal. 5:18); they receive the Holy Spirit (Rom. 8:16; 1 Cor. 2:12; 12:8; 2 Cor. 1:22; Gal. 3:14; Phil. 1:19); the Holy Spirit works as a power of energy within humans (1 Cor. 2:4; 12:11; 2 Cor. 3:17; Gal. 3:5); and even "dwells" in humans (Rom. 5:5; 8:2, 9, 11; 1 Cor. 3:16; 6:19; 12:11). Consistent across this range of witnesses is the conviction that *pneuma* is something real, powerful, and capable of bridging the gap between the human and the divine.

With various changes in emphasis and conception, the robust understanding of spirit found in Scripture continued within Christian piety and theology up to the time of the European Enlightenment. And something close to the New Testament language about spirit still flourishes uncritically in some contemporary forms of piety, especially those associated with the Pentecostal and Holiness traditions: God is spirit; the Holy Spirit is an active agent in human lives; Christian hope is for the salvation of the soul; cosmic opposition to God and the saints takes the form of spiritual beings; both exorcism and consecration effect genuine changes in humans. The conviction that spirit is real and important even finds significant expression in forms of modern philosophy. The entire system of the nineteenth-century thinker G. W. Hegel is an explication of *Geist im Welt* ("spirit in the world").[6] In a similar way, the theology of Karl Rahner, with its explicit philosophical roots in the Hegelian tradition, makes the capacity of transcendence that is implicit in spirit the key to thinking about human existence before God.[7] In parts of the world less affected by the Enlightenment, finally, language and perceptions concerning the reality of spirit in the world and in humans have more in common with antiquity than with modernity.

In those parts of the world most shaped by the Enlightenment, however, which are precisely the parts of the world inhabited by those I address in this book, language about the spirit and perceptions of the spirit have gone into a steep decline. The fault is not the Enlightenment's alone. The Enlightenment in Europe represented in many important ways both a positive and necessary development in human consciousness and in the practice of religion.[8] The liberation of the mind for critical inquiry; the posture of tolerance for traditions other than one's own; the turn to empirical data as the basis for and as the test for theories about the world — all these are Enlightenment advances that should not be abandoned. We do not want to return to a view of the world that the Enlightenment regarded as "superstitious," in which eccentric behavior or disease was instinctively linked to the presence of inimical spirits, and in which the execution of those condemned as heretics because of their allegiance to evil spirits was considered an act of faith.[9]

---

6. G. W. F. Hegel, *The Philosophy of History,* trans. J. Sibee, Dover Philosophical Classics (New York: Dover Publications, 2004 [1837]). See W. T. Stace, *The Philosophy of Hegel: A Systematic Exposition* (New York: Dover, 1955).

7. Karl Rahner, *Spirit in the World* (London: Bloomsbury Academic, 1994); see E. Johnson, *Quest for the Living God: Mapping Frontiers in the Theology of God* (London: Bloomsbury Academic, 2011), pp. 25-48.

8. See, e.g., J. S. Preus, *Explaining Religion: Criticism and Theory from Bodin to Freud* (New Haven: Yale University Press, 1991).

9. See A. Pagden, *The Enlightenment: And Why It Still Matters* (New York: Random House, 2013).

The fault for the decline in regard for the spirit is rather the systemic secularization of consciousness that was stimulated by the Enlightenment but has reached a totalizing state that could never have been conceived by the pioneers of Enlightenment. By the secularization of consciousness, I mean the kind of thoroughgoing materialism that not only appreciates the empirical, but considers the realm of the empirical to be exclusively real. In contrast to those ancients who considered spirit more real and true and worthy than matter, the modern secularist reduces everything to the material. Spirit is an unnecessary, and therefore imaginary, category. What can be seen, heard, touched, smelled, tasted — these alone count. All significant processes — that is to say, all material processes — are aspects of a self-contained and interlocking system of material causes and effects. Science, which engages precisely such material causes and effects, replaces religion as the privileged interpreter of the world thus construed. Science alone is capable of explaining, and together with technology, changing, a world understood in completely immanent terms, not dependent on or related to anything beyond itself, but explicable only through analysis of what can be engaged by the senses.

The successes accomplished by science and technology through such a reduction to the material are not only remarkable, they serve as the strongest possible argument that just such a materialistic reduction, and the corresponding hegemony of science, are necessary for genuine human progress. Who can argue with the techniques of measurement and manipulation when their practitioners can point not only to multiple conquests over sickness and disease, but have penetrated to the very core of human life itself; when they can claim to have improved the "standard of life" for millions around the world; when they need only point to journeys to remote outer space and the exploration and exploitation of the earth's depths; when the entire world is increasingly forming a global village linked through electronic communication?[10] What Pierre Teilhard de Chardin saw as the direction of increased complexification in human evolution, namely, the formation of a "noosphere," seems, with the ever-increasing reach of the digital revolution, to be on the verge of realization.

Compared to such positive accomplishments, the use of technology

10. Marshall McLuhan, who invented the term, was remarkably prescient concerning the effects of technology on the future shape of humanity. See esp. *The Gutenberg Galaxy: The Making of Typographical Man* (Toronto: University of Toronto Press, 2011 [1962]); and *Understanding Media* (Boston: MIT Press, 1994 [1964]).

71

for genocide, the persistence of poverty among the majority of the world's populations, the damage to the ecological balance of the earth, the spiral of narcotics addiction among the peoples of the most technologically advanced societies — all these can be dismissed by the committed secularist as the failure to have been sufficiently thoroughgoing in the application of scientific methods, or even the result of lingering superstition. For the secularist, the world is not a place of mystery, but merely a set of problems and solutions; the "problems" that remain simply need better solutions, and science will eventually find them. In a fascinating turn, the most rabid ideologues of secularity identify those who continue to think and speak in religious terms — that is, in terms of spirit — as the contemporary heretics responsible for impeding progress and therefore deserving of excoriation or even extirpation.

Secularism today is no longer simply one among many ideological positions. It has become the dominant cultural force of the modern age. The evidence is all around, and it goes well beyond the decline in explicit religious practice and implicit religious perspective wherever modernity rules. The mass media operate on the materialistic premise that human existence gains significance through the acquisition of pleasure, power, and, above all, possessions; thus they use a constant stream of entertainment to reinforce that perception of the world, seeking to create humans who are primarily consumers of material goods. In the world of mass entertainment, religion is mostly portrayed through parody or as a manifestation of neurosis; language about "spirit" tends toward vague spirituality (a form of self-care), or toward spiritualism and other kinds of charlatanism. Politics in Western democracies is part of the same process of commodification: candidates are produced and selected through the use of capital; candidates are elected on the basis of advertising in mass media, and are reelected on the basis of their success in delivering material prosperity. In American politics, language about religion represents a reassuring nod toward tradition, while language about spirit is at the level of a call to "school spirit" at pep rallies.

The world of the academy does its part to reinforce a secular outlook in the next generation of leaders, as universities themselves increasingly resemble corporations in their structure and outlook. The disciplines that are most honored within research universities (to some extent, liberal arts colleges provide some resistance to the tendency) are those that yield the most practical outcomes by the standards of technology; the disciplines most in decline are those devoted to the "useless" activities associated with arts and letters. The most powerful research universities in the United States are places where, even within departments of philosophy and psychology, discourse about spirit or soul or even mind has given way to language about brain chemistry. Within the cultural institutions that (together with religion) were intended to cultivate and encourage the life of the spirit, the secular flattening of humanity dominates.

The most spectacular success of science and technology has been the development of what has come to be called "information technology," the vast interconnected web of electronic devices that has made available vast resources of knowledge and virtually instant communication through computers and all the devices linked to the Internet, whose names change constantly, as one device makes another obsolete. Digital technology has not only revolutionized forms of entertainment — from hand-held video arcades of astonishing sophistication to photos and videos that become instantaneous worldwide sensations through "going viral" — but has profoundly affected the way in which manufacturing, commerce, and diplomacy are carried out. The comparatively clunky products of print (on paper) are everywhere in retreat, as Web-sites and blogs and Twitter make exchanges of information easily and cheaply available. Inevitably, a technology whose point is to enable the communication of information has also spawned various forms of what is termed "social media." By whatever name, and through whatever constantly altering digital instruments, people — most of all younger people — seek to make contact with others (sometimes almost constant contact) in the placeless space called "virtual reality."

So rapidly is digital technology changing, and so powerful are its effects on virtually every aspect of life — from paying taxes to buying groceries, from making a date to negotiating a contract — that its ultimate cultural impact is difficult fully to assess. This is especially true since we have not yet seen a generation that has been totally formed by the full flowering of the technology. But some worrisome tendencies are already evident. The above tendencies, I should emphasize, are not intrinsic to the technology itself, which can be used, and is being used, in remarkably productive ways. Think of the positive changes in the delivery of health care that digitalization has made possible.

The negative tendencies have to do, rather, with the ways humans always find to distort instruments that were intended to inform and to be enslaved by instruments intended to liberate. It is no surprise to find criminal minds using new technologies to misinform, defraud, steal (even steal "identities"), and dispense the sleazier forms of vice. More troubling in cultural terms is the creation of a generation that takes shape-shifting for granted within social media, that regards the spontaneous natterings of Twitter as significant, that thinks of Facebook exchanges as a form of genuine intimacy, and that is convinced that bodily presence is irrelevant to authentic human communication.

The perspective of secularism and the success of technology have together come close to forming what Mircea Eliade presciently called a "hominized" consciousness, in which humans are rarely in contact with the "otherness" of God's creation and live totally within structures made by humans.[11] They dwell in a closed system in which their brain circuits and the circuits of the machine together form a "virtual reality" that is so appealing, so alluring, that it can be mistaken for reality as such. Such cases reveal the idolatrous impulse implicit within secularism. Seeking to control all things, humans find themselves controlled by the machines they have fashioned. Secularism begins with the denial of spirit and ends with the body itself diminished and captive to forms of "intelligence" that make even imagining spirit ever more difficult.

Contemporary Christians are not immune to the power of secularism. Indeed, the argument can be made that in many ways contemporary Christianity has been coopted by secularity. At the very least, Christians today find the language of Scripture concerning spirit disconcerting if not utterly alien or even untrue. Talk about "unclean spirits," or the designation of the risen Christ as "life-giving Spirit," or references to the Holy Spirit "indwelling" humans make no more immediate sense to them than they do to their neighbors. For contemporary Christians, as for their neighbors, the world they inhabit is interpreted in language from which spirit has effectively been eliminated. Like their neighbors, they are more comfortable speaking of schizophrenia or personality disorder than of "unclean spirits"; they would rather think of Jesus as a moral teacher from the past; and as for "indwelling," well, that makes no sense at all.

For us to look for signs of the spirit in our world, to seek ways in which the human body might express spirit, even the Holy Spirit of God, we must make a choice to stand resolutely in tension with the world shaped by secularism, which also in profound ways shapes us who seek to resist it. Such a stance is possible, in turn, only because we allow ourselves to be

11. Mircea Eliade, *The Sacred and the Profane: The Nature of Religion* (New York: Harcourt, Brace, 1959), p. 204.

schooled by the language and perceptions given us by Scripture. We must be willing to imagine the world that Scripture imagines, and by so doing to find in our empirical world the basis for such imagination.

How then, as Christians shaped by modernity but also schooled by Scripture, can we begin to speak of spirit in a way that does not, on one side, represent a romantic reversion to a cosmology no longer our own, or, on the other side, does not capitulate completely to the dominant ethos of secularism? We can take our lead from Scripture, since the culture of secularity does not even provide the possibility of meaningful language about spirit. Therefore, we look for signs of an energy or power that is not itself available to the senses, but can be discerned through its effects. We look for such signs, not apart from human bodies, but in and through living human bodies as they act. On the basis of Scripture, we surmise that spirit is a dimension or aspect of the human person that displays itself indirectly through the human body. And since such display — the evidence for the spirit — is indirect, we are prepared, with Scripture, to recognize an inevitable ambiguity in the spirit's manifestations, demanding of us the art of discernment or testing.

Our search for signs of the spirit is thoroughly modern because it begins with empirical reality: no less than the scientist probes for DNA in human secretions do we probe the experiences of the living human body. But our search is also thoroughly counter to the secularism of modernity, because we insist that the human body yields evidence for a dimension of somatic existence that modernity has refused to acknowledge as legitimate. Our procedure is necessarily inductive. But it also necessarily resembles art more than it does science, for the simple reason that the dimension of somatic existence we seek remains elusive and unavailable to usual scientific methods and tools.

Our task demands of us that we carefully observe, not a slice of tissue or a broken limb or a cancerous mass, but the movements and behaviors of bodies as they live and love, suffer and die — apart from the controlled context of the laboratory. This means that we are in the realm of intersubjective learning, where controls are not available, where our own subjective experience must be used as part of the database we examine, and where the objectivity and dispassionate distance so admired in science are difficult to achieve and are not obviously helpful.

We need to start with a working definition of spirit. For this purpose, we must borrow a term that is not attested in Scripture, but one that is consonant with what Scripture says about spirit. The term *transcendence* denotes a "going beyond," and I use it here to identify that dimension of human bodies that is spirit: in humans, spirit is the capacity for self-transcendence. But transcendence does not mean simply "going beyond"; it suggests a going outside the body in order to get inside other bodies. The human spirit, therefore, is the ability of humans to get beyond their individual bodies and into other bodies.

Bodies considered simply as matter (apart from spirit) patently cannot get beyond themselves. The material body can be extended through tools, and can touch other bodies, can even be joined to other bodies through the interlinking of limbs or the application of adhesive. But all this is external: the bodies remain physically discrete. Considered in terms of spirit, however, human bodies show the capacity to get outside themselves and into other bodies. The preeminent examples of this capacity, as we know from our human experience, are acts of communication. Ideas, images, and even emotions find their way from one person to another. What is "inside" one body is now "inside" another. Such transmission is all the more remarkable because it is accomplished through instruments that are themselves material, such as gesture and sound and musical device. Through instruments of communication, one human body becomes interior to another human body.

Such transmission regularly crosses the boundaries of space. Words of a sermon enter the minds of those in the back pew and even those listening by radio or watching television; a tune from a distant concert enters and occupies the body of a passerby, who whistles the same tune and walks more briskly; words printed on a page in one city are read and remembered by a reader in another city. More remarkably, such communication also crosses the boundaries of time: ideas enunciated by philosophers in antiquity govern the thinking of philosophers today; notes put on a page by Mozart are "performed" by musicians and touch the heart of a listener. Our experience confirms over and over that such transmissions of the spirit, even across space and time, touch us intimately in a way that goes far beyond mere physical contiguity.

Such human experiences of embodied spirit encourage us to imagine, in turn, with Scripture, God as spirit. As in the case of human transcendence, we imagine God's spirit also as involving embodiment. Indeed, we can think of the relationship of God's spirit to the world as analogous to the human spirit's relationship to the body. All analogy involves similarity between the elements being compared: God's spirit transcends the physical world, and the human body expresses transcendence through spirit.

But analogy also involves greater dissimilarity: we catch glimpses of transcendent spirit through discrete human bodies, but must imagine God's spirit as transcending all bodies, as being indeed the unseen presence and power that holds all bodies in being. What is a finite capacity in humans is in God an infinite power.

Furthermore, in some way, as Scripture instructs us, God's spirit preeminently "gets inside" and communicates to the world through the instrumentality of the human body. Scripture speaks of prophecy and of incarnation. It speaks of the church as the body of Christ, who is life-giving spirit. These examples correspond to and confirm our experience of the spirit within and among human bodies: God communicates God's word through prophecy, and God's most intimate presence and love through incarnation and church.

That we can speak, following Scripture, of spirit with reference both to humans and to God complicates the subject. Can we apply the term "spirit" to God and to humans univocally? Our instinct is to respond in the negative, for as theologians we have been taught, quite properly, to apply the *via negativa* to all propositions about God. Analogical language is all we are allowed. And yet, the writers of Scripture and mystical writers through the ages have dared to imagine the meeting and even merging of divine and human spirit. Here is a case where the intuitions arising from experience may need to be taken seriously. Surely Scripture itself encourages us to think of the possibility of such intimate communion in the realm of the Spirit. In Romans, for example, Paul declares: "God's love has been poured into our hearts through the Holy Spirit which has been given to us" (5:5); and "[Y]ou did not receive the spirit of slavery to fall back into fear, but you have received the spirit of sonship; when we cry, 'Abba! Father!' it is the Spirit himself bearing witness with our spirit that we are children of God" (8:15-16).

In any case, the task we set ourselves as we seek to do theology inductively is to take seriously the reality of spirit in and among our bodies, and to find out what we can about how those manifestations of embodied spirit reveal the presence and work of the living God among us.

The Meaning of Body

Living within a secularized culture does not, paradoxically, make thinking about body any easier than thinking about spirit. In the case of spirit, to be sure, we must argue for its very existence and the legitimacy of taking it seriously, whereas, in the case of body, it is all too obviously real and important. But the place of the body in contemporary thinking and practice is far from the way body is spoken of in Scripture.

In the preceding chapter, I tried to show how Paul's discussion in 1 Corinthians 6:12-20 and other passages complicated the understanding of the body. Paul tells the Corinthians that "your [plural] bodies are members of Christ" (6:15), and that "you [plural] *are* the body of Christ" (12:27; see Rom. 12:5). He implicitly chides them for failing to be aware of what they already know: "Do you not know that your [plural] *sōma* is a temple of the Holy Spirit within you [plural], which you [plural] have from God? You are not your own; you have been bought with a price" (1 Cor. 6:19). When seeking to answer the question concerning the future resurrection ("with what sort of *sōma* do they come?"), he eventually answers in terms of a "spiritual body" *(sōma pneumatikon),* which he contrasts to the mortal body that is "sowed" *(sōma psychikon).* In other letters, Paul declares that believers have died to the law through the body of the Messiah (Rom. 7:4), that their mortal bodies would be brought to life (8:11), and that they could present their bodies to God as a living sacrifice (12:1). He says that he and his fellow preachers bear the death of Jesus in the body (2 Cor. 4:10) and declares of himself that he carries on his body the wounds of Jesus (Gal. 6:17).

There are a remarkable number of premises underlying these statements: that human bodies are intrinsically connected to others, to God, and to a crucified and raised Messiah; that the body can at once be singular and at the same time part of a collective or communion; that the body is not independent but dependent and interdependent; that the present empirical body can be offered in service to God and will be transformed in the future. Other passages in 1 Corinthians, in turn, make clear that bodies can profoundly influence others through sexual engagement, and can equally be profoundly influenced by others through common meals (see 1 Cor. 7:12-16; 10:14-30).

For Paul, the body as intersected by the power and presence of God participates in a *mystērion* (1 Cor. 15:51; Eph. 3:9; Col. 2:2), a mystery whose depths remain incalculable even when it has been revealed. Such premises are by no means shared by those whose culture has been thoroughly secularized. Indeed, the contemporary default mode for thinking about the body, inherited from Descartes and extended by science and technology, prevents us from truly engaging the language of Scripture, or imagining our own empirical world in the way Scripture imagines it.

The world of modernity has a completely different set of premises concerning the human body. In contrast to Paul, for example, we tend to think first of the individual human body. The pervasiveness of individualism, above all in contemporary American society, makes talk of a "social body" seem secondary and derivative, at best a political metaphor. The premise of the American experiment — derived from John Locke and other Enlightenment figures — is that society is formed by contract among independent individuals, who must "consent" to being governed by common rules or authority. The individual body, moreover, tends to be considered in isolation from the world and other bodies. This sense of separate somatic existence is expressed and reinforced by the development of distinct posture, clothing, housing, and variable zones of personal safety. A direct symbolic line runs from the "body language" of individualism to the acquisitive use of possessions: corresponding to the *noli me tangere* ("don't touch me") of political individualism is the NO TRESPASSING sign in front of gated "communities." In pathological cases, the bodies of others — whether those others are animals, people, microbes, or even food — are viewed essentially in terms of threat to the integrity of the individual body, which must maintain itself against dangerous entanglements.

Furthermore, the individual body is considered in purely physical terms. The progression in modern thought, as we have seen, has been from the ghost in the machine to simply the machine, or perhaps, more precisely, the workings of brain chemistry within the machine. The body is thought of in terms of problems to be solved: the dramatic exchanges of blood and vital organs through medical technology is extended through the regimens of exercise and diet, and even more dramatically through the kinds of body-engineering found in fetal harvesting, gender-changing, plastic surgery, and cloning.[12] In this construal, the body is considered a form of property. It is something I have; I own it and can dispose of it as I choose; I can sell my body for profit. I have rights over my body just as I have rights over my other property.

To some extent, cultural criticism has slightly modified such mechanistic views of the body, reminding us that ideological interests are at work in the social construction of the body in diverse cultures. Such analysis makes us aware that different cultures have different notions of what

---

12. It is unlikely that the irony of their titles occurred to J. Villepigue and H. Rivera when they wrote *The Body-Sculpting Bible for Men: The Way to Perfection* and *The Body-Sculpting Bible for Women* (New York: Heatherleigh Press, 2011).

is beautiful or admirable in human bodies, and that, conversely, body-typing has played a role in a variety of racist and sexist political programs. Obvious examples include the propaganda posters in Nazi Germany that depicted Jews with subhuman features, the stereotypical portrayals of African Americans during the era of segregation, and the pictorial representations of the "yellow peril" in Allied propaganda during World War II. The modification, however, is slight, for the body is still regarded as a problem to be solved, or as an object to be manipulated, or as a property to be negotiated. And it is still the individual rather than the social body that is of primary interest.

As in the case of spirit, better thinking about the body can begin with reflection on our own subjective experience of body. When I reflect bodily, that is, when I tap my foot, wrinkle my brow, sigh deeply, examine the itch on my left ankle, and, all the while, perform the amazing mental trick of remembering the former me — I realize that every sense of my self is of my bodily self. As long as I remember me, I remember my body. Indeed, I cannot truly conceive of me absent from my body. Although the cells of my body have sloughed off and been replaced endlessly, somehow what I call me has been borne through the years — and through entropy to ever greater corpulence — by the body. I realize, then, that whereas there is some truth to the claim that I *have* a body, since I can in fact dispose of it in a number of ways, there is at least equal truth to the claim that I *am* my body. I cannot completely dispose of my body without at the same time losing myself. In strict empirical terms, when my body disappears, so do I.[13]

If this is so — and all our experience confirms that it is — then my body does not lie outside myself as a problem to be solved, as if it were a sculpture to be carved or a project to be engineered. If I do objectify my body in that way, I alienate myself from my true somatic condition, which lies in the realm of the mysterious, that is, a reality in which we are inescapably involved as persons. A budget is a problem; marriage is a mystery; a broken timepiece poses a problem; but a dying friend involves us in mystery. Making budget decisions mysterious is simply silly, but treating marriage as a problem is tragic. Weeping over a stolen automobile shows confusion, but failing to weep for a dying friend reveals alienation.

---

13. See L. T. Johnson, *Sharing Possessions: What Faith Demands,* 2nd enlarged ed. (Grand Rapids: Eerdmans, 2010), and the fundamental insights in Marcel's *Being and Having.*

Furthermore, my body is by no means isolated from its physical environment; the world is just as much within as outside me. The microbes are not simply out there but are also in here, quietly doing their good work. I suck in and expel the world's atmosphere, in the process feeding the green things around me, which, in their turn, also feed me. Over some seventy years, in fact, I have eaten quite a considerable part of my environment. And while retaining some of it in storage, I have also returned an astounding mountain of body-stuff for the world's cycle of regeneration. Dung beetles, you are welcome! As I take, so do I give. As I eat, so am I eaten — while alive, and assuredly when I die. My body is not the exception to the world; it is the rule. It is not separate from the world; it is the world in concentrated form.

Reflection on my own experience of being and having a body also suggests that thinking first if not always in terms of my individual body rather than in terms of the social body is also a form of alienation. It is obvious that we are born out of the bodies of others and bear those bodies coded within our own, just as when we, in turn, give birth, our bodies are carried forth by our children and, in turn, by their children. And as we derive from other bodies, so are we dependent on other bodies, not only at birth but also at burial, not only in our first infancy but also in our second infancy. At the pivotal moments as we make our way through our own existence, we are utterly dependent on others. The moments of entry and departure, however, only accentuate the fundamental dependence of any individual body on the bodies of others throughout human life. When John Donne declared, "No man is an island" (*Meditation* 17), he spoke the soberest truth.

Such reflection on the lived experience of somatic existence does not by any means bring us all the way to Paul's perceptions and premises concerning the body. But it serves to call into question the default sense of the body peddled by radical individualism and cultivated by late-capitalist commodification. And it helps us appreciate the fact that notions of the body within secularism thrive not least because only the premises and perceptions — indeed only the instruments of analysis — given by modernity are allowed into consideration. As we move forward in the task of discerning the work of the spirit within embodiment, we must grow comfortable with the fact that the instruments available to us are above all those of subjective observation, intersubjective witness, and introspective reflection. Through these subtle means we can hope to catch a glimpse of the working of the human and divine spirit.

Reading Bodies

As we seek the signs of spirit within and through human bodies, we bear in mind the difficulties and ambiguities of the enterprise. Positively, we approach specific aspects of body in its states and activities with the expectation that careful observation will suggest the presence and work of the human spirit as well as intimations concerning God's Holy Spirit — and thus aspects of God's self-disclosure in the world. We are convinced that human bodies — alone and, above all, together — can express what speech cannot or dares not.

You and I may be engaged, for example, in what seems to be casual banter, but my rigidly crossed arms suggest another locution: "I am afraid of you; I resist you." My speech may be fluid and graceful, but my compressed lips and clenched teeth are declaring, "I am angry at you."[14] As much as I may speak about generosity and helping others, my closed fist says, "I am not letting go, and you must fight me to take this." Our bodies are symbols of our selves because they reveal, make manifest, our inner emotions and dispositions. Our bodies are more than mere "signs." Smoke signals the presence of fire, but smoke does not burn things up. The body, however, not only signals the state of my mind or heart; it also makes such thought or disposition real in the world. And the traffic moves both ways. Our bodies speak to our minds as much as our minds direct our bodies. Sexual arousal makes me aware of personal attraction. Scratching makes an itch real in a way that it was not before I started scratching.

Because the traffic moves both ways, because my body also speaks to my spirit, it is possible for me to place my body in witness to myself. We can become aware of our convictions and desires because of the place in which our bodies have put us. It is one thing for me to believe or confess that I believe in the resurrection life. But when I am willing to suffer martyrdom for that conviction, I place my body in witness to myself that my conviction is real. Likewise, when I remain celibate for the sake of the kingdom, my body bears witness, first of all to myself, that my longing for authentic life is not to be found in progeny but in the gift of resurrection. The disposition of my body not only expresses my conviction, it makes it real.

---

14. All such observations are now fairly common. The classic 1970 study of Julius Fast, *Body Language,* is not only in its third expanded and amended edition (Lanham, MD: M. Evans, 2002); it is now merely one of some five hundred books with similar titles listed on Amazon.com.

Our bodies make our attitudes actual most of all because we are social creatures, and our bodies speak within a language of social gestures. Facing each other's bodies, the signs and symbolic exchanges intensify and multiply and become mutually influential. Adopting a fetal position in my own bed is one thing; slipping into the same posture in the middle of a party has quite a different impact. I may smile to myself as I remember a pleasant moment, but if my smile is seen by a neighbor, it will in all likelihood evoke a smile in return, in the same way that extending the hand in greeting almost reflexively causes another to reach out his or her hand in response. Our bodily gestures are effective signs in the social context.

We are also aware that not all the language spoken by our bodies is of universal or immediate context of a cultural symbolic system. And these systems assign different significance to bodily gestures. The same wave of the hand that signals "good-bye" in the United States is, in Guatemala, the sign for "come here." Some biblical body language — the tearing of garments, the throwing of dust on the head — is probably rooted in the apotropaic gestures of the Ancient Near East and does not reveal universal significance. Even within the same culture, the smile on my face that elicited a smile in return from my neighbor can be read in other contexts quite differently: a smile can be sardonic and evoke worry; it can be cynical and evoke shame; it can be sadistic and evoke terror. An embrace, we assume, communicates warmth and acceptance, and elicits an embrace in response. But with a bit more pressure and force, an embrace can be experienced as a seizure or arrest, and can evoke a struggle for freedom. Unless the context is clear, the language of the body can be just as ambiguous, if not more ambiguous, than verbal language. Kissing another is probably as universal a symbol of affection as we know; but it, too, can have sinister significance, as we know from Judas's kissing Jesus in the Garden of Gethsemane (Matt. 26:49).

The analysis of body language is nevertheless of considerable help in reminding us that, with whatever historical and cultural variations, our bodies do express the movements of our ideas, emotions, attitudes, dispositions, and ideals. And the more elemental the impulse of the spirit involved, the more likely it is that the bodily expression will have general intelligibility, especially when the impulse is grounded in biological reaction. Our bodies instinctively and involuntarily recoil from danger, crouch in fear, flinch from pain. The surge of adrenaline accompanying fear and anger can cause our bodies to tighten, clench, and even shake — or evoke outbursts of energy that may deflect threat and overcome danger. Societal norms channel and camouflage these reactions, it is true, and part of the fascination in reading bodies is analyzing the ways our bodies can learn to express unacceptable ideas and emotions in socially acceptable ways.

The search for the work of the spirit in embodied human experience, then, works with two simple premises. The first is that our bodies do, inevitably, symbolize something of our inner attitudes, emotional states, dispositions. The body does give expression to spirit. The second is that the precise significance of that expression is not easily discerned. Even the "natural language" of the body speaks without ambiguity only within a clearly understood system of symbolic understanding. It should be obvious why we must think of this task in terms of an art rather than a science, for the bodily expressions that offer themselves to our consideration do not stand still or submit to laboratory procedures. The one who seeks the signs of the spirit — even and especially of God's spirit — in actual human behavior must abandon all pretense of control and must learn to respond flexibly and creatively to constantly changing phenomena, among which is the searcher's own embodied spirit.

There are some examples of human experience in the body worthy of the theologian's attention that I will not explicitly explore in the short studies that occupy the remainder of this book. Most obvious is the range of embodied manifestations of the spirit we call "religious," in which explicit claims concerning the power and presence of God among humans are asserted. Some such experiences can have an extraordinary character: healings and exorcisms, visions, speaking in tongues, and prophesying. Some of them are more ordinary, such as the regular practices of piety: the sacraments, the reading of Scripture, and acts of mercy. Christians certainly do not need to be told that God's Holy Spirit touches the human spirit in these embodied experiences, though theology has paid too little attention to the ways in which the human spirit undergoes transformation through such experiences, and still less to the narratives of those whose spirit has been touched and transformed in these ways.

Other embodied expressions of the spirit that demand consideration by theology are the developments of social movements and awareness that grow, perhaps, from small, even individual experiences, and that eventually take on proportions that command the attention of those seeking to discern how God is acting in the world today. In recent centuries, such movements have included, on the negative side, the Holocaust and other genocides, global warfare, and the pillaging of natural resources. On the positive side are the emancipation from slavery and the winning of civil rights; the liberation of women and the assertion of their full equality; the recognition of the dignity and rights of persons other than those who are traditionally heterosexual. Such movements have seldom begun in the realm of the religious, but they press on those who call themselves religious to discern how God's Holy Spirit might be at work in such social movements — and how the church is challenged by the divine activity.

I am not explicitly engaging these types of embodied experience in this book, because I have spoken and written about them and their importance for theology elsewhere. My neglect of them here is not in the least a withdrawal from the strong positions I have taken on them before. But here I want to push the analysis of the body as revelatory to an even more basic level by taking up very ordinary states and activities of human bodies, and by asking how such activities and states might disclose something of the human — and perhaps even something of the divine — spirit. I do this particularly because I think that, if theology is to become an inductive art, it must develop the capacity to discern the movements of the spirit in the small as well as the large things, because, almost always, the large things turn out to have numerous, intricate connections with small things.

CHAPTER FOUR

The Body at Play

To begin reflecting on the body's capacity to reveal spirit with the body at play makes sense for a number of reasons. Play is an almost entirely positive human activity (with cautions to be noted in due course). It is unusually transparent and accessible. It involves the communal as well as the individual body. So far as we can tell, play occurs in all human cultures. And while little is said about play in Scripture, valuable insights into this fundamental way of being human have been offered by philosophers,[1] anthropologists,[2] and theologians.[3]

Scripture, in truth, contributes virtually nothing on the topic. The majority of texts mentioning "play" refer to making music (Ps. 33:3; 1 Sam. 16:16-17; 2 Sam. 6:21; Ezek. 33:32; Luke 7:32; Matt. 11:17; 1 Cor. 14:7; Rev. 14:2). A handful of texts refer to the "playing" of animals (Job 40:20; 41:5; Ps. 104:26) or to the "playing" of a role (Deut. 22:21; 1 Sam. 21:15; Hosea 3:3; 4:15). The most famous passage uses play in a negative sense: in the wilderness the Israelites "ate and drank and rose up to play" before the golden calf (Exod. 32:6; see 1 Cor. 10:7). Otherwise, there is only Isaiah's positive image of the child playing over the hole of the asp (Isa. 11:8). Indirectly, perhaps, the love-making of Isaac and Rebekah in Genesis 26:8 can be construed as "play" (the LXX and

---

1. See E. Ryall et al., eds., *The Philosophy of Play* (London: Routledge, 2013).

2. See J. Huizinga, *Homo Ludens: A Study of the Play Element in Culture* (Boston: Beacon Press, 1971); R. Bellah, *Religion in Human Evolution: From the Paleolithic to the Axial Age* (Cambridge, MA: Belknap Press of Harvard University Press, 2011).

3. H. Rahner, *Man at Play, or Do you Practice Eutrapelia?* (New York: Herder and Herder, 1967); J. Moltmann, *Theology of Play* (New York: Harper and Row, 1972).

Philo so read it).[4] Similarly, the activity of the divine wisdom among humans — although it is explicitly called "work" — can, because of the note of delight, be understood as a kind of play (Prov. 8:30-31). But even when we stretch the data, it amounts to very little. For so extensive a literature that touches on so many fundamental dimensions of human existence, the reticence of Scripture on the topic of play is remarkable.

To learn how God's spirit might be disclosed in play, then, we must turn to the close observation of real life, paying attention to one of the most common, ordinary, and yet remarkable — and revealing — of human activities. We are invited to see, interpret, and assess the importance of what the writers of Scripture scarcely noticed, failed to interpret, and thought of little significance. The human body at play is thus the perfect test for the thesis of this book. If theology can build only on the words of Scripture, then nothing at all theologically important can be thought or spoken about an activity that is both fundamental to human existence in every known culture, and finds expression in multiple and complex ways. But if theology has to do first of all with what God is up to in the world, and what God is up to is disclosed first of all in the activities of human bodies, then the human activity of play must be regarded as potentially of the greatest significance for theological reflection.

I speak of a "human activity" — even though there is clear evidence that strikingly similar behaviors can be found among our fellow creatures, the animals. The case can be made, indeed, that patterns of play form — from an evolutionary perspective — one of the clearest links between humans and other animals. We have all watched with enjoyment as cats, large and small, puppies, porpoises, and primates engage in activities that we find appealingly similar to our own. It is easy to analogize the kitten batting at a string and a baby bouncing a ball, the puppies swarming one over the other with yips and yelps, and the little boys boiling together in a tangle of cries and shouts.

As we watch animals at play, several things strike us. First, we see that play is utterly engrossing, demanding a kind of concentration: the lion cubs are unaware of anything around their activity as they wrestle around and over their mother; only when she sounds the alert or paws them off herself irritably do the cubs break out of the spell of their shared activity.

---

4. The LXX of Gen. 26:8 translates: *eide ton Isaak paizonta meta Rebekkas tēs gynaikos autou.* See Philo, *Questions and Answers on Genesis* IV, 188.

Second, play among animals intensifies and becomes more complex as it moves from the individual to the group: the movements are not utterly random but form patterns that resemble choreography; the animals exchange roles as the pursuer switches and becomes the pursued, as the animal on top flips to become the one on the bottom of the scrum, so that the quality of concentration is one shared by all participants. Third, the play among animals is not immediately or obviously pragmatic: the kitten's stalking of a string does not catch a mouse; the crouching and chasing, the pawing and prancing, among wolves do not yield meat for the survival of the pack; play is something that seems to be done for its own sake, an expression of "animal high spirits."

Closer analysis, to be sure, suggests that from an evolutionary perspective, much animal play is actually intensely pragmatic, a form of training among the young for the adult activity that will dominate their short lives. This is particularly clear among predator animals: the crouching, chasing, mock-biting, sparring, and tracking — all find their goal in the eventual pursuit of food for the survival of the pack or pride. But also among nonpredators, such as herds of wild horses, the cantering and leaping, the nipping and butting seen among colts prepare them for the competition among males for dominance in mating. Outside the artificial context of domestication, play among colts is not only serious in itself, but it prepares them for the serious business of the survival of the herd. Still, there is in the disporting of some animals the sense of play that exceeds the merely useful: otters and seals, whales and porpoises seem at times simply to be having fun.

Aspects of Human Play

If attention to the body as disclosing the spirit is to become a factor in theology, it must begin with the theologian paying attention to his or her own body and the bodies of others. Only in this way can theology begin to be a truly inductive art. In the case of the body at play, then, I unabashedly begin with elements of my own experience in order to provide a lived context for the more analytic comments to follow.

When I look back from the age of seventy-one on the childhood I shared with my older brother in northern Wisconsin in the years 1943-1954, it appears as a world in which play was an almost constant feature. When we were children in that age and place of hardscrabble struggle for survival, play was an activity exclusive to children.[5] Adults were defined by the world of work. Adults knew little about our world of play and showed no interest in joining it or observing it; and we children certainly had no desire for adults to join us or to observe us. When children were done with their chores, they were free to find their own entertainment. There was no television in homes like ours in those years, and radio was for quiet evenings and Sundays. Apart from the occasional movie, our only other contact with technologically mediated entertainment was a handful of child-centered records: Bozo the Clown, Little Toot, Pecos Bill. Beyond that, we were on our own.

Between the ages of four and eleven, I experienced the rich round of play as one that was at once spontaneous and highly ordered. No great amount of planning ever seemed to be involved; as soon as a large enough group of kids got together, some sort of play simply evolved. The rules were set, not by adults, but by the oldest children in the group. We never asked where they learned the traditions that so strictly governed each activity. I cannot remember ever being taught any of the rules of baseball, for example, though there were many. It seems to me now that I always knew them, though I understand that this cannot be so.

Although certain solitary activities could count as play (catching fireflies, swinging at bats as they swooped through the summer evening air seeking insects, bouncing a basketball in intricate patterns while chanting), the addition of one or more kid led to more elaborate games, such as marbles and rope-jumping and hopscotch or "playing house" — which involved more discussion of roles and rules than actual activity. On rainy or snowy days, there were cards or checkers, Parchesi or Chinese checkers, or daylong marathons of monopoly. There was a whole set of games that my brother and I and our cousins played only when our delicate city cousin came north from Milwaukee — red-rover, captain-may-I, statues, hide-and-seek, tag — all games that were suitable to be played with girls.

As we grew a bit, we merged into the more elaborate games of the "older kids" that transported us out of the back yard. In the summer there were the almost daily treks on corduroy roads down to the Flambeau River to swim and to dive off the foot-bridge. Nobody drowned in that fast-flowing river despite the complete absence of adults. In the summer

5. Our small village of 400 survived on the basis of the traffic of hunters and fishermen from the big cities of Milwaukee and Chicago, and our mother was a widow raising six children.

afternoons and endless evenings, there was baseball or softball played with however many players could be gathered on whatever surface was available. For several summers, the field behind our house served for what then seemed an eternal baseball game in which every passing kid and adolescent played. Occasionally, we got organized enough to play something close to sandlot ball with kids in nearby towns — again, with not a single adult anywhere to be seen.

In the deep Wisconsin winter, the Flambeau River that ran through our village again served as the site for daytime and nighttime skating, with skaters gathering breathless and chilled around an astonishingly hot fire built with wood and discarded truck tires. I do not suppose that our experience of play in those years was in any way unique. But in its freedom from adult supervision and formal organization, I suspect that it contrasts sharply with the experience of my grandchildren and great-grandchildren, whose lives, by comparison, appear to be dominated by the presence of adults and organized "lessons" of one sort or another.

Such random observations on my own experience of play as a child agree with the more formal analysis of play classically provided by Johan Huizinga in *Homo Ludens: The Play Element in Culture*. Huizinga speaks of play as purposeless but meaningful activity. The term "purposeless" serves to distinguish play from all forms of work, which are carried out in order to accomplish something other than the activity itself: a product to be used or sold, a service tendered for payment, an effort expended for an effect. Work is essentially pragmatic. By contrast, play is engaged, not in order to accomplish something else, but for its own sake. The end of play is the means itself. To be purposeless, however, is not to be meaningless. Huizinga insists that play is intrinsically meaningful. The player finds satisfaction and pleasure in play, not because of an external reward or product, but because the pattern of movement and interaction in play involve both body and spirit. The body at play is content to be at play because play is deeply significant.

The meaningful character of play is connected to the highly regulated nature of this human activity. Play always involves rules. The rules serve, first of all, to set boundaries of time and space within which the play must take place. The boundaries are both arbitrary and absolute. The size of the circle within which marbles is played can vary, but the space must be a circle. There is no intrinsic reason why basketball hoops are set ten feet above the floor, but to play real basketball, they must be precisely that high. Sometimes the demarcation of space is most important while the rules for time are not. Such is the case with baseball, with its precise markings for what is fair and foul, for distances between the bases and between the pitching mound and home plate; but baseball games are not timed and could theoretically go on forever, because they are not over until the last batter is retired. In racing, the distance to be run is firmly set, while the length of time it takes to cover that distance constitutes the challenge. In boxing, the space is rigidly defined and the time of rounds is also set; but the bout can end abruptly at any moment. In some sports or games, time is of the essence: in football and basketball, everything has to be accomplished within sixty or forty-eight minutes, respectively. The effect of such boundary markers is to set apart the activity of play, above all in games, from the ordinary activity of life that has to do with work and the struggle to survive — efforts that have no set beginning or end. The boundaries help establish play as an alternative sphere of activity: here we do things this way.

Play always involves equally arbitrary yet absolute rules concerning patterns of activity within the boundaries of time and space. In board games, pieces can be moved only in the directions and distance prescribed. In diving, the body must twist and spin in strict conformity to the criteria that define a specific dive, and must enter the water at a particular angle of descent. Dance demands that certain steps and turns be done in regulated sequences whether alone or with a partner. Music requires the production of sound at predetermined pitches and tempos with voice or instrument. Movement with the ball in basketball requires dribbling the ball with one hand; in soccer, movement with the ball must use only the feet or head. Sometimes the rules are simple and straightforward: at the starter's signal, run in a lane until you reach the tape. Sometimes they are subtle and complex: to avoid a balk when trying to throw out a runner at first, the pitcher must come to a full stop in the pitching motion toward home plate before throwing the ball toward first base. What constitutes a "full stop" requires discernment. But simple or complex, play always involves rules. The rules constitute the game, and play demands observance of the rules.

How does the regulated character of play point to the way it is meaningful for participants? Here again, some sort of appeal to the actual experience of play is helpful. What I remember above all about the many forms of play in which I engaged as a child is the way in which they utterly absorbed me and those with whom I was playing so long as the game continued. This was the most important thing happening, and was completely satisfying — not because it met a basic need (food, drink, rest) but because it evoked a distinctive longing for ordered activity. Huizinga speaks of the seriousness of play: play is not silly or frivolous, and it is not a matter of "playing at" something casually and without care. Just the opposite: play demands of participants a genuine commitment of the body to certain movements in coordination with the movement of other bodies according to a script of what is allowed and what is not in that particular game. Such a commitment requires attentiveness and concentration. Players have to be aware of their own bodies and the bodies of others and the boundaries of time and space, as well as all the minute regulations for movement within the specific dance or game.

The more the rules of the game are internalized, the more "natural" and flexible is the interaction between bodies in motion. When players pay attention to the rules rather than to the movements, their participation is awkward and clumsy. Play reveals that a supposed opposition between order and freedom, between structure and spontaneity, is — at least in this privileged activity — illusory. The players whose mastery of the rules of the game is most complete are the ones who play with the greatest freedom of body and spirit. The strictness of rules, moreover, is a prerequisite to genuine spontaneity. Two examples illustrate the point. The game of chess is stringently governed by rules concerning the movement of the respective pieces; yet these basic moves can be marshaled within strategies of great complexity, and at the highest level, when grand masters face off, when attack, defense, and counterattack are mounted with astonishing virtuosity. Music is similarly governed by strict rules, but it is precisely the mastery of the basic forms that, through talent and practice, can give rise to free improvisation within the frame of the rules. Nowhere is this more splendidly displayed than in the virtuosic play of jazz musicians, whose seemingly spontaneous and even formless riffs are actually worked out within the framework of music's strict rules. When a jazz ensemble is truly "cooking," the complex interactions among the musicians — and the music they are making — represent play at the highest level.

The need for attentiveness and concentration is revealed by the disturbance the players experience when a distraction from the outside breaks that concentration and causes the body to break step, the goal to be missed, the wrong note to be struck. Play is so deeply satisfying — and even relaxing for both body and spirit — just because it distinctively engages both body and spirit in rhythmic and coordinated movement. It is thus "meaningful" precisely because, in a way not matched in ordinary time and space devoted to work, it gives a sense of being part of something larger within which the presence and activity of our body and spirit is an essential part. If we quit the game, the game is diminished, and we experience ourselves as diminished as well. In some way, play enlarges our existence in a distinctive fashion.

We recognize the role played by arbitrary yet absolute rules in play by the universal experience of revulsion at cheating. If we understand cheating, then we understand that a commitment to play means a commitment to "playing right." Cheating is a fundamental distortion of the character of play precisely because it bends or breaks rules in order to gain an advantage. In effect, cheating turns play into work: the point of cheating is winning at any cost; the meaningful character of play has been reduced to the purposefulness of work. But the cheater is abhorrent because she or he bends or breaks the rules surreptitiously, under the guise of playing the game the right way. As a parent, I remember the family fracases that arose when our children were home from school on snowy days and we settled in to play Monopoly. Some of us wanted to "play right," according to the rules of the game: dealing real estate only when it was our turn, making fair deals. For us, the game was mainly a matter of chance — to get a lucky roll of the dice, to land on the best property, to get sent to jail — and we expected games to last a whole day, in patient expectation of the moment when we each counted our assets and declared who won. But other family members considered the point of the game to be winning through the early elimination of others from the game, and they engaged in the kind of business practices associated with raw capitalism: dealing out of turn and seducing younger siblings into bad deals. They saw themselves as good players; but for those who left the game "beaten," they were cheaters who "did not play the game right" because of their willingness to bend or break the written rules. A game that should have been a peaceful "pastime" became the occasion for bitter disagreement.

One of the most distinctive aspects of human play at its best, and also one of the most difficult to describe, is the sense of participation in something larger than the self that it engenders. Once again, an appeal to common experience is helpful. I am speaking of those moments when, in the midst of the movements of our bodies with those of others, we experience a state that is at the same time profoundly embodied and outside the body, a state that can legitimately be called transcendence. This condition, I note, does not take place alongside or apart from the play, in a moment of contemplation or retrospection, but arises from within the movement of bodies during play. The experience of transcendence happens as a dimension of play itself, but if play were undertaken in order to have that experience, it would not be available, for play would have then become "purposeful" — and thus a form of work.

Here, I think, is the magic moment that play does not always bring about but always provides the basis for happening. Here also is the heart of what makes play, in its finest realization, "meaningful." My own experience of play as participation in a larger reality that also heightened my own sense of being came most often when singing in choir. Voicing song even alone provides an expanded sense of one's body: one's chest fills with air, and one's breath expands into the air with the added weight of sound. But when one sings with others, the engagement of mind and emotion and body with the music and with the sound being produced by the other singers in the chorus provides a sense of at once being a specific body making a specific sound and a part of a larger body that together makes a sound that none of the chorus members can produce alone.

At this point it might be helpful to ask how these aspects of human play help us think about the ways in which the body is revelatory, how it discloses spirit. Most obviously, perhaps, the pervasiveness of play among all human cultures suggests the deep pleasure that humans find in activity that is set apart and formally ordered. Play provides the most visible evidence that structure and freedom are not opposed but mutually dependent. The willingness of humans to commit themselves gladly to the "made-up" worlds of play with total concentration, moreover, supports the notion that humans long for a mode of existence that is not utterly defined by the search for survival, and that leisure is not an aspect of life that can be eliminated without great cost. Play also points to a sphere in which the primacy of the individual body is less significant than the interactions between many bodies, in which the sense of participation in a larger "body" is precisely the point. Finally, play shows us, in common human experience, how "transcendence" is a natural occurrence as spirit leaps beyond the confines of the individual body and enters into the larger sphere of body-spirit interactions that constitute play. There are even moments, we see, when the transcendent spirit becomes aware simultaneously, in a kind of ecstasy, of an almost timeless presence to one's own and others' bodies both above and within the movements in which the individual body participates.

The Elevation of Play: Art

Given the description of play as purposeless but meaningful activity, it is easy to see how art falls more squarely within the realm of play than of work. Although the slogan *ars gratia artis* ("art for its own sake") is seldom perfectly realized in a world of patronage and commerce, it nevertheless represents an ideal. At its best, art is done for its own sake, not for some pragmatic end. Even when the production of art is caught up in the world of patronage and commerce, the actual artistic process requires the concentration and transcendence characteristic of play. For the artist, the rules set by the art being practiced provide the necessary structure for free expression and creativity; the expectations of patron and audience represent (unfortunately) necessary distractions.

For those participating in artistic performance, above all in performances involving many bodies, everything already said about the experience of play applies perfectly. Those singing in the chorus, as I have said, experience a heightened sense of bodily existence through engagement with the music and the voices of others in the chorus. More complexly, because they are playing individual and diverse instruments, the members of a string quartet or symphony orchestra find themselves caught up in an effort that transcends and elevates the sounds made by the individual musician. In both musical examples, the strict rules set by the music itself provide the structure within which this mingling of body and spirit can take place. Actors in a drama likewise find the space for their own creative interpretation both in the words of dialogue and in the stage direction dictated by others, and in the play of voice and emotion between actors. Dancers can find themselves caught up into a form of communion with other bodies through the complex movements dictated by the choreography; so intense can this sense of communion be that dancers often keep at their art even when the body no longer is able to meet the rigorous demands made on it. Opera enjoys a special place among the performing arts because it combines all these elements with the highest degree of difficulty and the least tolerance for distraction. In all these cases, the musical composition or the written drama or the choreography provides the framework for participants both to enter and co-create an alternative space and time that is not defined by any immediate biological need, but which distinctively satisfies both body and spirit.

But what about the ones who *create* the musical compositions, the dramas, the choreography? I use the term "create" advisedly, because the transcendence of spirit in such artistic "bringing into being" can be seen as the expression of and even extension of the creative spirit of God constantly at work to create in the world. It is no surprise that poets above all were thought to be led by a *daimon,* or Muse, so extravagant and powerful is the work of spirit in their bodies. More recently, the designation "genius" has been applied to those whose inexplicable leaps of imagination and ability to translate those imaginative visions into physical expression astound those of us with only ordinary capacities. From the side of those who create art, however, the actual experience of artistic expression seems to be a form of play.

I can speak personally here only of a very low level of literary effort that has occasionally yielded verse and more often prose of a not exceptional character. But I know that nothing so inhibits even this level of creativity as the extrinsic demands imposed by deadlines or publisher standards, and nothing so liberates my imagination as the intrinsic demands of genre or thought. When I am able to deflect the distractions of extrinsic demands and enter into the alternative universe that is the argument I am trying to develop, my spirit experiences the peace and contentment that comes from the distinctive form of concentration and awareness that we associate with play. My wife, Joy, has frequently noted that I am a better person when I am engaged in a truly large literary effort. The engagement with this alternative world serves to connect me to a greater sense of being than is available, for example, in correcting papers or in attending committee meetings. And if such is the case with a mere professor, how much more must it be true of those capable of inventing out of their own body and spirit entire imaginative worlds within which others might temporarily dwell.

The creative spirit working in and through the body is even more evident in the case of the plastic arts. Once more, allowing for the necessary distractions of patronage and commerce, the actual making of art in material things resembles play more than work. To be sure, great and strenuous physical exertion is sometimes required: the making of a statue demands an exhausting effort by the sculptor. But this is the case also in the playing of vigorous games. In the act of sculpting itself, however, the aspects of play dominate. The sense of time and space is defined by the sculptor's interaction with the material she seeks to shape; the rules of engagement are set by the intrinsic task rather than external forces; the body of the sculptor interacts with the inert matter of the body being brought into being. In a way even more dramatic than the composer of music or the playwright, the sculptor's imagination (spirit), working through her body, brings another kind of body into being. The same can be said of the artists working in paint and other media: through the play of their spirit and body, new and beautiful things enter the world, often things that the world never expected to see and sometimes things that require some time to recognize and appreciate as works that elevate the spirits of others. The artist imagines a world that does not yet exist, and through his body's skill he brings it into being.

These very brief observations enable us to ask some questions pertinent to the practice of theology as an inductive art rather than a deductive science. My remarks only suggest some ways in which attention to play might yield insight into the revelatory body through which God's spirit is disclosed. The theologian is called to attend to the specifics of the exercise of human liberty within the ruled activity of play. We learn from the analysis of play the ways in which we might begin to fill in the concept of being created in the image of God. Might it involve a desire for entering a larger world than that of constant work, a place where there is a hunger for leisure, a love of contemplation, a thirst for communion with other bodies in a context of free exchange? Might we learn from the ways in which the artist creates something new from the depths of the artist's spirit how to think analogously about God's relationship to the world God creates out of nothingness every moment? More critically, we can ask what play teaches us about what God is up to in the world. We can also ask how the creative expression of artists tells us — in visual displays, in music, in literature — something about the condition of play in our culture, and thus something of how we bear the image of God in our individual and communal lives.

The Elevation of Play: Liturgy

That human play and religious ritual share many features is a commonplace for anthropologists and sociologists.[6] They note that communal ritual involves a commitment to gathering in a specific place at a specific time, and that the ritual itself helps establish time and place as "sacred" or "other"

6. See C. Bell, *Ritual: Perspectives and Dimensions* (New York: Oxford University Press, 1997), p. 154; see also R. Bellah, *Religion in Human Evolution* (Cambridge, MA: Belknap Press of Harvard University Press, 2011), pp. 89-116.

than the space and time that is undifferentiated and hence "profane."[7] They note that ritual involves rules governing what is to be done *(ta drōmena):* kneeling, genuflecting, standing, processing, sitting — all these must be done in the appropriate sequence either by designated players ("offici-ants") or by all worshipers together. Rules equally govern what is to be said *(ta legomena):* these hymns and chants and prayers and readings rather than those, and in this stipulated order. Breaking these rules represents a "distraction" from the ritual action that is more fundamentally fatal than interrupting ordinary games, for it represents an intrusion of the secular into the time and space designated as sacred.

In religious ritual, however, the sense of participation in a reality larger than the individual self — that element of transcendence we observed in all play — reaches a new level, because ritual involves communion with the divine as well as with other worshipers. The concentration and aware-ness characteristic of games here become an attitude of awe appropriate to creatures in the presence of the power or powers that are perceived by humans to be ultimate. Ritual is far more compelling than ordinary games precisely because the elusive sense of communion that gives game-playing its meaningfulness is elevated to an entirely new realm. The ecstasy of spirit that is momentarily experienced in games is, within religious ritual, understood to be a participation of the individual's human spirit — and the spirit of all participating in the ritual — in the spiritual energy field that is the presence of ultimate power. In this sense, religious ritual can be regarded as an intensification of human play as well as an elevation of it.

The analysis of religious ritual as a species of play is particularly helpful as a way of understanding and assessing practices in Christian liturgy. My observations here are based primarily on my personal experience of liturgy within Roman Catholicism (throughout my life, pre- and post–Vatican II) and Orthodoxy (I served as a deacon for a year in the Liturgy of St. John Chrysostom) and on my participant-observer status in Protestant wor-ship in interdenominational seminaries (Yale Divinity School and Candler School of Theology) over a period of some thirty years. The very first thing that must be said is that it is much easier to think of Roman Catholic and Orthodox worship in terms of the analysis of play than it is to view most Protestant worship from this perspective. To be sure, all Christian worship displays some of the elements of play. The boundaries of sacred time and

---

7. J. Z. Smith, *To Take Place: Toward Theory in Ritual* (Chicago: University of Chicago Press, 1987).

sacred space set the frame within which the action must take place. Patterns of sitting and standing are prescribed and predictable. The singing of hymns joins all participants in a choral experience of "becoming one body"; such hymns are composed specifically for worship and are — or have been — carefully distinguished from the music of the secular world. The language of prayer and response tends to be formal and elevated above the rhythms of ordinary speech. Sermons are discourses that can also be distinguished from lectures and informational presentations by their rhetorical character, above all in the use of *pathos* appeals that are absent from most secular discourse. The "kiss of peace" (even when in the form of a handshake) links body to body, and spirit to spirit, in a moment of communion. To the degree that Christian liturgy maintains these formal elements of play, it enables participants to experience a form of transcendence. Worshipers so internalize the patterns of liturgical play that they can move in spirit beyond their individual bodies and into the larger body of the community, in a form of "going beyond" that does not eliminate but enhances the significance of the individual as part of a meaningful whole.

Such transcendence is even more available in Catholic and Orthodox traditions — for two reasons. First, worship is even more highly formal and regulated, so that the "holiness" of the action — in the sense of being "different" — is greater. The adornment of the sacred space with stained glass windows, frescoes, statues and icons; the use of musical instruments and chants for music; the wearing of specialized liturgical garments; the appeal to the senses in the exotic smell of incense and the flickering light of candles; the intensified forms of movements both around the altar and among the people; the dialogical exchanges between ministers and worshipers, especially when sung — all of these mark the liturgy even more decisively as play of a distinct and elevated kind. Such elements also encourage the worshiper to let go of secular preoccupations and enter into the alternative world constructed by liturgy. They also serve to focus the concentration and attentiveness so critical to the "seriousness" of play, and to that extent, provide the element of deep relaxation that is characteristic of play even when it involves strenuous effort.

Second, in the Catholic and Orthodox liturgies, the Eucharist occupies a central place in worship. To take only the example of the Roman Catholic Mass, the solemn words of the *anaphora,* the gestures at the act of consecration, the display of the elements to the congregation, and the prostration by the celebrant serve to concentrate the attention of all participants on this central action. Even more, the sharing of the bread and wine — understood to be the sacramental body and blood of the Lord — by those moving in procession to the altar and then back to their places, provides a profound sense of actual participation, not only in the communal body as in other forms of play, but in the actual body of Christ that is available through the presence of the Life-Giving Spirit in the body, that is, the congregation gathered in the name of Jesus. Such sacramental awareness, I should emphasize, comes about, not through instruction or explicit interpretation, so much as through the traditional gestures and movements that congregants have internalized through lifelong repetition. Precisely because the "rules of the game" are formal, established, and not open to negotiation, they liberate worshipers from self-consciousness and free them to enter joyously into the common action that unites them all in a body that is greater than they are, yet embraces each of them bodily.

In contrast to the freedom enabled by the formal rules of traditional liturgy, the forms of worship that are constructed *de novo* by seminary "worship committees" tend to move liturgy in the direction of work rather than of play — in two ways: first, such efforts often focus on a pragmatic end, and second, the absence of traditional rules serves to inhibit spontaneity of spirit rather than to enable it. The planning sessions dedicated to a specific worship service seek to integrate all elements to make a single point or to create a single effect among participants, and that effect is shaped according to a certain moral lesson or disposition. Such pragmatism is the opposite of play. It is instructive that such constructed services are necessarily "scripted" in the form of bulletins or brochures that enable participants to know what elements come next and what their responses should be. Concentration is necessarily turned to getting the words of the song right rather than to a reality that memorized formulae and movements open to free contemplation in action.

Play Distorted: Sports

Sports are so obviously an aspect or derivative of play that one can be tempted to identify the two, especially when one form of sport or another is constantly being shown and discussed on television and radio around the world, and its athletes are competing with the stars of music, cinema, and politics for celebrity. Indeed, many of the examples of play I cited earlier in this chapter come from recognized sports: baseball, basketball, tennis, golf, soccer. Yet there are aspects of sports, above all in the contemporary world, that should caution us against such a simple identification. Sports may be a form of play, but in some instances, it appears most of all as a species of work.

All of the elements of play that I have identified are present in sports: the boundaries of time and space are strictly drawn and vigorously maintained. The movements within the game are highly regulated — indeed, often monitored by officials (referees, umpires) rather than by the players themselves. The separation of these sports from ordinary activities is signaled by special uniforms, the use of specialized language (among both players and referees), and highly formal ceremonies at the beginning of the event (introduction of players, flags, music, dance, moments of silence, etc.). Most of all, as all participants in sports attest, this kind of organized play enables moments of transcendence, when the body of an individual player is experienced as being elevated to a level not available outside the game.

Players speak of being "in the zone," when, for a short period within a game, their bodies and minds seem to work in such harmony that all their movements are perfect: every shot at the basket goes in, every strike of the golf ball finds the fairway or the green, every forward pass is caught by a receiver, every pitch looks hittable. Even more rarely, players testify, there are moments when the movements of all the members of a team seem to be "in the zone" together: players anticipate the movements of other players with uncanny accuracy, and they speak of a sense of being a single multimembered body rather than individual bodies. Indeed, players of sports often relish the sense of communion with other players as much as, or even more than, the often painful and difficult actions on the field or court. Such fleeting but powerful moments of spiritual awareness and transcendence keep athletes playing a sport even when their bodies have long since stopped deriving any pleasure from it.

Sports can be distinguished from the simpler forms of play by the addition of complicating elements. The first of these is a higher degree of organization: games not only have rules, but the rules are, as I have noted, monitored by referees. In sports at the collegiate and professional levels, games are played by organized teams, and these teams have managers. Teams are gathered into leagues. Games are played according to set schedules rather than when the opportunity arises. Leagues, in turn, can be organized into conferences, and these conferences oversee the entire structure of the sport, often assessing penalties on players and teams and even leagues for failure to observe, not the rules of the sport itself (baseball or soccer, say), but the rules of the organization itself. The vast structure of the Olympic Games, where thousands of athletes from around the world meet every four years in intricately structured performances under the supervision of national and international committees who qualify and disqualify participants, shows how sports represents an elaboration of play far beyond sandlot baseball or schoolyard basketball.

The second way in which sports complicate simpler forms of play is through the emphasis they put on competition among players. Certainly there is some element of this in games generally: no one begins a game of chess or checkers seeking to lose, and even in "captain-may-I" getting to the finish line first is important. But competitive and structured sports make competition a central and indeed all-important dimension of play. There is certainly a positive aspect of competition: athletes, by competing, hone their skills to a higher level and achieve a degree of excellence that would not be reached were they not pushed by other players. It is difficult to argue against such excellence, and we must acknowledge that it is an aspect of other forms of play as well: music competitions lead musicians to excel at their chosen instruments, and archers seek ever-greater accuracy when they are pitted against other archers. But there is also a negative side to the emphasis on competition that sports fosters, when the quest is less for excellence and almost exclusively for victory. When "winning becomes the only thing," then play shifts slightly from its nature as "meaningful for its own sake" to "purposeful": the game is worth playing only if victory is the result.

A third way that sports complicates play is through specialization: whereas in ordinary games any player can take up any role required, in sports the emphasis on excellence and competition tends to limit the freedom of players' movement among roles. Now a participant plays this role because he or she has developed the specific skills required to play a certain position. Body size, speed, hand-eye coordination, stamina — all are assessed by coaches when they assign this player to be a lineman and that one to be a running back, this one to be a defenseman and that one to be a goalie. Specialization often reaches the point that participants are able to play only one position, and they don't even understand the demands of other positions. They are less players of the game than players of a position.

The fourth complication is the introduction of spectators. Here we can make a comparison to artistic forms of play such as drama and dance, which also assume the presence of those who hear and see the "play" being performed by actors and dancers. The size of crowds viewing sports varies tremendously, from the handful of folks faithfully waiting at the finish of a cross-country run to the hundreds of thousands attending international soccer matches. Likewise, the degree of spectator participation varies, from the polite attention given tennis and golf, to the raucous (and sometimes violent) venting found among football and soccer fans. Indeed, the term "fans" reminds us of the avid, almost fanatical following of sports that dominates the lives of many who do not themselves play the game but for whom the outcome of competitions has become of almost ultimate importance. The comparison between basketball fever in Indiana or Kentucky and religious ritual is not far-fetched, nor that between the liturgical year and the schedule of high school football games anywhere in the southern United States. Sports function for many in today's world as the functional equivalent of religion, a thesis that can be tested by observing which set of rituals displaces the other on a regular basis.

Sport becomes a distortion of play, above all, through its entanglement with money. When a sport becomes professional, it exhibits the features of work more than of play. The turn toward work is most obvious in sports that candidly identify themselves as "professional." Highly organized leagues and associations pay athletes astounding amounts of money to play games that in their fundamental shape are continuous with those played by children on sidewalks and playgrounds. The money paid to athletes places them under obligations as "professionals" to regard and treat their training and performance as a form of work rather than play. Because athletes' salaries are computed statistically in competition with others in their field or position, it is not a great surprise that they seek an edge through the use of performance-enhancing drugs, even though, within the framework of play, such enhancements amount to outright cheating.

The salaries and bonuses paid to such athletes are at a level matched only by the stars of music and cinema, but they represent only a portion of the wealth gathered and controlled by team owners via stadiums, ticket sales, concessions, advertising, and other exploitations of the team brand. Professional sports are "serious" in a way that is distinct from the seriousness that is inherent in all play. Today, an athlete's future can be jeopardized in a moment's collision, a coach's career can tip on a few wins or losses, an owner's franchises can rocket or plummet because of a winning or losing season. In all of this entanglement with commerce, it becomes more difficult to discern the elements of play within sports.

Professionalization has moved steadily downward to encompass the playing of sports in colleges and even in high schools. The ways in which

"Big Time Sports" (above all football and basketball) can dominate and distort universities is patent as well as painful. Coaches are paid salaries and bonuses far exceeding those of professors, or even presidents, of universities. "Student athletes" are recruited in fierce competition with rival universities and are "signed up" through means that are often suspect. These star athletes are rarely real students, and they frequently leave college after only a year to enter explicitly into the professional ranks. Competitive recruitment has even reached into the ranks of grade-schoolers who show exceptional athletic promise. But, in this regard, major sports actually lag behind sports that long branded themselves as amateur, but have recently been revealed as equally coopted by commerce. That is certainly the case with Olympic athletes, who are regularly recruited and trained and financially supported — either by their countries or by corporations — from the time their talent is first detected. Olympic champions with equal regularity "professionalize" themselves as both athletes and advertising spokespersons for commercial products.

Conclusion

As with the other short essays that make up the second part of this book, this set of reflections on the body at play is meant to be suggestive rather than exhaustive. It would betray the entire argument I am advancing to pretend to "close the book" on any aspect of human embodiedness. My point throughout is to encourage a certain way of observing real life for the signs of God's self-disclosure, in the conviction that theologians must learn to think inductively. Therefore, my conclusion to this chapter does not amount to a fixed set of *theologoumena*. Rather, it leads to my further observations and reflection — and perhaps yours as well.

Observing the body at play confirms for me, first of all, the importance of the topic. Play is so pervasive, and has so many manifestations, that failing to think about it means removing a great deal of human behavior from theological consideration. In contrast, paying attention to play in all its manifestations means widening the arena in which the work of God in the world can be seen and engaged. Three aspects of play strike me as being of great importance for theological reflection. The first is the apparent paradox that the human spirit experiences a distinctive and joyful freedom when constrained by rules to which the human has freely consented. There is much to think about on this point. Second, play provides a place where we can observe the interplay between the individual body and other bodies that emphasizes the coordination (even in competition) among them in the making of a greater "body." Third, connected to the previous point, play is a readily available example of the experience of transcendence, when, even momentarily, an individual has the sense of being both in one's own body and present in the bodies of others. Because many can acknowledge such an experience in their lives — whether in "games" so designated or in the arts or in worship — the theologian has a basis on which to think with others about the bodily expression of spirit in ordinary life.

The closer we examine any phenomenon, in turn, the more complexities that were not initially evident come to light. Play helps us see how the body reveals spirit. But in my analyses of "play elevated" and "play distorted," we can also see how bodily activity can obscure spirit. I have suggested that art and liturgy represent intensifications and elevations of play, but as art is enmeshed in commerce, its revelation of spirit can be diminished, and as worship tilts toward the pragmatism of work, it likewise weakens the capacity for transcendence. I have suggested that the same is true even more emphatically in sport: in its most basic forms it elevates play through excellence, but as actually manifested in our world, it is deeply problematic as a place where body reveals spirit. These are complexities that I have suggested. Some people may not only find others, they may also challenge my classifications of elevation and distortion, and even argue in a way opposite my own. Such discussion would actually be good, for it would take seriously the premise that, in some form, play is a dimension of human behavior that deserves the closest possible attention.

Finally, I am not in a position to speak definitively on how the observation of play enables us to speak of God. I am left, instead, with a number of questions. This is by no means a bad thing: questions serve better than answers to open up possibilities of discovery. But the asking of questions also means that the conversation on the topic must continue outside the confines of this or any other book, for the data keeps coming in. Two questions, above all, preoccupy me at the end of this essay. The first is most basic: How is the spirit of God at play in the play of human bodies and spirits? Can play in its purest manifestations be regarded as exemplary of God's creative activity as such? In this regard, the universality of play among humans — as well as the evolutionary links between the play of animals and that of humans — is richly suggestive. Is the creative God "playful" in the proper sense of the word? Does God seek bodies for God's own self-expression, and does the play among those bodies God creates (at every moment) signal the presence of a God who is about play more than work?

The second question is related: What can we learn from the close examination of human play about the conviction — this one deeply embedded in Scripture — that humans are created as *imago Dei* (in the image of God)? This question turns in two directions: perhaps play tells us something, as I have suggested, about the character of God and how to understand God's "seriousness"; and perhaps play also tells us something about the kind of human activity that is, as a reflection of God, most properly human. Is the deep satisfaction or contentment that humans tend to experience in play — the combination of rest and action, of contemplation and action found intensely in art and worship — an indication of when humans are most fully human?

There is a last question I might pose, if theology is thought to have a prescriptive as well as a descriptive function: How can theology speak clearly and convincingly about the forms of play that ennoble the body and enhance the spirit — and serve thereby to disclose the activity of the playful God — and those that degrade the body and diminish the spirit? Asking this question leads to others concerning such issues as violence and severe injury or death in games, such as the corrupting potential of commerce and commodification in art and sports, and such as the distorting effect of pragmatism in liturgy. It enables us to ask about the presence or absence of leisure that is the presupposition for play in any form. It allows us to ask whether forms of "games" that pit a "player" against a mechanical or electronic system (whether we think of slot machines and roulette wheels or computer and video games) do not, in fact, exacerbate the privatization of the body and the confinement of spirit, and represent the opposite of the play that discloses the spirit of God through human bodies.

CHAPTER FIVE

The Body in Pain

A fundamental truth about human existence is that humans hurt in both spirit and body. The experience of pain is not optional. Pain can be avoided for a time, delayed, and soothed, but ultimately, to be embodied means to be in pain. The subject of the suffering body thus requires close attention for any effort to discern the presence of God's spirit in the world. The topic of the suffering body seems to stand in neat opposition to the topic of the body at play. Whereas play appears to be almost entirely positive, suffering seems to be almost entirely negative. We associate play with pleasure and suffering with pain. While play is something freely chosen, suffering is experienced as something imposed. Play is widely pervasive in all human cultures. But suffering is certainly more universal than play: that is, it is conceivable that humans could live and die without ever engaging in play; it is unimaginable that humans could live and die without suffering. And whereas Scripture pays scarcely any attention to the subject of play, the theme of suffering receives considerable attention in Scripture. So that is a good place to start.

Suffering in Scripture

The strength as well as the weakness of the scriptural witness concerning human suffering is the way it connects suffering to the great themes of sin and salvation.[1] In the Old Testament, suffering is not considered

---

1. There are any number of theological works that, working within the framework of Scripture, deal with human suffering either as a problem of theodicy that requires solving, or

something neutral or natural. Instead, it is the tragic consequence of bad human choices. This perception is stated most clearly in Deuteronomy. Moses presents before the people in the wilderness the choice of blessing or curse. Blessing follows from obedience to the commands that God has revealed to them: "Blessed shall you be in the city, and blessed shall you be in the field. Blessed shall be the fruit of your body, and the fruit of your ground, and the fruit of your beasts, the increase of your cattle, and the young of your flock. Blessed shall be your basket and your kneading trough. Blessed shall you be when you come in and blessed shall you be when you come out" (Deut. 28:1-6). In contrast, cursing follows from the refusal to obey God's commandments: "Cursed shall you be in the city, and cursed shall you be in the field" (28:15-16).

Among these curses is every form of suffering, enumerated in the same passage: "The Lord will send upon you curses, and confusion, and frustration, in all that you undertake to do, until you are destroyed and perish quickly, on account of your doings, because you have forsaken me" (28:20). The list continues in great detail: pestilence will consume the land and them; they will experience consumption, fever, inflammation, fiery heat, drought, blasting, mildew; they will be smitten with the boils of Egypt and ulcers and scurvy and the itch from which they cannot be healed, as well as with madness and blindness and confusion of mind. They will be oppressed by other nations and taken into exile. So great will be their deprivation that they will be reduced to cannibalism (28:27-57). "He will bring upon you again all the diseases of Egypt, which you were afraid of, and they shall cling to you" (28:60). All of these afflictions, we note, are sent by the Lord as punishment for disobedience: "As the Lord took delight in doing you good and multiplying you, so the Lord will take delight in bringing ruin upon you and destroying you" (28:63).

The principle is given mythic expression in the account of human origins in Genesis 1–3. Adam and Eve dwell in a garden of delights, but their

---

as an existential crisis for which pastoral advice is needed; see, e.g., A. C. McGill, *Suffering: A Test of Theological Method* (Eugene, OR: Wipf and Stock, 2007 [1982]); Dorothee Sölle, *Suffering* (Minneapolis: Fortress, 1984); C. S. Lewis, *The Problem of Pain* (San Francisco: HarperOne, 2009 [1940]); J. Piper, ed., *Suffering and the Sovereignty of God* (Memphis: Crossway, 2000); H. Van Zeller, *Suffering: The Catholic Answer; The Cross of Christ and Its Meaning for You* (Manchester, NH: Sophia Institute Press, 2002). Neither of these approaches is mine in this chapter; but see L. T. Johnson, "Suffering, Sin, and Scripture," *Priest and People* 13 (1999): 87-90; "Sickness and the Stoic Sage," in *Voices in Our Midst: Spiritual Resources,* ed. G. R. Gary (Atlanta: Scholars Press, 1996), pp. 9-11.

transgression of God's command leads to their banishment from paradise. The human experience of suffering and death follow as a consequence of disobedience. Women will experience pain in childbirth and be subordinate to their husbands (Gen. 3:16). Men will survive only through struggle, and then will die: "In the sweat of your face you shall eat bread till you return to the ground, for out of it you were taken; you are dust and to dust you shall return" (3:19). In this mythic account, the principle enunciated by Deuteronomy for the people of Israel is given universal application. Suffering and death are not necessary dimensions of embodied existence; they happen only because the first parents rebelled and were expelled from the place where they could eat from the tree of life and live forever (Gen. 3:22).

In this sense, Torah is God's response to the human condition, for if the disobedience to God's commandments now brings curse, obedience also brings the possibility of blessing. Israel can attain posterity, prosperity, safety, even life itself, from the keeping of the commandments: "I have set before you life and death, blessing and curse; therefore choose life, that you and your descendants may live" (Deut. 30:19). Leviticus 18:5 states it succinctly: "You shall therefore keep my statutes and ordinances, by doing which a man shall live. I am the Lord."

The deuteronomic principle, in turn, dominates the narratives of the Old Testament that relate the story of Israel. The success or failure of Israel's judges and kings is measured by their degree of fidelity to God's covenant, and the experiences of national defeat and exile are seen as punishments from the hand of God for apostasy from the commandments (Josh. 24:19-28; Judg. 2:11-15, 19-23; 8:33-35; 13:1; 1 Kings 11:1-13; 15:25-30; 16:15-20; 2 Kings 3:1-3; 10:28-36). The prophetic literature reinforces the equation between suffering and sin. The calamities that threaten the people are a direct consequence of their disobedience. Amos declares the constant refrain: "'They do not know how to do right,' says the Lord, 'those who store up violence and robbery in their strongholds.' Therefore, thus says the Lord God, 'An adversary shall surround the land, and bring down your defenses from you, and your strongholds shall be plundered'" (Amos 3:10-11; see also 2:1-16; 4:1-13; 8:4-14; Isa. 1:21-26; 3:1-26; Jer. 3:6-25; 4:8-31; Ezek. 13:1-23; 16:1-63; Hos. 8:1-14; Mic. 3:1-12; Zeph. 1:2-18). In sum, the Old Testament is dominated by a powerful and rigid conviction concerning human suffering (and death). Every negative experience of the body must be seen in terms of a curse, a form of punishment from God for disobedience to God's commands. The prophet Ezekiel simply intensifies the conviction when he insists that punishment and reward are not inherited but are the consequence of each individual's behavior: "The soul that sins shall die. The son shall not suffer for the iniquity of the father, nor the father suffer for the iniquity of the son; the righteousness of the righteous shall be upon himself, and the wickedness of the wicked shall be upon himself" (Ezek. 18:20).

A variation on the theme with great future potential is offered by Isaiah's extraordinary depiction of God's servant (Isa. 52:13–53:12). The servant is innocent of wrongdoing — "he had done no violence and there was no deceit in his mouth" (53:9); he is "the righteous one, my servant" (53:11) — but he nevertheless experiences suffering and oppression (53:3-7) and is "cut off from the land of the living" (53:8). Remarkably, however, the suffering of this innocent man does not alter the fundamental equation. Suffering is still a punishment from God for sin ("it was the will of the Lord to bruise him," 53:10); but it is a punishment that is carried for the sake of others by the one who is God's servant: "He was wounded for our transgressions, he was bruised for our iniquities . . . the Lord has laid on him the iniquity of us all" (53:5-6). Therefore, the servant suffers for the sake of others — by taking upon himself the punishment that is due them for having "gone astray" (53:6). He has made himself an "offering for sin" (53:10), bearing the sin of many and making intercession for the transgressors (53:12). By "bearing their iniquities" and by "pouring out his soul in death," the servant "makes many to be accounted righteous" (53:11). Second Isaiah thus offers a modification of Ezekiel's insistence that each person's sin accounts for each person's suffering, and points to the possibility of salvific and vicarious suffering. But this vision does not alter the fundamental link between suffering and sin.

In the Psalms, however, we catch a glimpse of how actual human experience can pose a challenge to the rigid ideology that links human suffering to God's punishment. The pious singer of the psalm observes how wicked people appear to prosper and escape punishment, while the righteous person is afflicted (see Pss. 10:1-18; 22:1-31; 37:40; 69:1-36). The emotional and mental pain caused by this realization is real: "My feet had almost stumbled, my steps had well-nigh slipped. For I was envious of the arrogant when I saw the prosperity of the wicked. For they have no pangs; their bodies are sound and sleek. They are not in trouble as other men are; they are not stricken like other men" (Ps. 73:1-5). In the face of the dissonance between experience and ideology, however, the response of the psalmist is not to reject the ideology but to reassert the conviction that God will reverse the situation: "Wait for the Lord, and keep to his way, and he will exalt you to possess the land; you will look on the destruction of the wicked" (Ps. 37:34). Again, "O Lord, thou wilt hear the desires of the meek; thou wilt strengthen their heart, thou wilt incline thy ear to do justice to the fatherless and the oppressed, so that the man who is of the earth may strike terror no more" (Ps. 10:17-18). Even when such a reversal is not in view, unjust suffering makes the pious one place his faith even more on the Lord: "Whom have I in heaven but thee? And there is nothing upon earth that I desire besides thee. My flesh and my heart may fail, but God is the strength of my heart and my portion forever" (Ps. 73:25-26).

It is often supposed that Job and Qoheleth represent challenges to the deuteronomic equation of sin and suffering, and to some extent, they do. Job's protest against the suffering inflicted on him and his resistance to the simplistic applications of the deuteronomic principle by his visiting friends are powerful. He is not, in fact, an unrighteous person; rather, he exemplifies fidelity to God and care for the neighbor. He is, by such measures, free from blame. Nor does he abandon God even when he himself feels abandoned by God. Within the narrative framework of the book, the suffering of Job is understood as a testing of his faith rather than a punishment for any sin. In this sense, the rigid ideology of Deuteronomy is altered. But not entirely, for at the end of the story Job receives all the magnificent rewards that faithfulness to God ought to win, and from beginning to end, the book of Job operates within the premise that suffering is something that should not happen to those faithful to God. It only suggests in passing the perception that suffering is natural to humans simply because they are human: "Man that is born to woman is of few days, and full of trouble. He comes forth like a flower, and withers; he flees like a shadow and continues not" (Job 14:1-2).

Qoheleth (Ecclesiastes) comes closer to challenging the deuteronomic principle in a fundamental way. The Preacher retains the conviction that God will judge the wicked (3:17), but his observations based on the experience of life — which he summarizes as "vanity of vanities" (1:2) — tend to work against that confident assertion. He notes that suffering is a part of living (2:23) and that everyone suffers (4:1-3), with no reference to suffering as punishment for sin. Indeed, he notes that the righteous man perishes while the wicked man prolongs his life (7:15), even though no one can really control the length of life (8:8); and he observes that all face the same destiny (of death), whether wise person or fool (2:14-15), beast or human (3:19): "One fate comes to all, to the righteous and the wicked, to the good and the evil, to the clean and the unclean, to him who sacrifices and him who does not sacrifice. As is the good man, so is the sinner; and he who swears is as he who shuns an oath" (9:2). Qoheleth's deep ambivalence toward the traditional equation is indicated by the series of statements in 8:11-13: "Because the sentence against an evil deed is not executed speedily, the heart of the sons of men is fully set to do evil. Though a sinner does evil a hundred times and prolongs his life, yet I know that it will be well with those who fear God, because they fear before him; but it will not be well with the wicked, neither will he prolong his days like a shadow, because he does not fear before God."

Despite these few challenges to the link between suffering and sin — all of them based more on the experience and observation of actual life than on ideology — the deuteronomic principle dominates the pages of the Old Testament, and it is given particular force by being located anthropologically in the sin of Adam and Eve. The equation continues to dominate the minds of many contemporary believers. When those in distress are heard to say, "I must have done something wrong" as an explanation for their suffering, or when preachers account for sickness or disaster, even meteorological events, by appealing to the vice of the local population, or when children blame themselves for the divorce or death of parents — and we hear this sort of thing every day if we are paying attention — then we learn just how powerful this ancient conviction continues to be.

To an impressive degree, the New Testament continues to assume a link between sin and suffering, between sin and death. The connection between Jesus' healing and the forgiveness of sins is implied by Mark 2:5-11 (see Matt. 9:2-13; Luke 5:20-24). But Jesus explicitly controverts the assumption in John's account of the healing of the man born blind. When the disciples ask whether the blind man or his parents had sinned, thus accounting for his condition, Jesus responds: "Neither this man nor his parents sinned; he was born this way so that God's works might be revealed in him" (John 9:1-3). The statement is of great potential significance for our reflection, since it speaks of the body as the arena for the revelation of God's works, and suggests that suffering can be a profoundly polyvalent reality.

The New Testament makes a more powerful link between sin and death. Paul appropriates the connection established by Genesis 1–3 when he says that "sin came into the world through one man and death came through sin, and so death spread to all because all have sinned . . . death exercised dominion from Adam to Moses, even over those whose sins were not like the transgression of Adam, who is a type of the one who is to come" (Rom. 5:12-14). Paul's real interest, however, is in "the one who came," namely, Jesus, whose faithful death in behalf of others (Rom. 3:21-26; 1 Cor. 8:11) brought about a new dominion of grace and of eternal life (Rom. 5:15-21). For Paul, death is the last enemy to be destroyed (1 Cor. 15:26), and this will not be fully accomplished until God's reign is fully established and "God is all in all" (1 Cor. 15:28). He makes the connection: "The sting of death is sin" (1 Cor. 15:56).

Because Christ "died for our sins" (1 Cor. 15:3; 1 Pet. 3:18), the dominant attention to suffering in the New Testament is given to the suffering of Jesus and to the salvation from sins that it accomplished. In this regard, the influence of Isaiah 52–53 is unmistakable. Christ is understood as the Messiah who "had to suffer" before entering his glory (Luke 24:26, 46; 1 Pet. 1:11), and whose sufferings were endured for the sake of others (see Mark 10:45; 14:24). Clearly echoing Isaiah 52–53, First Peter declares: "He himself bore our sins in his body on the cross, so that, free from sins, we might live for righteousness; by his wounds you have been healed" (1 Pet. 2:24). All of this dramatically reverses the deuteronomic principle of the Old Testament, especially the individual application given it by Ezekiel 18. Now, the suffering of the "righteous one" (Luke 23:47; Acts 3:14) shatters the premise that human suffering must be a punishment for sin. The suffering Christ, moreover, is the source of the new blessing that is eternal life, the seal of which is the gift of the Holy Spirit (Gal. 3:6-29; 2 Cor. 3:12–5:21). And all this is mediated through the body of Jesus Christ, both the suffering and the glory; in his body, the definitive revelation of God for human salvation is displayed.

The intense union between the risen Christ and those living by the gift of his Holy Spirit means that something of the significance of his suffering can be shared by believers as well. First Peter states it in terms of imitation: "Christ also suffered for you, leaving you an example, so that you should follow in his steps" (1 Pet. 2:21). Paul, in turn, thinks in terms of a participation in suffering and salvation that unites both Christ and believers, and believers to each other: "I am now rejoicing in my sufferings for your sake, and in my flesh I am completing what is lacking in Christ's afflictions for the sake of his body, that is, the church" (Col. 1:24; see esp. 2 Cor. 1:3-7). Indeed, for Paul, the "sufferings of the present time" that are endured by those led by the Holy Spirit "are not to be compared with the glory about to be revealed to us." Human suffering here is a participation in the cosmic process by which the Spirit frees creation from its present bondage to decay and reveals the "freedom of the glory of the children of God" (Rom.

8:18-21). The Letter to the Hebrews also connects the suffering of Christ and those who follow him. Christ "offered himself" to bear the sins of many (Heb. 9:28), but his suffering is also part of the mysterious process by which God perfected the humanity of Jesus into full sonship (2:10-18). Jesus "learned obedience from the things he suffered" and became the perfect son (5:7-9). Those who follow him in obedience likewise endure suffering as part of an educative process from God: "You endure for the sake of an education" (Heb. 12:7; see 12:3-11).[2] The same participation with the sufferings of Christ experienced by believers (13:12-13) enables them to identify with the sufferings experienced by others (13:3).

The witness of Scripture concerning suffering is complex and not totally consistent. But the experience of a suffering and exalted Messiah completely revised the dominant view of the Old Testament that an individual's suffering resulted from a punishment for sins. Nevertheless, the understanding of Christ as the innocent sufferer, who died for the sins of others, also clearly responds to this notion. But the fundamental shift is from suffering as a mark of sin to suffering as a means of salvation. Even more dramatically, the suffering of Jesus is seen as an ingredient in the process by which his followers also become conformed to his image (Rom. 8:28-30). Suffering is now capable of bearing a positive valence it did not previously have. Suffering can be, as Jesus declares in John 9:3, an opportunity for "God's works to be revealed."

The Experience of Suffering

The strength of the scriptural witness, I have suggested, is that it so powerfully connects human suffering to the great themes of sin and salvation. Throughout Scripture, suffering is given meaning through an explicit theological perspective: human suffering is consistently linked to a human response to God's will and God's response to human freedom. The deuteronomic principle thus holds that suffering results from human apostasy from God's covenant, as the punishment that God inflicts on the unrighteous. Likewise, the suffering of Jesus is understood as his bearing the sins of humanity as the means of God's saving humans from sin. Paradoxically, this explicit theological linkage is also the *weakness* of Scripture's witness,

---

2. For a defense of this translation, see L. T. Johnson, *The Letter to the Hebrews,* New Testament Library (Louisville: Westminster John Knox, 2006).

for two reasons. First, it floats above the actual experience of human suffering as an abstract interpretation that often has little pertinence to ordinary embodied existence. Second, sin and salvation do not adequately comprehend the full range of sufferings actually experienced by humans. A nonreflective application of a theological interpretation derived from Scripture can distort the experience of suffering itself. If there is a way forward to more authentically engaging Scripture, it must go through a more adequate examination of human suffering in the body.

Such a fresh examination of the experience of human suffering is made more difficult by certain contemporary ideological positions that are as abstract as those proposed by Scripture. If many believers are still haunted by the conviction that their suffering is a punishment sent by God for some sin, at least as many people, including Christians, view suffering from a perspective far removed from Scripture's. Especially for those living in the comfortable circumstances of "First World" modernity, where prosperity, safety, and success tend to be regarded as "natural," a form of human entitlement, suffering can be regarded as "abnormal," an exception to the way life ought to be. Such a view is prevalent, to be sure, only among a small portion of the world's population. For most people throughout history and around the world today, suffering is built into the very structure of existence: hunger, exposure, illness, violence of every kind, and early death are not exceptions but the very rule of life itself.

But the small minority that enjoys a level of wealth, medical advancement, and comfort unparalleled in human history — so that an ordinary urban dweller in the USA has more varieties of food and luxuries available virtually on demand than even the most privileged rulers had in ages past — can afford to regard any form of suffering as "tragic" (the favorite term of the news media) or even "evil." Language that is appropriate only for deliberate moral action (evil) is misapplied to phenomena outside the moral order.[3] No matter the magnitude of the loss of life and property caused by a tsunami, for example, the shift of tectonic plates and the birth of new volcanoes that cause such tidal phenomena cannot in any sense be termed tragic or evil. Indeed, a tsunami is better viewed as a corollary of God's continual creation of the world that in metaphysical and moral terms should be called

3. Thus, in discussions of theodicy, the "problem of evil" is often another way of speaking about "the problem of suffering." Beyond the fact that neither evil nor suffering is properly a "problem," but they are mysteries (in the sense of Gabriel Marcel), evil is always a moral category — whereas suffering, I argue here, only occasionally falls within the realm of morality.

"good." But the moral category of "evil" is attached without critical pause to various forms of human suffering, ranging from poverty to war, with the attendant moral responsibility asserted that humans must work to "eliminate suffering" in the same way that they are obliged to "resist evil." Once this moral equation is made, it is impossible to think about any positive valence that might be attached to human suffering.

The behavioral corollaries of such premises include an approach to parenting that seeks to remove any possibility of suffering from one's children, as though it were, in fact, something intrinsically evil. Parents don't want their children to go through the hard things they did when they were young, so they cater to their children's every whim and seek to remove from their path any possible pitfall. The avoidance of suffering is at least as pervasive among adults: the present generation (in affluent parts of the world) seems dedicated to eradicating pain from life. It is no shock that this is also a generation distinctively devoted to agents of anaesthesia and addiction. In some circles, a life without chemical additives is unthinkable. Even those committed to a "green" lifestyle do so with the assistance of supplements and potions guaranteed to relieve every twinge of pain.

The most dramatic example of a departure from Scripture's witness concerning suffering is theological. Working with the assumed identity of suffering and evil, and locating evil (sin) above all in social structures that keep certain classes of people (persons of color, women, peasants) in conditions of oppression, certain forms of liberation theology speak of salvation in terms of liberating people from the conditions that cause their suffering. For some theologians who adopt this approach, the writings of the New Testament are particularly problematic, for they seem to provide meaning to the suffering of the innocent, and thus they can be regarded as supporting the forces of oppression within society. Such suspicion of Scripture's perspective reaches an extreme when a womanist theologian declares that the cross can no longer be a viable symbol for believers.[4]

We can begin to recover contact with the actual suffering in the body by attempting a definition that is both neutral — that is, not driven by ideology — and corresponds to real-life experience. Beginning with a simple definition, we can then offer some important qualifications. Suffering, then, can be considered as the pain of a sentient system in disequilibrium. Each term requires some elaboration. By "sentient system," I mean that

---

4. See Delores Williams, *Sisters in the Wilderness: The Challenge of Womanist God-Talk* (Maryknoll, NY: Orbis, 1993).

an ability to *feel* is required; we can assume that rocks and gravel do not suffer because they are not sentient. The more sentience there is, in turn, the greater and more complex the capacity for pain. Hence we are rightly more willing to grant the experience of pain to animals, especially mammals, than we are to vegetables.

By "pain," I mean simply that suffering involves some sort of "hurting" across a wide range of physical, mental and emotional states, and with varying degrees of intensity — from "discomfort" to "agony." As pleasure is ordinarily sought, pain is instinctively avoided; a sentient system prefers soothing to stress. Although it is distressingly abstract, I use the term "disequilibrium" in an effort to be neutral. A sentient system in stasis does not hurt, but one that is undergoing change, movement, or stress can experience pain and thus can be said to "suffer."

This simple definition is helpful, but it stands in need of immediate qualification. First, even at the physical level, pain does not necessarily reveal itself bodily in a clear or unambiguous fashion. People can experience great pain even when no clinical signs or tests can confirm it; conversely, the body can be in great danger — even near death — without the presence of pain. Severe trauma often brings on shock, with pain occurring only after the traumatized body emerges from shock. And it has often been observed that the moans and groans that can signal pain can also signal sexual arousal and climax, the experience of the most exquisite physical pleasure.

Second, we know that the several kinds of "sentient systems" in humans are interconnected and influence each other. The phenomenon of psychosomatic or psychogenetic illness is well-documented: a condition of acute emotional distress can affect the physical organism so that pervasive bodily pain can be felt, and even organic pathologies develop. The traffic can move both directions. Conditions of depression and anxiety can, it is true, cause a chemical imbalance in the brain; in the same way, chemical imbalances in the brain — caused by tumors or drugs — can create anxieties and depression, as well as other emotional conditions. Similarly, great mental stress can give rise to both emotional and physical reactions. Ancient and modern healers alike share the wisdom that states of forgiveness, acceptance, and peace can relieve symptoms of physical pain, just as the relief of physical pain can soothe the agitated spirit.

Third, the experience of pain is intensely subjective. What is sometimes called "tolerance for pain" varies greatly. Or at least we think it does. But is it a matter of being able to *feel* more (with one sentient system less or more sensitive than another), or is it a matter of being able to *bear more pain* (for whatever reason)? The subjectivity of pain befuddles medical practice. Physiological conditions that "should" be accompanied by acute pain sometimes do not — or at least patients say so. But then, other patients whose observable physiological state "should not" give rise to pain claim it to be present and beg for relief through medication. To some extent, then, since pain is not measurable by clinical means, the experience of pain is revealed to others only through the testimony of those experiencing it. Such testimony, in turn, demands of others the willingness to hear and to trust the words "I am hurting" spoken by another. Here is a form of self-revelation that entrusts the self in a condition of great vulnerability to the care and concern of others.

Just as with physical pain, so also with mental and emotional pain: I cannot know what you are suffering unless in some way you make your pain known to me. Paradoxically, as we shall see, one of the effects of pain is to make such vulnerability difficult, which means that by the time such pain is expressed verbally to another, it has already become so great as to break through the barriers of self-protectiveness. Consequently, when those told of such pain refuse to believe it, the pain itself is compounded.

With a more neutral definition of suffering and with these important qualifications in mind, we can see that both the biblical connection between sin and suffering and the contemporary identification of suffering with evil are simplistic. Suffering can be a negative thing, but it can also — and emphatically — be a positive thing. Negatively, pain is a signal of something gone wrong in the sentient system, or that the system is under threat — as when I touch a hot stove and the pain helps me avoid a serious burn. Pain in the body can result from injury, or illness, or the process of aging. Likewise, mental pain can indicate a variety of brain disorders, or only the common if sometimes horrifying experience of cognitive dissonance. Emotional pain can point to conditions of confusion, disorientation, or shame. But do such negative aspects of suffering also point to something wrong religiously or morally?

My review of the Old Testament evidence on the subject of suffering has, I think, made clear my refusal to accept a straightforward link even between the above negative forms of suffering and sin — as though such suffering resulted from God's punishment for the sin of an individual or nation. The fact that the wicked prosper and the innocent suffer stands as perennial and powerful rebuttal of that ideological position. At the same time, however, it would be obtuse to deny that a closure of the human spirit to the presence and power of God in the world — what Paul especially means by "sin" — could not have negative consequences on the one so refusing to acknowledge God's claim on creation, not in the form of a punishment inflicted from the outside but as a corollary of the choice of closure itself. Paul's speaking of a "darkening of the mind" that results from disobedience to God (faithlessness) and that leads to further distortions of human freedom (Rom. 1:18-32) is not without pertinence. It is possible, I think, to speak of a suffering that is specifically religious and that points to sin, a suffering that humans bring upon themselves. To think otherwise would be to remove sin from the realm of experience and to detach it from embodied human existence. If *faith* can open a person to the healing power of God in body and spirit, then sin correspondingly can show the effects of closure to God in both spirit and body.

Equally difficult and ambiguous is determining the moral aspects of suffering. I will argue shortly that some suffering has a positive moral valence, and I have rejected the proposition that suffering should be equated with moral evil. Nevertheless, I agree with those who hold that the unjustified imposition of pain on other sentient beings, especially humans, is a moral evil. Thus, doing violence to another must ordinarily be considered morally wrong. However, it is more difficult to determine the degrees of pain involved: not all exercise of power or even coercion, after all, can necessarily be considered violent. Similarly, when is the inflicting of pain "justified"?

It is easy to condemn both sporadic and systematic expressions of oppression that treat other humans as objects and targets for disdain and abuse. More ambiguous are those ways of making others suffer that can be construed as at least potentially beneficial. Such might be a teacher's imposing difficult assignments on students; certainly, some degree of mental and even physical pain may be involved, but such is the cost of education. Is acquiescence in ignorance morally better? For a teacher to refrain from imposing such suffering is to despise students and condemn them to ignorance. Similarly, the practice of mutual correction among friends may involve mental and emotional pain, but both the intention for such correction and the consequences of such inflicted pain are salutary. The example of parenting is most telling. The raising of children involves making decisions in their regard that they regard (and experience) as painful. Sometimes such pain takes the form of correction, or of withholding approval, or even of punishment. But to consider the suffering children experience from parental discipline as morally wrong — a signal that the "family system" is broken — is to miss the point. In such cases, the inflicting of pain (intentional or not) may be a signal that the family system is in fact working properly.

The discussion of what can be called "pedagogical suffering" leads naturally to a consideration of the ways in which the experience of pain points, not to something wrong in the sentient system but to something very good, such as growth and new life. Here it is necessary to concede that suffering can and often does have a positive valence. At the physical level, pain can indicate something wrong in the body, it is true, but it often also signals a positive process. The classic example is the pain of childbirth (see John 16:21): such pain can be both intense and frightening, yet mothers gladly endure it for the sake of bringing a new child into the world. The physical pain experienced by those going through adolescent growth spurts is similar: young men who grow six to nine inches in a year can hurt in all their joints and find themselves unexpectedly clumsy and accident-prone. The slogan "no pain, no gain," in turn, is popular among those engaged in intense physical training that seeks to increase muscle mass or aerobic capacity. Running or swimming long distances and lifting weights produce pleasant endorphins, to be sure, but such activities also cause sore muscles and aching joints.

Mental growth also frequently involves pain, a form of suffering. The disequilibrium in this case is caused by the effort to assimilate new ideas, or even more, new paradigms of thought. Breaking out of former frameworks and stretching to grow into new insights involves a kind of mental pain that is acknowledged by the ancient maxim *mathein pathein,* which can be rendered either as "to learn is to suffer" or "to suffer is to learn."[5] So daunting is the suffering attached to serious learning that many people choose not to pursue it beyond what is strictly necessary for citizenship. Yet ignorance can also bring on suffering of a different kind, as a lack of learning disables a person from full participation in society. The pain of learning to read is real but positive; the pain of illiteracy is real and completely negative. Suffering in the first instance is temporary, but in the second instance it is lifelong.

Emotional maturation likewise involves pain. When the lyrics speak of young love in terms of "heartache," we recognize and can remember the pain that accompanied our own first infatuations. The experiences of shame and rejection are also painful, as are, in their own ways, anger and

---

5. See C. H. Talbert, *Learning through Suffering: The Educational Value of Suffering in the New Testament and Its Milieu* (Collegeville, MN: Liturgical Press, 1991).

sexual desire. The grief that we feel at the loss of one we have loved is universally acknowledged to be among the most powerful and threatening experiences of pain. As with physical and mental pain, the first human instinct is to avoid or deny emotional pain in an effort to stabilize the system. The disequilibrium seems too great and too frightening to endure. But in the emotional realm above all, the capacity to embrace the pain that signals loss or rejection is the key to growth to a new and larger (and more capacious) self and the possibility of new life and love. Conversely, the refusal to allow the pain of grief to be truly experienced means that it can never truly be transcended.

Even so cursory a catalogue of sufferings as this one suggests that the human experience of pain is universal and unavoidable. It does not result from a punishment sent by God for sin; it is not an evil that can be eliminated. Instead, suffering is a necessary component of embodied human existence. Where there is body, there is movement, and where there is movement, there is pain. Suffering, moreover, has both negative and positive dimensions. Therefore, the meaning of suffering in any specific circumstance can only be discerned by the careful consideration of the context in which pain is experienced. But because the experience of pain in virtually all circumstances does not reveal itself to others in a clear or straightforward manner, extraordinary care must be taken to weigh all factors, to consider all the possible levels of interaction among the physical, mental, and emotional, and above all, to take seriously the testimony of those who claim to be suffering. Although the experience of suffering is universal, there is nothing abstract or universal about the experience itself: suffering remains highly individual and subjective. It is possible, nevertheless, to say a few general things about what we can learn about body and spirit — and the Spirit of God at work in human bodies — through the experience of suffering.

Suffering and the Diminishment of Spirit

One of the obvious effects of every kind of suffering, and a reason why we think of suffering in negative terms more than positive terms, is the diminishing of the human spirit it brings with it. First of all, suffering seems to shrink rather than enlarge us. The physiological condition of shock provides a metaphor: when the body experiences a great trauma, its systems tend to shut down so that available resources can be dedicated solely to the task of survival. The person in shock is "not available" to the larger world. I do not think that I am unusual when I attest that my experiences of physical pain (in sum an embarrassingly small number given my seventy-one years of life) seem to focus all my available attention on the spot that hurts.

In this sense, my physical pain is, to all intents and purposes, absolute. I "become" my aching tooth, my throbbing head, my bleeding finger, and, in my particular case, my aching back. When I have a cold or the flu or pleurisy, I cannot pay any attention to larger realities. I have no horizons larger than the one established by what hurts in my body. I am even tempted to the wildest sort of projection: I hurt, and the world is evil! My pain demands all my concern, and I tend to resent any interruption to the attention I am giving to what hurts in my body. When I am hurting, I am also irritable and often irascible, insensitive to the needs or concerns of others, outraged often at their insensitivity in asking anything of me. (Don't they know I am hurting?) The book of Job captures such self-preoccupation nicely, showing how Job and his friends talk past each other. The friends want to offer meaningful interpretations of Job's pain, but Job just wants them to shut up and go away so he can be alone with his pain. I learned this lesson the hard way, when as a young and insufferably smug husband, I stupidly tried to read the book of Job to my wife while she was in the acute phase of her chronic-periodic sickness. Those who are suffering pain, I discovered, are not concerned with the meaning of suffering; they only want the pain to go away.

The experience of mental suffering is even more diminishing of the human spirit. In the common psychological condition called cognitive dissonance — the tension created between conviction ("I know I left my keys right here") and experience ("the keys are not here") — can be tormenting and totally preoccupying, leaving us literally walking in a circle in the effort to resolve the conflict, unavailable to any other concern and unable to move forward. When the cognitive dissonance is even greater, so is the mental pain we suffer, and so is the sense of our spirit's diminishment to a single point. My conviction is that members of the clergy are trustworthy and that the church seeks to protect the helpless; my experience is that my child has been abused by a priest and the church has sought only to protect itself. The mental torment of such conflict often turns the one experiencing it into a concentrated point of fury, fear, and frustration. No larger vision is possible because of the myopia imposed by the experience of dissonance.

The point is made from the other direction when the mental suffering involves states of dissonance, especially in conditions of untreated schizophrenia. It would seem that here there is almost too much enlargement of spirit, as the afflicted person hears voices and sees visions that are little attached to the ordinary run of existence. Focus on such transcendent realities is often connected to the neglect of quotidian matters having to do with the body, even to the point of abandoning basic hygiene. Indeed, persons suffering such conditions often resist taking medications that could "bring them back to earth," precisely because they see those drugs as making them dull and sluggish, earthbound, removed from those fantastic communications that they find so fascinating and preoccupying. Yet, though schizophrenia appears to the one with the condition to enlarge the spirit, it actually diminishes the spirit by removing it from any but idiosyncratic and circular forms of communication. Schizophrenia is solipsism of the spirit. By listening only to voices from within his own head, the schizophrenic loses the capacity to hear any other voices.

Those who have lived with persons afflicted with Alzheimer's disease, or some other form of dementia, understand how the very essence of the condition is the diminishment of the human spirit, which seems to disappear progressively before our concerned gaze. The loss of memory for those so afflicted means, as we know, the progressive loss of self. The demented person becomes increasingly disoriented, dislocated, deranged, lost in the world. The spirit within seems reduced to a few poor remnants of memory, and then nothing at all. For those committed to the care of such persons, the experience of the diminishment of spirit is all too real, as they see a loved person retreat from in front of them moment by moment, in the end leaving only an animate body that still requires care.

The way that emotional suffering can seem to diminish the human spirit is perhaps best illustrated by forms of obsessive-compulsive behavior. The circle of obsessive thoughts and the round of compulsive rituals serve as mechanisms to provide some sense of control over a pervasive and powerful anxiety that makes a person feel out of control and in danger. Both those who have suffered such emotional disorders and those who have lived with those who suffer them recognize how these patterns reduce a person's availability to any reality beyond the circle of self-preoccupation and protection. The need for constant vigilance means that the person's spirit is focused utterly on those patterns of thought and practice that provide such protection. Little outside the closed circle can get in, and one imprisoned by anxiety and obsession has great difficulty paying attention to anything else.

A similar kind of emotional captivity is found among those on whom great emotional pain has been inflicted through the physical or sexual abuse suffered when they were children. The imposition of such pain on innocent children can never be justified, and stands as a prime example of the infliction of pain as morally evil. The effect of such trauma on the very young is often to imprison the child within the adult. Although the grown men or women appear in the eyes of others to be adults, their spirits are confined by the early trauma; they are inhibited in their efforts to form stable and creative relationships with other adults because of this diminishment of their spirit. Sometimes psychological therapy, sometimes the mediation of a loving and patient relationship can help heal the childhood wound and enable full growth to adulthood. Sometimes the trapped child never finds release. In its ugliest manifestation, this abuse can be carried forward, as those once molested by exploitative adults in turn inflict the same damage on others.

Suffering and the Enlargement of Spirit

The natural effect of pain, I hope I have demonstrated, is the diminishment of the human spirit and the imprisonment of the creative self. Against the backdrop of these examples of how suffering can cause the human spirit to contract, we are moved to wonder at the mysterious ways in which suffering provides the occasion for the expansion of the human spirit. Specifically, I speak here of the ways in which humans show themselves able to move past every kind of physical, mental, and emotional limitation, and past the experience of pain itself, in manifestations of spiritual creativity. Simply as evidence for the human spirit as transcendent, they demand attention; but as pointers to the activity of the God's Holy Spirit, they require of the theologian particular consideration.

From antiquity there is the case of Epictetus, a slave, exile, and cripple — possibly made so by an abusive owner — whose daily homilies to his students on the noble life reveal a spirit that has transcended all these limitations and combines perseverance in the face of suffering with a sweetness of demeanor that moved even the satirist Lucian to call him "that marvelous old man."[6] In the contemporary world, perhaps the most

---

6. Lucian of Samosata, *The Ignorant Book Collector* 13; for an appreciation of Epictetus, see L. T. Johnson, *Among the Gentiles: Greco-Roman Religion and Christianity* (New Haven: Yale University Press, 2009), pp. 64-78.

notable example is provided by Stephen Hawking, whose crippled body, which makes him dependent on technology and the care of others even to survive — and who, in addition, has allegedly suffered abuse by at least one of his helpers — has not prevented his amazing mind from leaping to the furthest reaches of theoretical physics or his indomitable will from publishing books that have been read by millions.[7]

Closer to home, my academic colleague Nancy Eiesland demonstrated an indestructible and creative spirit that transcended a life of constant pain and endless surgeries, enabling her before her early death from cancer to compose a truly landmark book on disability studies.[8] In my own life, there is, above all, the constant example of my dear wife, Joy, whose entire life has been marked by chronic pain and a body that has severely limited her, yet has been a faithful and creative spouse, a mother of seven children, and a woman whose care for others always triumphs over her own physical limits and pain.

Indeed, as we look around us, we see many examples of people who overcome their own limitations and pain in order to serve others: the mothers whose lives are defined by the sacrifices they make for their children; the soldiers who overcome their own fear for the sake of their "band of brothers" to step into the line of fire even when they are themselves injured; the firefighters who not only enter burning buildings but endure serious injuries in order to rescue those trapped by flames; the policemen who enter places of extreme danger in order to protect the innocent, often at the risk of their own safety; the caregivers who fight fatigue and ignore their own needs in order to be present for the needs of those in their charge; the doctors and nurses who risk serious illness and even death by caring for patients in conditions of infectious disease and plague; the teachers who spend countless hours losing brain cells in the correcting of papers in order to improve the work of their students. In all these cases — and many others — we observe the astonishing capacity of the spirit to transcend the natural tendency of pain to diminish the spirit and confine it to self-preoccupation. Included in the list must be many of the mystics in the Christian tradition. A remarkable number of those whose ecstatic prose and poetry concerned the ascent to God wrote out of conditions of severe suffering.[9]

---

7. Stephen Hawking, *My Brief History* (New York: Bantam Books, 2013); L. Lawson, *Stephen Hawking: A Biography* (New York: Prometheus Books, 2007).

8. Nancy Eiesland, *The Disabled God: Toward a Liberatory Theology of Disability* (Nashville: Abingdon, 1994).

9. For example, Hildegard of Bingen (1098-1179), Mechtilde (1241-1298), Julian of Norwich (1342-1416), Teresa of Ávila (1515-1582), Simone Weil (1909-1943).

Compassion and the Suffering God

The capacity of the human spirit to extend itself beyond the bounds of the body set by suffering is demonstrated most remarkably by the miracle of compassion. As the term suggests, this disposition involves a "suffering with" another, which requires of us a kind of imaginative leap into the embodied spirit of another, and a generous embrace of their pain as though it were our own, making it, indeed, our own.[10] I refer to compassion as a "miracle" because against the backdrop of our tendency to be confined and defined by the self-preoccupation caused by our own suffering, the power to accomplish such identification with the pain of another seems to require more than the power of the individual human spirit on its own. I consider the presence of true compassion as a sign of the presence of the spirit of God at work with the human spirit. The Letter to the Hebrews recommends that believers "remember those who are in prison as though in prison with them, and those who are ill-treated, since you also are in the body" (Heb. 13:3). Such remembrance and such a disposition are possible only within certain premises governing a shared existence in the body.

Compassion, we know, is also recognized as crucially important in Buddhism: *Karuna* is a key component of enlightenment and is the essential characteristic of the Bodhisattva, who seeks to liberate all sentient beings.[11] Compassion, then, is not uniquely Christian; it is a powerful expression of the human spirit discerned by the other world religions in which suffering plays a central role. But while compassion is not at all unique to Christianity, it does have a specific and distinctive understanding within Christianity.

The term *sympathēs* is used only once in the New Testament, when 1 Peter 3:8 exhorts, "Finally, all of you, have unity of spirit, sympathy, love of the brethren, a tender heart and a humble mind." But the term *splanchnistheis* is used by the Gospels specifically for the human Jesus' response to those in need before he reaches out in care (Matt. 9:36; 14:14; 15:32; 18:27; 20:34), and the reality of compassion is clearly present in texts that speak of a "fellowship of sufferings" (*koinōnia tōn pathēmatōn;* see 1 Pet.

---

10. See H. Nouwen, *Compassion: A Reflection on the Christian Life* (New York: Image Books, 2005).

11. For example, see Sangharakshita, *The Bodhisattva Ideal: Wisdom and Compassion in Buddhism* (Cambridge, MA: Windhorse Publications, 2004).

4:13; Phil. 3:10; 2 Cor. 1:7). These passages give us a sense of the distinctive Christian understanding of compassion, and possibly a new lens for reading Scripture's witness on suffering.

For Christians, compassion is not a matter of a universal disposition of one who has transcended the suffering of the body (associated with change and corruption) toward all sentient beings (who still struggle within the cycle of somatic existence). It is, rather, both embodied (the one with compassion also experiences pain and is subject to all the vicissitudes of the flesh) and particular: the object of care is not the universal cycle of being and becoming, but the neighbor. The model for such "participation in suffering" with those around us is Jesus himself.[12] The Gospels do not portray Jesus as one above or removed from suffering; just the opposite, his destiny is to experience human suffering to the fullest, even to the agonies of a shameful and violent death. His suffering and death, moreover, are the final expression of an existence in which he gave himself as a ransom for all (Mark 10:45). In his particular and vulnerable body, Christ reached out to touch and heal and restore to community those who were experiencing physical, mental, and emotional pain. The New Testament bears consistent witness to the conviction, furthermore, that such suffering for and with others in the body by Jesus is the revelation of "God with us" (Matt. 1:23), the "word made flesh" (John 1:14). Jesus' suffering with and for others is recognized not only as the expression of human compassion, which it is, but also as the expression of God's compassion for humans, God's "love for the world" (John 3:16).[13]

The deepest meaning of suffering within Christianity, then, and the most profound understanding of compassion, is found in God's participation in the suffering of creation, first through the incarnation itself and then through Jesus' life for others, and finally through the innocent Jesus' death on the cross suffered for the sake of others. God's full participation in human embodiedness through the incarnation of the Word does not remove human suffering, for the experience of pain, as I have suggested, is ingredient to embodied existence. But it transforms suffering by revealing its positive capacity: suffering is not first of all a punishment for sin nor only a means of saving from sin: it is an expression of God's own willing-

12. See S. Kierkegaard, *Works of Love,* trans. H. V. Hong and E. H. Hong, The Works of Kierkegaard, vol. 16 (Princeton: Princeton University Press, 1998).

13. L. T. Johnson, *Living Jesus: Learning the Heart of the Gospel* (San Francisco: HarperSanFrancisco, 1998).

ness to identify with God's own creation, and the means by which that creation can be transformed according to the image of God (Rom. 8:18-39).

When Paul declares that "God was in Christ reconciling the world to himself" (2 Cor. 5:19), he understands this as God's entering into the fabric of human existence in order to transform it, through a pattern of participatory exchange. The one who did not know sin, God made to be sin, so that in him we might become God's righteousness (2 Cor. 5:21); though Christ was rich, for our sake he became poor, so that through his poverty we might become rich (2 Cor. 8:9); "Christ was crucified in weakness yet lives by God's power, so that though we are weak in him, by God's power we will live with him" (2 Cor. 13:4). The power of such transformation has been made available to believers through "the love of God that has been poured out into your hearts through the Holy Spirit which has been given to you" (Rom. 5:5). This gift of the Holy Spirit, we saw in a previous chapter, changes dramatically our understanding of the body — and therefore of suffering in the body. Because of God's gift, we are all implicated in each other's bodies. Paul says in the blessing of 2 Corinthians 1:3-7:

> Blessed be the God and Father of our Lord Jesus Christ, the father of all mercies and the God of all consolation, who consoles us in all our affliction, so that we may be able to console those who are in any affliction with the consolation with which we ourselves are consoled by God. For just as the sufferings of Christ are abundant for us, so also our consolation is abundant through Christ. If we are being afflicted, it is for your consolation and salvation; if we are being consoled, it is for your consolation, which you experience when you patiently endure the same sufferings that we are also suffering. Our hope for you is unshaken, for we know that as you share in our sufferings, so also you share in our consolation.

We are, indeed, a single "body of Christ." Compassion, then, is not merely a moral option; it is the reality in which we participate through the Holy Spirit. It is not by accident, I think, that Paul develops the image of the church as the body of Christ in this way:

> For the body does not consist of one member but of many. If the foot should say, "Because I am not a hand, I do not belong to the body," that would not make it any less a part of the body. And if the ear should say, "Because I am not an eye, I do not belong to the body," that would not

make it any less a part of the body. If the whole body were an eye, where would be the hearing? If the whole body were an ear, where would be the sense of smell? But as it is, God arranged the organs in the body, each one of them, as he chose. If all were a single organ, where would the body be? As it is, there are many parts, yet one body. The eye cannot say to the hand, "I have no need of you," nor again the head to the feet, "I have no need of you." On the contrary, the parts of the body which seem to be the weaker are indispensable, and those parts of the body which we think less honorable we invest with the greatest honor, and our unpresentable parts are treated with greater modesty, which our more presentable parts do not require. But God has so composed the body, giving the greater honor to the inferior part, that there be no discord in the body, but that the members may have the same care for one another. For if one member suffers, all suffer together; if one member is honored, all rejoice together. Now you are the body of Christ and individually members of it. (1 Cor. 12:14-27)

How is any of this pertinent to the way we perceive our everyday experience of pain, our local and all-too-present suffering? Not easily or directly. The theological task that I see as constantly pressing upon us is to understand what we experience as transparent to the realities of which Scripture speaks, without in the least suppressing all the all-too-human aspects of pain that I have tried to elaborate. I hope that I have established three basic aspects of that theological task:

1. A simplistic application of the explicit scriptural witness concerning suffering in terms of punishment for sin or means of salvation can both be too abstract to be helpful and in some cases serve to suppress or distort the actual experience of suffering.
2. Close attention to all the dimensions of the experience of pain is necessary as well to break through harmful contemporary ideologies that block the way to seeing suffering as having any positive dimension.
3. The understanding of God's compassion for humans expressed through the sharing of human suffering in Jesus Christ, and the appreciation for the shaping of a body of Christ through the gift of the Holy Spirit, open the way for thinking about our own suffering that is faithful to the ambiguities of experience yet is open to the possibility of larger meaning.

CHAPTER SIX

The Passionate Body

The ambivalence toward the body within much of Christian theology — and before that in ancient philosophy — is based on the conviction that the human mind (or soul) is a much more reliable instrument for perceiving reality and for guiding behavior than is the body. The mind, it is thought, is made for contemplation and control. It is the "image of God," the spark of the divine within humans.[1] In contrast, the body is enmeshed in the confusion and turmoil of materiality. If the mind's natural tendency is upward toward the divine, the body's natural tropism is downward toward the animal. The best we can expect from the body is for it to obey the mind. But the body's submission to the mind is made difficult by those feelings and drives, the emotions and passions that, being sensual rather than rational, drive the body toward the merely animal and away from the higher things of the mind. The tendency is to think of virtue as the passions being guided by the mind, and vice as the passions controlling both body and mind. The passions, as representing the animal body, stand in opposition to the mind, which strives toward the divine. The path of moral progress and the way of mystic ascent to God alike, therefore, demand as the first step the "controlling" or the "overcoming" of the passions.[2]

Within Christianity, the starkest form of such despising of the body's natural instincts occurred in the dualistic heresies that began in the second century CE with Marcionism and Gnosticism.[3] These forms of Christianity

1. As in Thomas Aquinas, *Summa Theologica* I, 93, 6.

2. See, e.g., M. Nussbaum, *The Therapy of Desire: Theory and Practice in Hellenistic Ethics* (Princeton: Princeton University Press, 1994).

3. For the Greco-Roman roots of religion as "transcending the world" and for its full

saw the human body as part of the material world that came into being either as a malicious trick played by a secondary deity or as a disastrous error. In either case, the spark of light in humans that fell from the realm of the divine now found itself trapped in the body and subject to the body's vagrant passions of desire and fear, rage and jealousy; only the revealed and saving knowledge of the soul's true origin and ultimate destiny in the light could, through self-realization and through eschewing all that pertained to the flesh, speed the human spirit back to its source and goal. The Gnostic germ within Christianity found a welcome host in Manichaeism, the dualistic religion to which the great Saint Augustine owed allegiance for some time, and from whose ideology he worked so hard — and some would say, with only partial success — to free himself.[4] The mature Augustine robustly affirms the goodness of the body as part of God's creation; but he also remains deeply suspicious of the impulses of "the flesh" as the arena where sin can do its best work.[5] Both Gnosticism and Manichaeism were opposed and condemned by orthodox teachers as heresies, it is true, but mainly because of their radical ideas about God and the world. The orthodox teachers did not entirely disagree with the radical dualists concerning the danger of the senses and the peril that the passions posed to the soul. As a result, a negative view of the passions continued in Christianity, not only in overt forms of Christian dualism, such as the Albigensian heresy, but also in the ascetic and mystical teaching advanced by the most orthodox of theologians.[6]

The Bias against the Passions

Christianity did not invent such hostility toward the passionate body; rather, it drew on a dualistic element in Greek philosophy. The most familiar version is that of Plato, who himself was influenced by Pythagorean and Orphic ideas. In his writings, Plato has his mentor Socrates declare

flowering in second- and third-century forms of Christianity, see L. T. Johnson, *Among the Gentiles: Greco-Roman Religion and Christianity* (New Haven: Yale University Press, 2009), pp. 79-92 and 214-33.

4. See his anti-Manichaean treatises, including *On Two Souls; Against Fortunatus; Reply to Faustus; Concerning the Nature of the Good.*

5. See *On Continence; On Holy Virginity; On Marriage and Concupiscence; On Nature and Grace.*

6. See Johnson, *Among the Gentiles,* pp. 268-71.

that the soul *(psychē)* alone is immortal, alone capable of grasping truth rather than mere opinion, alone able to ascend through knowledge to the divine. The body, in contrast, is a prison, or even a tomb *(sōma sēma)* from which the soul longs to be free.[7] Bodily urges must be purified of their physical characteristics in order to be worthy of the soul's quest; thus, the eros that at the physical level desires sexual intimacy must be transmuted into the drive that impels the soul to seek unity with ultimate truth.[8] Plato imagines the passions as powerful but unruly animals that must be brought under the control of the mind, as a driver can direct, by using the reins, the powerful beasts pulling his chariot.[9]

Although philosophy after Plato took a number of forms — and a number of competing schools — Greco-Roman moralists were virtually unanimous in their suspicion of the passions. The Platonic influence is most obvious in the Hermetic literature, which makes the dualism between spirit and body absolute,[10] imagining the liberation of the spirit in terms of escaping the passions of the body.[11] The highest form of virtue among the Stoics, for example, could be expressed in terms of a state of *apatheia,* a freedom from passions that enabled action completely in accord with the "governing principle" that is the mind, which, because it is free from such lower impulses, can act "according to nature" rather than according to craven desires.[12] Even Epicurus, who in contrast to other philosophers held pleasure in high regard,[13] saw the most desirable condition to be that of *ataraxia,* a freedom from the turbulent passions that Epicurus attributes to an ignorance of natural causes.[14]

The Old Testament does not thematize the passions in the way Hellenistic philosophy does. To be sure, biblical characters display a variety of strong human emotions: anger (Gen. 4:6; 27:41-45; 34:7; Exod. 11:8; 32:19, 22), contempt (Gen. 16:4-5), lust (Gen. 19:4-9; 39:7-12; 2 Sam. 11:2-5), jealousy (Gen. 37:11), and fear (Gen. 45:26). Such negative emotions lead to disastrous actions: Esau's hunger enabled him to trade away his birthright (Gen. 25:29-34), and his rage made him seek to murder Jacob (27:41-45);

---

7. Plato, *Gorgias* 493C; *Cratylus* 400C; *Phaedo* 62B-67A-B.

8. Plato, *Symposium* 199C-212C.

9. Plato, *Phaedrus* 246C-247C.

10. *Aeclepius* 22, 26.

11. *Poimandres* 24-26.

12. Epictetus, *Discourses* 1.1; 3.2.1-2.

13. Epicurus, *Sovereign Maxims* 5.

14. Epicurus, *Sovereign Maxims* 14.

similarly, the anger of Joseph's brothers leads to attempted murder (Gen. 37:4, 5, 8). Israel's God also displays strong emotion: the Lord is "sorry" that he has created humans (Gen. 6:5-8), and even though he declares himself to be "slow to anger" (Exod. 34:6), the Lord's wrath burns hot against Israel (Exod. 32:10, 12; Num. 11:10, 33; 12:9; Pss. 78:21, 31, 49-50, 58-59; 79:9; 80:4; 106:29, 32, 40; Jer. 6:9-15; Ezek. 16:26, 38; 23:25). But no attention is given to the nature, causes, or consequences of such human and divine passion.

Traditional wisdom instruction in the Old Testament is likewise perfectly aware of the full range of human frailty: the book of Proverbs speaks of the love of pleasure (21:17), the desire for loose women (5:20-23; 7:1-27), laziness (6:6-11; 19:15; 24:30), crooked speech (5:12-15), haughtiness (6:17; 21:4; 27:1), false witness (6:19; 26:28), stealing (6:30), drunkenness and gluttony (23:20-21), envy (24:1; 27:4), adultery (6:32), greed (15:27; 28:25), pride (16:18; 29:23), and anger (14:29; 16:32; 19:19; 29:22). But nowhere are such dispositions and actions attributed to specific passions, and no real analysis is dedicated to them, apart from such vague generalizations as "a tranquil mind gives life to the flesh, but passion makes the bones rot" (14:30), and "never satisfied are the eyes of man" (27:20).

A partial contrast is presented by the book of Wisdom, precisely because in this composition, biblical traditions meet Hellenistic language and sensibilities. Although Wisdom speaks of specific acts such as slander and lying (1:11), and fornication (14:12), it also generalizes: "jealous ears" (1:10), pleasure (2:6-8), roving desire (4:12), arrogance (5:8), envy (6:23), sexual perversity (14:25-26), and greed (15:12-13). The more general characterization of vice corresponds to a more generalized sense of "virtue" (4:1; 5:13), as "the way of truth" or "light of righteousness" (5:6) as a manifestation of "wisdom" (6:12-22), which has a divine origin (7:22; 8:1). Wisdom can even cite the classic fourfold division of virtue in Greek philosophy: self-control, prudence, justice, and courage (8:7).

The same Hellenistic sensibility directs the interpretation of the biblical material by Philo of Alexandria. Philo fully approves of Plato's image of the mind controlling the passions as a charioteer controls horses.[15] He virtually equates passion and vice.[16] He declares: "Every passion is blameworthy. This follows from the censure due to every 'inordinate and excessive impulse' and to 'irrational and unnatural movements'" — he is citing

---

15. Philo, *Decalogue* 60; *Allegorical Laws* 3.223.
16. Philo, *On Husbandry* 22-25.

Stoic definitions — "for both these are nothing else than the opening out of a long-standing passion. So if a man does not set bounds for his impulses and bridle them like horses which defy the reins, he is the victim of a well-nigh fatal passion."[17]

In *The Sacrifices of Abel and Cain,* Philo constructs a contest for mastery between a personified pleasure *(hēdonē)* and virtue *(aretē).* Pleasure seduces humans and makes them do what reason says not to do: the desire for food that led Esau to trade his birthright is his prime example. Philo says: "For when the life of man begins, from the very cradle till the time when the age of maturity brings the great change and quenches the fiery furnace of the passions, folly, incontinence, injustice, fear, cowardice, and all the kindred maladies of soul are his inseparable companions." Only when the body grows weaker do the passions quiet, enabling wisdom and virtue to flourish.[18] Similarly, the Jewish composition entitled *The Testaments of the Twelve Patriarchs* reinterprets the biblical stories concerning Jacob's sons in terms of Hellenistic vices and virtues. Vice is closely connected to desires and passions (*TJos.* 7.1-8), which manifest themselves in a "spirit" of greed (*TJud.* 17.1), anger (*TDan.* 2.2), hatred (*TGad.* 3.3), arrogance (*TReub.* 3.5), and envy (*TSim.* 4.8).

The moral discourse in the New Testament draws from the Old Testament, to be sure, but also from Greco-Roman and Hellenistic Jewish traditions. As a result, references in the epistolary literature to the "passions" — most often translating the Greek *epithymiai* (desires) — are negative. As I have shown above, the apostle Paul has a complex but mostly positive appreciation of the body. And his language about "flesh" and "spirit" should be read, not in terms of a body-spirit dualism, but in terms of a conflict between attitudes closed to God and dispositions open to God. Nevertheless, Paul speaks of those who have rejected the claim of God in their lives and whose minds have been darkened (Rom. 1:18-25) as being driven by "dishonorable passions" when they engage in sexual practices "contrary to nature" (1:26-27); and he calls on his readers to "cast off the works of darkness" such as reveling and drunkenness, debauchery and licentiousness, quarreling and jealousy (13:13).

Similarly, Paul identifies the "works of the flesh" as "fornication, impurity, licentiousness, idolatry, sorcery, enmity, strife, jealousy, anger, selfishness, dissension, party spirit, envy, drunkenness, carousing, and

17. Philo, *The Special Laws* 3.4.
18. Philo, *The Sacrifices of Abel and Cain* 15-20.

the like" (Gal. 5:19-20). Such dispositions are associated especially with Gentiles before their conversion; so Ephesians speaks of those who "once lived in the passions of our flesh, following the desires of body and mind, so we were by nature children of wrath, like the rest of mankind" (Eph. 2:3; cf. 4:31–5:13; Col. 3:5-10). He says, "We ourselves were once foolish, disobedient, led astray, slaves to various passions and pleasures *(epithymiai kai hēdonai)*, passing our days in malice and envy, hated by men and hating one another" (Titus 3:3). Paul exhorts his male readers to take a wife "in holiness and honor, not in the passion of lust *(pathei epithymias)* like the heathen who do not know God" (1 Thess. 4:5).

Such language is not restricted to Paul. James 1:14-15 ascribes sin to "desire" *(epithymia)* or "passion." And 1 Peter instructs his readers: "As obedient children, do not be conformed to the passions *(epithymiai)* of your former ignorance" (1:14). He said that they should not live by "human passions but by the will of God," letting go what they used to do as Gentiles: "living in licentiousness, passions, drunkenness, revels, carousing, and lawless idolatry" (4:2-3). The Gospels even have Jesus declare that "out of the heart of man come evil thoughts, fornication, theft, murder, adultery, coveting, wickedness, deceit, licentiousness, envy, slander, pride, foolishness. All these evil things come from within, and they defile a man" (Mark 7:21-23; Matt. 15:1-20). The First Letter of John declares the conviction succinctly: "All that is of the world — the desire of the flesh, the desire of the eyes, the pride in riches — comes not from the Father but from the world. And the world and its desires are passing away, but those who do the will of God live forever" (1 John 2:16-17).

It is no surprise at all that those Christians also shaped by the rhetoric and philosophy of the Greco-Roman world should read this language from that perspective, and take it as axiomatic that the passions are both negative and dangerous, needing to be brought under control by the mind. Nor is it shocking that such language could be read by Marcionites and Gnostics as supporting their more radically dualistic views. But it is important to ask whether the dominant way of understanding the passions needs to be challenged.

Another Perspective on the Passions

It would be foolish to deny that the traditional perspective on the passions has some merit. More than simply an ideological bias in favor of the mind helped shape that perspective. Observation of plain human behavior also led to the conclusion that human passions are frequently at the root of those moral dispositions considered to be vices rather than virtues. Who does not agree that envy can lead to rivalry, social unrest, and even murder (James 4:1-2)? Who would argue that unchecked anger does not have the capacity to do harm to others as well as the self (Matt. 5:21-22)? Who would object to the condemnation of covetousness (Exod. 20:17; Deut. 5:21; Rom. 7:7-8) and avarice (Luke 12:15; Eph. 5:3) as drives that are destructive of human community? When Aristotle defined envy as "a certain sorrow [*lupē*]" experienced because another has something that we do not, he shows himself to be a magnificent psychologist. So does the saying attributed to Socrates, that envy is the "ulcer of the soul," suggest a shrewd appreciation for the gnawing and aching character of the chronic combination of longing and frustration that constitutes envy.

My effort to provide another perspective on the passionate body is not by any means intended to overturn all that is legitimate and true in such traditional teaching. I agree wholeheartedly that sobriety is almost always superior to drunkenness, and that moderation is ordinarily to be preferred to excess. I concur that satisfying every itch by scratching is not the measure of human greatness, and that a life defined by the pursuit of physical satisfaction is more to be pitied than admired. But I do want to ask why forbidding the scratching of all itches is thought to be an ideal, or why drunkenness cannot sometimes be better than sobriety. I want to ask why pleasure seems so problematic in the moral tradition. In short, I want to suggest another way of thinking about the body's impulses and appetites. Are they always the portal to perdition? Must they always be mistrusted? Is control the only moral attitude toward the passions?

We can remind ourselves first that the bias against the body's passions has also involved a bias in favor of the mind. The more the mind is in control, this bias has it, the more humans are likely to be virtuous rather than vicious. The passions are problematic because they challenge and threaten the mind's control over the body. But is the mind, even apart from the passions, really such a powerful instrument that it can provide so reliable a guidance? Experience tells us that the mind is itself limited in any number of ways, through inattention, through ignorance, through misinformation, through false principles. To borrow Plato's image of chariot and horses, if the charioteer does not know the way home, it does not matter if he has a good grip on the horses; he will still wander around in ignorance of his destination. Or if he is convinced that his home is in another sector of the city than it actually is, the fault is not with the horses if he ends up in the wrong part of town. Even the ancient moral philosophers agreed that bad behavior often had its source in bad principles.[19]

Indeed, the mind is capable of directing the body to do great evil based on a passionless embrace of abstract principles. More harm has come to humanity, as the experience of the preceding century has demonstrated, through the ruthless application of ideology than through the excesses of physical pleasure. The cold dictator who in the name of racial purity or social engineering orders the exportation, enslavement, or murder of millions does more evil than the sad drunk who orders the drink that damages his liver. The calculating head of a drug cartel, who has no attachment to his product but thinks solely in terms of production and sales, is responsible for more misery than the meth addict whose family is being destroyed by his addiction. Those military minds in hidden bunkers who play hypothetical "war games" on computers and prepare scenarios for mutually assured nuclear destruction are all the more frightening because their calculations are rigorously removed from any human passions. In short, if the mind completely controlled by the passions is a dangerous instrument, no less dangerous is the mind that is uninformed by passion.

From the other side, the body's drives and appetites have their own kind of logic, their own ability to point toward truth. "The heart," as Pascal famously noted, "has reasons of which reason knows nothing."[20] Human emotions may not provide directions where we should go, but they are wonderfully accurate in telling us where we are. There even are cases, as we all have experienced, when our passions precede our minds in reaching places we really want to be — and consider it right to be. To borrow Plato's image again: even when the charioteer is too sleepy to remember the way home or is confused about which turn in the road to take, if he gives his horses their head, they will take themselves and him back to the place where there are shelter and food.

But if the passions have a logic all their own, and can speak truth to us about the state of affairs in which we find ourselves, why should our first moral obligation be to suppress them, or control them? Wouldn't it make more sense to pay attention to the passions and to learn from them? I say

---

19. L. T. Johnson, "The New Testament's Anti-Jewish Slander and the Conventions of Ancient Polemic," *Journal of Biblical Literature* 108 (1989): 419-41; see also Epictetus on Epicurus: "Your doctrines are bad, subversive of the state, destructive of the family, not even fit for women" (*Discourses* 3.7.20).

20. Pascal, *Pensées*, no. 277.

this while completely agreeing that our lives would not be properly human if we were totally defined by our drives and desires. But being "totally defined by" is a long way from "allowing to be heard"; it is almost certainly the fear of being "totally defined by" that leads us to suppress these aspects of our embodied selves.

In many ways, the passions have been regarded as unruly children and our minds as the adult self that must take charge lest the household be destroyed. In its anxiety to avoid ruin, the mind tries to exercise total control over the children. The greater the effort at control, however, the more the children's energies flourish in all kinds of inventive and — yes, often ruinous — ways. The mind increasingly sees the emotions as enemies to be suppressed, and the emotions increasingly fight the rigid control that threatens their very existence. Even when the "adult" mind succeeds in getting the emotional "children" under absolute control, it is at too great a cost: the mind that should be seeking the stars spends its time tracking mud on the carpets, and the "good children" in starched shirts and precise manners lack all life and spontaneity. The children have lost their fun, and the adult has missed its joy.

Yet, quite another approach to child-rearing is possible — and quite another approach to our human drives and desires. It is possible for parents to listen to and learn from the energetic but not entirely rational children in their care. It is possible for parents to enter into genuine partnership with their children for the improvement of relations within the household. It is even possible for the adult to gain in wisdom and compassion through steady attentiveness even (or especially) toward those children whose energies appear at first to be least well-directed and disruptive. In similar fashion, the mind that is attuned to the movements of the emotions, that attends to them, understands them, and even learns from them, can work in a more relaxed and discerning way in the face of life's complexities.

The objection might be made that recent generations, especially in the so-called First World, have not only long ago abandoned the ancient tradition of repressing the passions, and have not only allowed the children complete freedom of self-expression but have actually put them in charge of the household. Such an abandonment of self-control may in fact characterize contemporary society as a whole; it certainly is found among segments of society. But two observations are appropriate. The first is that such capitulation to the passions is least to be found among those seriously committed to religion and theology, precisely you, my readers. The second is that turning the household over to the children is exactly contrary to the dialogical and cooperative relationship between the mind and the body that I advocate. If totally suppressing the emotions blocks the way to understanding them, so does a total submission to the body's drives and desires.

The issue concerning the passions for my project, however, is not a more adequate psychology, but a more inductive theology. If we adopt a posture toward human drives and desires that is fundamentally attuned to learning what they can teach us about ourselves, we are also in a position to learn from the impulses of the body something of what God is up to in the world. In contrast, the effort to suppress or eliminate such drives and desires can mean missing out on what God seeks to display in and through the experience of the human body — and how God might disclose his will for human discernment.

In the paragraphs that follow, then, I will take up two of the topics that have proven most troublesome and resistant to a positive appreciation — pleasure and desire. And I want to suggest how openness to the revelation of God's spirit through the human body might alter the way we think about and act toward the passionate body.

The Problem and Potential of Pleasure

The moral tradition has been suspicious of pleasure above all. The nouns *hēdonē* in Greek and *voluptas* in Latin are the basis for the derogatory terms "hedonist" and "voluptuary" applied to people whose lives are defined by the pursuit of pleasure, whose moral maxim, if it can be called that, is: "If it feels good, do it." In its pleasures above all, the body seems to draw the spirit away from higher things. But just as pain is a universal experience of sentient beings, so do all bodies experience pleasure, and in how many ways is the body attuned to what feels good! Each of the senses of taste and touch and smell and hearing and sight pleases the body in a distinctive — and sometimes converging — way. Viewed negatively, the spirit is under assault from the body at each of these points of entry, for when the sense is pleased, it desires more of its specific kind of pleasure. As Qoheleth notes, "The eye is not satisfied with seeing, or the ear with hearing" (Qoh. 1:8). The fear is that pleasure leads inevitably to sensual addiction and the captivity of the spirit by the senses. Moral anxiety concerning pleasure focuses above all in the realm of venery: the body seems to be one large erogenous zone, with ground zero represented by the astonishingly sensitive cluster of nerves in the genital area, capable of pleasure so intense and potentially addicting that it has been regarded alternatively as divine and demonic.

It is because of his wholehearted embrace of pleasure as a governing principle for life that Epicurus was so enthusiastically condemned by all other moralists in antiquity. Even though he was himself far from being a hedonist and was even something of an ascetic in his personal life,[21] the very affirmation of pleasure as a fundamental good was enough for him to be condemned as a corrupter of the morals of society.[22] For Stoic philosophers like Epictetus, indeed, pleasure was the enemy of virtue: it was pleasure above all that needed to be eschewed if the seeker after wisdom was to achieve an authentic and admirable manner of life.[23] Epicurus continued to attract positive attention, however, even among some Stoics like Seneca, because his affirmation of pleasure corresponded with a basic human experience: feeling good is preferable to feeling bad.[24] And his teaching was far from the caricature sketched by critics: he acknowledged that some pleasures were not worth the trouble, that some pleasures were of a more noble and uplifting character than others, and that the best of all pleasures is the release from pain, whether physical or mental.[25]

With the subtlety typical of him when analyzing human experience, Aristotle also distinguishes between kinds of pleasures. Although he has nothing but contempt for those "lower" pleasures attached to the body — pleasures connected to those the philosopher considers to be among "the herd" — he recognizes that the soul can also experience genuine pleasure in the things proper to its endeavors.[26] Above all, Aristotle approves of those forms of pleasure that are attached to contemplation.[27] Although his distinction exemplifies the bias in favor of the mind against the body, it is important that Aristotle, together with Epicurus, recognizes pleasure as a basic human good.

Because of his dependence on Aristotle in the analysis of virtues and vices, Thomas Aquinas likewise makes a distinction between those

---

21. Diogenes Laertius, *The Lives of Eminent Philosophers,* 10.11.

22. Plutarch, *Against Colotes* (Mor. 1107D-1127); and *A Pleasant Life Impossible* (Mor. 1086C-1107C).

23. Epictetus, *Discourses* 3.23.30; 3.24.37-39.

24. See Seneca, *Moral Epistles* 8.8; 21.9; 33.2.

25. Epicurus, *Sovereign Maxims* 7, 10, 18, 20; Diogenes Laertius, *Lives* 10.123, 10.131.

26. Aristotle, *Nicomachean Ethics* 1095B.

27. Aristotle, *Nicomachean Ethics* 1176A-B.

pleasures that are noble and those that are base.[28] Scripture also provides some significant if muted support for a positive evaluation of pleasure. Most notably, the book of Qoheleth repeatedly says: "There is nothing better for mortals than to eat and drink, and find enjoyment in their toil. This also is from the hand of God; for apart from Him, who can eat, or who can have enjoyment?" (Qoh. 2:24; see also 3:12-13, 22; 5:18; 8:15). Similarly, Paul warns against depending on riches, saying that the wealthy should instead depend on God, "who richly provides everything for our enjoyment" (1 Tim. 6:17). The tradition, then, provides some warrant for viewing pleasure in a more positive way.

Appetite, Addiction, and Anhedonia

For the ancient moralist, pleasure appears to pose a danger particularly through the appetite for food and drink, not least because some amount of eating and drinking is necessary for sustaining life, and thus cannot altogether be avoided. But human delight in food and (especially) strong drink goes far beyond what is necessary for maintaining existence. Such delight can lead to consumption that far exceeds the body's basic requirements, and such consumption can become an all-encompassing form of addiction. Gluttony and drunkenness appear on all ancient lists of vices, and are regarded as vices that reduce humans to a level below that of the beasts. Animals who are constantly in search of food, after all, still manage to raise their offspring and protect their herd. But the glutton cares only for stuffing the self and disregards any duty toward family and friends. Animals organize their lives around the availability of drink, but when they have drunk the needed water, they move on to other activities. But the drunk not only organizes life around the availability of strong drink, but does so in order to obtain the altered consciousness or oblivion that the alcohol alone can provide.

So powerful are the human appetites for food and drink, and so difficult to control, that fasting from food and abstinence from drink other than water are regarded as necessary starting points for the moral life. The best way to resist the temptation to excess is to reduce appetite, and the best way to reduce appetite is to eliminate — as much as possible — the pleasure given by food and drink. Bread and water and a few vegetables — these

28. Thomas Aquinas, *Summa Theologica* I, 2, 31-39.

simple elements that are necessary for life provide absolute protection against gluttony and drunkenness. Meats, delicacies, and condiments of every kind are regarded both as luxuries, and, insofar as they please the palate, a danger to the soul. Those who sought to free the spirit from the body would therefore begin with severe regimens with respect to food and drink. In 1 Timothy, Paul warns against teachers who "demand abstinence from foods, which God created to be received with thanksgiving by those who believe and know the truth. For everything created by God is good, and nothing is to be rejected, provided it is received with thanksgiving; for it is sanctified by God's word and prayer" (1 Tim. 4:3-5). In the same spirit, he told his delegate: "No longer drink only water, but take a little wine for the sake of your stomach and your frequent ailments" (1 Tim. 5:23). Despite these affirmations, the regnant dualism of the Christian tradition made fasting from food and abstinence from strong drink the marks of the ascetic on the way to spiritual maturity.

By paying attention to the way the body actually responds to stimuli, we have learned much more about the actual roots of addiction. We find that the physical pleasure at the taste of food is not the cause of overeating; the physical pleasure of wine on the palate is not the cause of overdrinking; the dependence on a variety of drugs does not result from their good taste. The experience of pleasure is not the cause of addiction; rather, it is the lack of pleasure, or anhedonia. The person who chronically stuffs food in her mouth is the person least likely to actually enjoy — indeed, to even taste — anything she consumes. Addiction to food derives not from the pleasant taste of food, but from a complex of other factors: an inner emptiness or sense of unworthiness, forms of dysmorphia, a need for control, and a profound lack of pleasure in anything that life has to offer. At the heart of human depression is anhedonia, an inability to find savor or sweetness in anything.

The compulsive behavior that we call addiction — whether to food or alcohol or sex or drugs or gambling or danger — arises not from the presence of pleasure, but the absence of the experience of pleasure in the ordinary round of life. The addict's need for higher doses does not come from pleasure but pain: the "fix" of food or alcohol or drugs provides only the pleasure that is the cessation of pain. Strikingly, though, the ascetic who seeks to suppress appetite and addiction does not altogether escape the same trap, for vigilance against the dangers of pleasure must also be constant and even compulsive. And the ascetic can also find himself caught in anhedonia, with unfortunate consequences. As Thomas Merton once commented, "The false ascetic begins by being cruel to everybody because he is cruel to himself. But he ends by being cruel to everybody but himself."[29]

In contrast, pleasure plays a positive role in the ancient moral ideal of contentment. The term *autarkeia* is sometimes translated as "self-control," and the etymology of the word supports that rendering. But *autarkeia* does not suggest the rigid and suppressive control of the ascetic so much as the balanced appreciation for life's gifts that accompany wisdom. The person who is content takes pleasure in what is at hand, and therefore does not need to compulsively seek more. As Paul puts it, "If we have food and clothing, we shall be content with these" (1 Tim. 6:8). When I was in my forties, I was restless and unhappy, feeling overworked, underpaid, underappreciated. I found no pleasure in my life. I was thoroughly discontented. And since my emotions have always tended to work themselves out through food and drink, my discontentment expressed itself in frantic cycles of overeating followed by obsessive dieting. Indeed, I had little idea of what contentment actually could be. So I decided to make a study of the most contented man I knew, Sam Randazzo, my father-in-law.

Sam was a simple and straightforward man who had worked hard his entire life, and he was enjoying simple and straightforward things in his retirement: fishing, gardening, and watching football on TV. Since he never seemed to want anything more than these things — plus his regular meals — he was a difficult target for his children's gift-giving. What can you give a man who is still happy with what you gave him ten years ago? Therefore, since my own discontent found expression in addictive patterns of eating, I decided to pay close attention to the way Sam handled the meals provided him by his wife. Sam would accept a heaping plate of hot food; he would look neither to the left nor the right, but would dedicate himself fully to the enjoyment of what was before him. He ate every bite, and would wipe his plate with a morsel of bread to get all the goodness available. Then he would sigh, push his plate forward, and say, "thank God" — and he never went back for a second helping.

It was not difficult to contrast his mode to my own. I never really tasted what was in front of me because I was already thinking of another helping of food; I was constantly aware of what others had on their plates, as though I was in a race to get seconds first! Sam's contentment — the pleasure he experienced in life — was perfectly expressed through his

---

29. Thomas Merton, *No Man Is an Island* (New York: Harcourt, Brace, 1955), p. 96.

healthy appreciation of the food God provided: he ate it all, he enjoyed it all, and he never sought more. Precisely the pleasure the food gave him, I learned, enabled him to have *autarkeia* ("self-control") with regard to that food. The pleasure in his simple (but hearty!) food satisfied his appetite. He did not need more and did not seek more. It was an important lesson, one that I am still learning.

From this perspective, the body's capacity for pleasure does not appear as a threat to virtue that must be battled, but seems much more like an element in genuine virtue that should be embraced. The path to excess and to the destruction of self and others through the bodily appetites and addictions does not run through pleasure but through the absence of pleasure. In the first chapter above, I criticized the failure of Pope John Paul II to pay any attention to this element of human sexuality within marriage. By focusing on sex only as a means of procreation and by failing to appreciate the role of giving and receiving intense bodily pleasure through sexual engagement, the pope's teaching misses the dimension of married love that is at once most obvious (to those who experience it) and most subtly in service to authentic sexual virtue. Certainly, the widespread patterns of sexual addiction (voyeuristic and otherwise) in contemporary culture arise, not from an excess of sexual pleasure, even in the marriage bed, but rather from a widespread anhedonia.

Pleasure and Discerning God's Call

The moral tradition was so suspicious of pleasure's ability to seduce the body, and thereby deceive the soul, that the idea of pleasure as providing guidance for moral and theological discernment would seem to be laughable to that tradition. Moral and religious discernment had to do with duty, what one should do, while pleasure had to do simply with satisfaction, what felt good. Pleasure and duty, it would seem, are diametrically opposed. Such was certainly the conviction of the ancients, and such was the premise that governed those who were raised Catholic in my youth. The thinking went this way: in every choice between good and evil, one must choose the good. But what if one is presented with two goods? Then one must choose the good that is "more perfect"; to choose the less perfect over the more perfect was, in effect, the same as choosing evil over good. But how, in every circumstance, could one know which option was the more perfect? The answer: the option that we didn't want to do, the option that promised us no pleasure, was almost certainly the option that was more perfect, more pleasing to God. In such thinking, pleasure plays a role only by indicating what we should not do.

Our actual human experience, in contrast, suggests the opposite, namely, that pleasure is an important indicator of what we like to do and thereby becomes a critical factor in discerning what we should do. Two aspects of this position need to be noted. First, it is clear that pleasure, or enjoyment, leads humans to engage in certain activities and to excel in them. I don't have in mind here the basic bodily pleasures that we all share — the enjoyment of eating and drinking and sleeping and having sex. Instead, I have in mind the choice to engage the world in certain ways rather than others. The more I enjoy the activity in which I am engaged, the more likely I am to persist in it, and seek to devote even more time and energy to it. Athletes excel in sports not only because they have physical ability beyond the norm but because the exercise of those abilities brings them intense pleasure.

The same is true for musicians and artists: despite the degree of effort and suffering that such activities demand — and, like athletics, they do demand effort and suffering — it is the pleasure of making music or making art that binds them to these activities. No less is the pleasure given by the cultivation of living things a factor in people devoting themselves to serious gardening. Men and women become architects not simply because they can draw precisely, but because they take delight in drawing a vision of what a building might be. There are many who are able to read and write, but only those who find intense and enduring pleasure in the reading of many books and the writing of many papers pursue the life of scholarship. The pleasure experienced in and through such activities is a central element in the human choice to engage in them.

Second, it is clear that delight in diverse activities is highly particular. Not everyone gets equal (or sometimes any) pleasure from the same activity. Laying bricks with precision or tuning an engine to optimal performance provides genuine enjoyment to some people, but not to others. The solving of mathematical problems seems the height of pleasure to some and sheer torture to others. Training for athletic competition brings deep satisfaction to some but appears to be pointless labor to others, who in turn consider the baking of the world's finest cakes to be a supreme source of enjoyment. Observation of the lives around us suggests that people tend to enjoy doing the things they are good at (thus mathematics is torture, not pleasure to me) and tend to seek to become even better at doing those things because of the pleasure they derive from them. Pleasure makes a task seem more like play than like work because it does not sap our energy but increases it: "I could do this all day!"

It does not follow, to be sure, that pleasure in an activity necessarily correlates with excellence in it. Plenty of young men love to play baseball, but their abilities limit them to mediocre (if enthusiastic) participation in the game. Many students take pleasure in their learning, but not all have the ability to translate such delight into a lifetime commitment. After saying that, however, how foolish we would be to ignore the factor of pleasure when we try to discern the vocation to which God calls us. Paul says with regard to marriage and celibacy: "Each has a particular gift from God, one having one kind, and another a different kind" (1 Cor. 7:7). But if it is the gift of God to each one of us that should shape the way we commit our energies in the world, shape our particular way of serving others in the world, should not the pleasure that we take in doing some things rather than others be considered as part of the gift that God has himself placed within us?

The pleasure principle cannot be absolute, for other factors must always be considered. I may find the greatest pleasure in the pursuit of knowledge, but the needs of my family or of my community may require of me that I fasten bolts or lift bales. Pleasure is often necessarily trumped by duty, as experience also shows us. But to ignore the possibility of pleasure in our life's activities is to miss part of the truth that our bodies can teach us.

Is Desire Deceptive?

The topic of desire is closely linked to that of pleasure. Humans seek after things, and usually do so because they expect to find them pleasurable. I desire food because I am hungry but also because food tastes good. I seek a sexual partner not only to beget children but also because sexual intercourse is intensely enjoyable. But the influence of the Greco-Roman moral tradition on the Christian perception of the passions is perhaps most evident in the New Testament's use of terms that are variously translated as desire, passion, or lust.

In ordinary usage, the noun *epithymia* and the verb *epithymein* are neutral: they derive a positive or negative connotation from the object of desire rather than the desire itself. The Septuagint translation of the Old

Testament for the most part observes this common usage. Thus desire can attach itself to positive or morally neutral objects: water (2 Sam. 23:15), a former home (Gen. 31:30), land (Exod. 34:24), and meat (Deut. 12:20). People can also desire holy things: instruction (Wis. 6:17); the Lord's commands (Ps. 119:20, 40), God's words (Wis. 6:2), God's wisdom (Wis. 6:12, 20; Sir. 6:37), or the Lord himself (Amos 5:18; Isa. 58:2, 11). Such desires of the righteous, Scripture declares, God will grant (Deut. 14:26; Ps. 20:4; 140:8; Prov. 10:24; 11:23).

Desire gains a negative connotation when the object desired is unlawful or harmful. Thus, most famously, God's commandment not to covet *(epithymein)* a neighbor's wife or house (Exod. 20:17; Deut. 5:21; see also 4 Macc. 2:5). It is not desiring a woman or a household that is wrong, but the fact that the wife or household already belongs to another. "Coveting" in this case involves the intention to take away what properly belongs to the neighbor. Similarly, the Israelites are told not to covet *(epithymein)* the gold and silver of idols (Deut. 7:25) or delicacies (Prov. 23:3) or an evil woman (Prov. 6:25), or to be with an evil man (Prov. 24:1). In such cases also, it is the object that makes the desire bad. The most famous instance of "coveting" is the Israelites' craving for meat in the wilderness, a sign of their faithlessness (Num. 11:4, 34; see Ps. 106:14; 78:18; Wis. 16:3; 19:11). The nearest thing to a generalization concerning desire is that the "desires of the godless are wicked" (Prov. 12:12), and that "all day long the wicked covets" (Prov. 21:26). But in the traditional wisdom texts, *epithymia* is not isolated as a problem in itself.

Only in the wisdom writings that derive from the Hellenistic period do we find *epithymia* as such considered problematic — quite apart from its object. Therefore, the book of Wisdom declares that "roving desire perverts the innocent mind" (4:12). Sirach commands: "Do not follow the desire of the heart" (5:2), and "do not follow your base desires but restrain your appetites; if you allow your soul to take pleasure in base desire, it will make you the laughingstock of your enemies" (18:30-31). Even more direct is 4 Maccabees, which states in 1:3 that "reason rules over those emotions that hinder self-control, namely gluttony and lust *(epithymia)*." Now we are in the realm where "the passions" are themselves the problem. The author declares: "Desire precedes pleasure and delight follows it" (1:22). Fourth Maccabees is indeed an encomium to self-control *(sōphrosynē):* "Self-control, then, is dominant over the desires. Some desires are mental and some are physical, and reason obviously rules over both" (1:31-32). Reason rules over sexual desire and every desire (2:4); proof of this is

God's commandment: "Since the law has told us not to covet *[epithymein]*, I could prove to you all the more that reason is able to control desire" (2:6). Although no one can escape bodily desires entirely, "reason can provide a way for us not to be enslaved by desire" (3:2).

Such sentiments are clearly influenced by the tendency in Greco-Roman moral discourse to deprecate "desire" as such. Already in Plato, *epithymia* is sometimes used as roughly equivalent to "lust,"[30] and Epictetus exhorts his students to resist all desire.[31] Hellenistic Jewish texts apart from the LXX adopt this completely negative view. Philo speaks of the soul "driven by desire or enticed by pleasure."[32] The link between desire and vice is drawn explicitly (see 4 Macc 1:25-26),[33] as shown by the appearance of *epithymia* — without any qualification — in vice lists.[34]

The New Testament sometimes uses forms of *epithymia* with a positive object; Paul, for example, desires to see his communities (1 Thess. 2:17; Phil. 1:23); Jesus desires fervently to share Passover with his disciples in Luke 22:15 (see also Matt. 13:17; Luke 17:22; 1 Pet. 1:12; 1 Tim. 3:1; Heb. 6:11). Other times, desire has an inappropriate object — such as another man's wife (Matt. 5:28) or silver and gold (Acts 20:33). And Paul alludes to the "desiring" of the wilderness generation that tested God (1 Cor. 10:6). In other cases, the verb "to desire" appears without a specific object as a human impulse that is dangerous or destructive or deceitful. Thus Paul says that the flesh desires against the spirit (Gal. 5:17), and James speaks of "desiring and not getting" (James 4:2). Strikingly, when Paul cites the Decalogue in Romans, he does not supply the object that the Old Testament had, stating only "do not covet ['desire']" in 7:7 and "do not steal, do not covet" in 13:9.

Overwhelmingly, though, the noun *epithymia* appears throughout the New Testament with thoroughly negative connotations (see Mark 4:19; John 8:44; 1 Pet. 1:14; 2:11; 4:2; 2 Pet. 1:4; 2:10; 3:3; 1 John 2:16-17) so that "following one's own desires" can stand alone as a moral condemnation (Jude 16, 18; 2 Tim. 4:3). Above all in Paul's letters, the "desires of the heart" (Rom. 1:24) or "vain desires" (1 Tim. 6:9; 2 Tim. 3:6) or "passions of desire" (1 Thess. 4:5) or "desires of the flesh" (Rom. 6:12; 7:8; 13:14; Gal. 5:16; Eph. 2:3) are put in opposition to the work of the Spirit, so

30. Plato, *Phaedo* 83B; *Phaedrus* 232B.
31. Epictetus, *Discourses* 2.16.45; 2.18.8; 3.9.21.
32. Philo, *Every Good Man Is Free* 159; *Special Laws* 4.93-94; *Contemplative Life* 74.
33. See Philo, *On Husbandry* 22-25; see also *Testament of Joseph* 7.1-8.
34. Philo, *Preliminary Studies* 172; *Migration of Abraham* 60; *Contemplative Life* 2.

that believers are those who have "crucified the flesh with its passions and desires" (Gal. 5:24). Such passions or desires — both terms translate *epithymia* — are "deceitful" (Eph. 4:22) and "worldly" (Titus 2:12), and they serve "various pleasures" (Titus 3:13). In language similar to Paul's, the Letter of James speaks of humans being "led astray by their own desires" (James 1:14), declaring that such desires reach their end in sin (1:15). In short, the New Testament, sharing the outlook of the later Wisdom writings affected by Hellenistic philosophy, provides abundant grounds for Christians to consider desires, passions, and lusts to be, by their mere existence, deceitful and destructive of humans. But are they?

Sexual Desire and Divine Delight

The desire that moralists hold in greatest suspicion is sexual desire. Scripture notoriously has little positive appreciation of the erotic. The Old Testament at least has the Song of Solomon to celebrate lovers' delight in each other, but the New Testament pays absolutely no attention to the human desire (eros) that among the Greeks was considered either divine or a stage in the ascent to the divine. And the dualistic tendency within Christianity, represented most prominently by Gnosticism, has regarded the passion driving humans to seek sexual partners as truly deceptive.

At the very least, the desire to join physically with another is a distraction from the ultimate human task of seeking to be joined to God, spirit to spirit. At its worst, the children produced by sexual engagement offer a deceptive hope for the continuance and enhancement of life, an illusion that can induce ignorance of the fact that real life is to be found only in the realm of the spirit. Best, then, if sexual desire cannot be suppressed completely, to view any of its manifestations with the highest caution, and to direct it as quickly as possible within the relatively safe bounds of matrimony, and even there, restrict its legitimate expression to the procreation of children. I complained in an earlier chapter how in this way John Paul II's *Theology of the Body* effectively eliminated eros from theological consideration — even within marriage.

But what might we learn theologically if we took seriously the premise that God seeks to disclose God's spirit through the body? Here we must resist at all costs the tendency to disembody sexual desire in order to make it "spiritual." Eros has to do first of all with bodies seeking to be physically joined through an act which, while seeming beautiful to those engaged in it, appears most often to observers as resembling the rutting of animals. The Shakespearian phrase "making the beast with two backs" (*Othello* 1.1) captures the impression nicely. The experience of physical pleasure in sexual contact is sufficiently intense as to make it desirable quite apart from any consideration beyond its feeling really good.

Two aspects of human sexual desire especially deserve attention. The first is the mysterious character of sexual attraction among humans. To focus on this dimension, we must locate it between two extremes. It is true that some deranged sexual desire can be utterly indiscriminate in the search for partners: eros is not really a factor here, only biological urges in overdrive. At the opposite extreme, humans can mate for a variety of reasons that have little to do with eros: they have an arranged marriage, they seek to merge property, they want security. In such cases sex is an element within negotiations. Between the extremes is the kind of physical/emotional attraction we are all familiar with from our own experience and that we find as a feature of literature from antiquity to the present: this one person, and only this one, is the object of my desire. Eros is the love of preference based on attraction.

The basis for such sexual attraction, however, remains mysterious, almost always to outside observers, and frequently to those caught up in the passion themselves. What is it in him that makes me want to be with him at every moment, that makes me excited simply to hear his voice or touch his hand? What quality is there in her that makes my eye seek only her in every room, my ear long to hear only her voice, or makes me delight in her specific way of standing and sitting and laughing and turning her head? We know from our experience that we don't have the slightest understanding of why we are sexually attracted to some people and not to others, why we seek to be in the presence of, to touch, this person but are repelled by that person. Yet we also know from experience that such desire simply *is;* we cannot argue ourselves to it or dissuade ourselves from it. Rather, we experience such attraction as a form of recognition: "Of course, you are the one." The recognition does not mean that we will marry or even mate. In fact, you may not be attracted at all in the same way to me. But it is an undeniable fact of my existence: I am powerfully drawn to you; I desire you and you alone.

The fact that we experience eros as a power beyond our control, that is, beyond our calculation or manipulation, is a reason why the ancient Greeks thought of it as divine. Humans are swept by it to places they did not anticipate, find themselves in situations they could not have foreseen.

It is not inappropriate, I think, for us also to think of sexual desire as one of the ways in which the Spirit of the Living God exercises its freedom in our human existence. A power that is so great and so outside our calculation, that moves us in a moment from one place to another without warning, indeed, that can change our lives completely in an instant, must at least be taken seriously as a force by which God might be disclosing Godself in the world.

Thinking this way becomes more plausible because our experience of human eros enables us to better grasp an otherwise puzzling dimension of God's self-revelation in Scripture, namely, the language expressing God's preferential love for Israel. It should not be surprising that the relationship between God and Israel — a relationship based on God's choice that is inexplicable in ordinary terms — is often couched in terms of passionate, sexual love. Both the positive (Jer. 2:1-6; Hos. 1:2–2:23) and negative (Ezek. 16:1-63; 23:1-49) aspects of that relationship can use such language, precisely because in no other aspect of human experience is there so intense a desire for intimacy and union, and in no other aspect of human experience can the breaking of such intimacy and unity appear so tragic.

Taking our lead from Scripture, then, we might be so bold as to say that the aspect of God's character that enables God to desire unity with humans, among all creatures, is also the aspect that God has implanted within humans — a dimension of God's image — leading them to seek complete unity with each other. When the language of human sexual love is also used for the incarnation, as when we call Christ the bridegroom and the church his bride, then we again signal the mystery by which God has shown such preference for humans among all his creatures as to seek total bodily union with them.

Human sexual desire is not only particular and preferential; it also has a kind of transcendence that distinguishes it from the mating of animals. Animals are attracted to each other to mate (and sometimes form families); we suspect that they do not thereby form new worlds of meaning. But such a search for a larger world is an integral part of human sexual desire. When people seek sexual intimacy and union with others, there is almost always — apart from the crassest and most casual sexual encounter — a desire for spiritual intimacy as well. Part of the mystery of human sexual desire is this plus factor: our search for complete physical unity is also a search for a meeting of minds and emotions. The biblical use of "knowing" for sexual intimacy effectively captures this dimension: we want to know the other and to be known, and in this quest we risk a vulnerability to the other and an openness to him or her that is rare in any other aspect of human interaction.

The other whom I desire is not simply a combination of attractive physical properties, but she is uniquely other in a more profound sense: she is an embodied spirit who invites me to the sharing of ideas and ideals. The one whom I seek, then, is also mystery in this sense, that she refuses to be reduced to an object, to be a problem that I can solve, but remains always elusively and intriguingly apart from my control, and as such, beckons me to another and (I am convinced) a better place. I find myself in a communion that is at once intensely physical and intimately spiritual, where it becomes impossible to distinguish adequately among the communication that passes between us by touch, by sight or smell, or by spoken word, or by simply being together alone, rather than by being (as before this) alone together, in an alchemy that makes of "you" and "me" a "we."

Moreover, just as God's preferential love for humans can legitimately use the language of human sexual passion, so can the human search for the face of God use the same kind of erotic speech, as the writings of the mystics have demonstrated. This is not, once more, a matter of forsaking the body in favor of the spirit. It is rather a matter of body and spirit together reaching beyond what they can grasp into the mystery of the one who remains always hidden behind the veil of appearances and in his manifold beauty always entices us further than we ever planned to travel. Sexual desire, in short, is a dimension of somatic experience that both impels us on a quest for the other and enables us to think about the one who is truly Other in a deeply satisfying way.

Desire and the Pursuit of Excellence

The fear of being out of control that has led to the suppression of sexual desire within the Christian tradition has had the side effect of making any kind of desire appear dangerous. This suspicion also has its roots in the philosophical preference for *apatheia* — lack of passion or desire — as the ideal state for the wise person. If vice was automatically connected to unruly passions, then not to desire at all seemed self-evidently a path to virtue. The impossibility of that ideal, however, is revealed by the fact that seeking such a state is itself a form of desire — to be such a wise person — and that without such a desire, the goal would never be reached. The desire to be a good and wise person is not an "evil desire," but it is just as much a desire or passion, energizing and directing our body in just as powerful a way as other, less elevated, desires do. Nobody in antiquity, for example, was as passionate about the need to have *apatheia* as Epictetus, or showed more passion in his effort to inculcate this ideal among his students.

This realization reminds us of the important, indeed indispensable, role that passion plays in any significant human project. Desire is the motor that pushes us past our inertia and resistance, enabling us to overcome obstacles in order to accomplish something in the world. We speak of a passion for sport, a passion for art or music, a passion for learning, for science, or for social justice. What we mean when we use the term passion in such contexts is a disposition that declares this arena of activity as of such importance that we are impelled both in body and spirit to engage it in a way that surpasses any other activity in our lives. Passion of this sort, like sexual desire, is a form of love that seeks intimacy and union, not with a single person, but with an entire realm of activity. The relationship of spirit and body in this case, however, is the opposite of that in sexual desire. In sexual passion, the body is drawn to the other first through a complex process of attraction, and the spirit follows after. In a passion for art or learning, by contrast, the imaginative spirit leads and the body follows. Because my embodied experience of this activity delights me in the first place — gives me pleasure — my imagination leaps ahead to the possibility of expanding such activity in my life.

It need not be the specific experience of pleasure that begins to form the passion; in the case of a passion for social justice, for example, the experience may be one of outrage at the sight of those abused in society or one of satisfaction at the sight of wrongs being made right. In any case, I begin to fantasize a life centered in and organized around such activity. My mind begins to try out possible avenues of access to such activity. My passion for music, a level of love far greater than my simply liking or admiring music, may lead me to become a musician, or a producer, or a publisher of music. My love of drama may lead me to become an actor or director or a publicist, anything connected to the theater. My passion for social justice may lead me to desire the life of a lawyer, or a social worker, or judge, or community organizer.

In each of these cases, we notice, the broad and inclusive passion for the activity as a whole precedes and impels the specific desire for a place within that realm of activity. Desire is not enough, to be sure; talent and opportunity come into play. But without passion, no specific desires would be formed, and it is this passion that moves our bodies and "brings them under control" — not by suppressing them, but by directing them to a goal. The stronger the passion, the greater our willingness to push our bodies beyond what we first thought was possible. My passion for teaching drives my body, despite its fatigue, to meet with students, prepare lectures, grade countless papers, write endless letters of recommendation, and even sit through interminable committee meetings. Your passion for football leads you to discipline your body through exercise, diet, workouts, and arduous practices, overcoming fatigue for your "love of the game." Here indeed is the link between passion and excellence in any endeavor. Excellence requires the discipline of body and mind directed to any activity, whether it be kayaking or composing, modeling in clay or mountain-climbing. Our bodies resist such effort, but are energized by the fierceness of our passion. Desire, passion, and healthy ambition are the keys to excellence in any endeavor.

Such passionate desire is not contrary to the faithful obedience we owe to God but rather an integral part of such obedience. As instinctually impoverished creatures — meaning that, within the confines of contingency, we are free to choose who we will be — we are obliged to form projects for our lives that we treat as though absolute, just to provide direction to our lives.[35] Failure to form such projects is not virtue but a kind of "will-lessness" that both makes us subject to the projects of others and contributes nothing to challenge or elevate the projects of others. Because we are convinced that the Spirit of the Living God challenges and elevates us, in turn, through the passions and projects of others, we also seek to be open to the call of God to us in each specific circumstance, aware that God can call us beyond or even outside our life project (our passion) to step into a space that we have not anticipated. If we perceive such a call and insist nevertheless on making our own passion (project) absolute, then we are revealed as willful and have failed to respond with the obedience of faith. But for our faith to be truly obedience to the call of God, having a desire or project of our own is critical. The pattern is displayed perfectly by the prayer of Jesus in the Garden before his death: "Father, all things are possible to you. Take this cup away from me. Yet not what I will, but what you will." Jesus' project was to live, and he passionately desired it. He prayed that he might live. Yet he was willing to die if that is what God demanded of him.

---

35. For the argument here, see L. T. Johnson, *Faith's Freedom: A Classic Spirituality for Contemporary Christians* (Minneapolis: Fortress, 1990).

Authentic faith, then, operates in the tension between forming legitimate human projects based on desire, and responding to the call of God in specific circumstances that can confirm or challenge those projects in unpredictable ways. Two aspects of this dimension of human passion thereby become pertinent to theology as an inductive art. The first is the need to cultivate such passionate projects, if faith is not to be mere will-lessness. Humans need to risk committing their freedom to passionate desires that may not, in fact, be realized precisely because God asks something else from them. The second is the revelatory value of our human passions and the projects we form from them. We learn much about how God is at work in our bodies by paying attention to the projects we are forming on the basis of our passions, and how these are being challenged by the projects formed by the passions of others.

CHAPTER SEVEN

The Body at Work

The best way to enter a discussion of work as a form of embodied activity that can disclose (or hide) the Spirit of the Living God is through contrast to the human experience of play. If in play we see humans "taking time off" or "marking time" in a special way, in work we see humans in ordinary time. Play seems to be an arena of freedom, while work is the realm of the necessary. Play constructs an alternative reality, and work responds to the demands of everyday life. If play is liberty, work is necessity. If play is an activity engaged in for its own sake, work is most often what we do to reach a definite result. It is easy to see the role of transcendence in play, where the spirit is allowed to leap; it is difficult to find transcendence in work, where the spirit often appears to be crushed or absent. It is easy to portray play in the bright colors of joy, elation, excitement; it is equally easy to paint work in the drab colors of depression, sorrow, and boredom. The body language of play is upright, with head held high and eyes bright; the body language of labor is bent, with head bowed and eyes dim. Pain and fatigue can occur in play as well as work, but they are experienced quite differently. In play, soreness and tiredness suggest accomplishment and satisfaction; in work they are experienced as injury and exhaustion.

Defining Work

Work is so much a part of everyday life that — in contrast to play, which is essentially "set apart" from the everyday — it is difficult to define precisely. Work is not simply doing something that is difficult, for difficulty attaches to activities such as art and sport as well; it is not something from which we derive profit, for sport and art can profit us in a variety of ways. The best place to start in defining work is by way of contrast to play. If, as Johan Huizinga proposes, play is "purposeless but meaningful activity," work is by no means always "meaningful," but it is always purposeful. We engage in play for its own sake; but we work for the sake of something else. Work has a goal, a definite end. And if we engage in play by free choice, we work because we must. If we do not play, we are impoverished spiritually; but if we do not work, we perish physically. Work is therefore marked by necessity. Someone must be working for me to live out my life, either myself or someone who supports me.

Necessity and purpose go hand in hand. Thus, I plant seed in order to grow a crop, and I grow a crop in order to feed my family. I prune my vines in order to produce grapes, and I produce grapes in order to make wine. I do not prune my vines as an aesthetic exercise. I water and feed chickens so that they will give me eggs, and eventually meat. I do not water and feed chickens because I love chickens but because of what chickens can provide me. In short, I do not farm because I enjoy the rhythms of planting and weeding and scything, or the beauty of cows scattered on the green field in the golden light. I farm in order to gain a crop that will support me and my family. The work of agriculture illustrates other basic aspects of work simply and directly. The crop I grow, for example, is governed by the condition of my land and the climate: What will this soil support, and what do the cycles of rain and drought allow? The kind and number of beasts I raise likewise depend on the size of my property, the availability of herbage, the severity of the seasons.

In farming, possibility is severely circumscribed by conditions outside my control: success and failure depend not only on my skill and effort, but even more on the vagaries of heat and cold, of wet and dry. Too much rain is as disastrous as too little; too little sun is as damaging as too much sun. The growth of a crop, moreover, means overcoming resistance. I must clear stones and stumps from the field if I am to plow and plant. I must fight weeds and insects and vermin if the plants are to grow. The successful herding of animals such as sheep and goats and cattle similarly must overcome a variety of diseases to which they are prey and the many predators that threaten to make them prey.

Making a living from the land means observing and creatively responding to the rhythms imposed by nature rather than imposing my will on nature. I need to learn when to plant, when to weed, when to harvest. Failure to pay attention can lead to utter loss and destruction. Chores that are part of farm labor are dictated rather than chosen: vines must be pruned in order to yield; cows need to be milked in order to stay healthy. On a productive farm, there is too much work for one person: the tasks of the outdoors and the tasks of the household make marriage and the procreation of children a blessing. On a working farm, there are no debates over appropriate gender roles: all hands must pitch in as needed. A rough gender equality, in fact, is established by the never-ending demands on both man and woman, girl and boy, in the running of a farm. And though farmers may rejoice and find play in seasonal festivals, it is only when and if all chores have been done, all stock secured, all harvests safely in.

Agricultural labor itself represents a development toward stability and predictability beyond the catch-as-catch-can efforts of hunters and gatherers, whose tribal existence depends on ceaseless movement in the search for killable game and edible plants. Whereas with agriculture and animal husbandry it is possible to distinguish at least moments of intense labor and relaxation from labor, hunters and gatherers have so small a margin between subsistence and starvation that an almost constant vigilance and movement is required of them. Agriculture and animal husbandry, in turn, give rise to other basic forms of human work, such as logging and mining and manufacturing (simple as in crafts, complex as in factories), milling, trade, and the travel that trade demands. On the basis of these activities, still more elaborate forms of work develop, such as banking, financial speculation, a variety of personal services (voluntary and involuntary), and ultimately the structures and systems of government.

Who can enumerate all the things that humans do to occupy themselves and provide a living? And who can adequately delineate the varieties of purpose, pleasure, and pain in each endeavor we call work? In my chapter on the body at play, I spoke of music, art, and drama as forms of play. But they can also be — and have been — forms of work in both the ancient and modern world. In my discussion of desire, I noted the pleasure attending the life of learning, but no one who has graded student papers will deny the physical and mental exhaustion, that is, the cost in labor, of that mode of life.

Appreciating Work

The first point of this brief inventory of human occupations is to support a definition of human work as involving (across a wide range of activities) purposefulness, effort, and a degree of seriousness, dictated by necessity, that is also in some degree costly. The second point to my listing all these activities is to note the degree to which it escapes notice in the religious and moral literature of antiquity. I do not mean to suggest that the various forms of work were entirely ignored. We have extant from the Greco-Roman tradition any number of tractates that treat various occupations in considerable detail. The eighth-century BCE *Works and Days* by Hesiod, for example, sees work as a consequence of the decline of the human condition from the golden to the iron age (II, 170), but considers that "work is no disgrace; it is idleness that is a disgrace" (II, 293-313). Each one should do the work that the gods have ordained (II, 381-82), but agriculture is superior to trade (II, 646). Hesiod provides detailed instructions to the ancient landholder with slaves concerning the proper seasons for farm activities (II, 383-828).

Greek writers like Theophrastus of Eresos (387-287 BCE) and Xenophon (after 362 BCE) continued to pay close attention to the specific demands of agriculture and household management. Romans in particular always held agriculture in honor, and substantial attention was given it by Cato the Elder (234-249 BCE), Varro (117-27 BCE), Virgil (ca. 38 BCE), Columella (first century BCE), Celsus (first century CE), and Pliny the Younger (23-79 CE). Although these writings contained much solid information about farming and other occupations, however, they remain at an aristocratic distance from the activities they describe. Plato and Aristotle considered physical labor as "servile" and unworthy of citizens, who should be dedicated to the life of the mind.[1] The story of how Cincinnatus left his farm to save Rome, and then returned to his farming, was certainly an emblem of antique republican virtue.[2] But in fact, such work was most often observed from the perspective of leisure. Thus Cicero declares, "Of all the occupations by which gain is secured, none is better than agriculture, nor more profitable, none more delightful, none more becoming in a free man."[3] He says further that farming is "the teacher of economy, of industry, and of justice."[4] But such idealized affirmations not only come from a "gentleman farmer" whose land was actually worked by slaves and hired hands, but they fail to pay specific attention to the actual experience

---

1. See Aristotle, *Politics,* Books 1 and 7.
2. Livy, *History of Rome* 3.14-26.
3. Cicero, *On Duties* 1.42.
4. Cicero, *Pro Roscio Amerino* 75.

of those carrying out such labor. It is doubtful that those actually laboring on Roman *latifundia* were equally appreciative of the educative and pleasurable dimensions of their sweat-filled days. For classical antiquity, it can be safely said, work was always best when carried out by others; the ideal was the life of leisure that was considered both necessary and the due of aristocratic souls.

The Old Testament likewise shows little positive appreciation for work. Although Adam is placed in the garden to "till it and keep it" (Gen. 2:15), one of the effects of the first couple's sin is that work is defined in terms of a curse: "Cursed be the ground because of you; in toil you shall eat of it all the days of your life . . . in the sweat of your face you shall eat bread" (Gen. 3:17-18; see also 5:28). The stories of Genesis note that Cain was a tiller of soil and Abel was a shepherd (Gen. 4:2); that Noah was the first keeper of a vineyard (Gen. 9:20); that Ishmael and Esau were hunters (Gen. 21:20; 25:27). Abraham and his son Isaac and his grandson Esau were all managers of flocks and enjoyed great prosperity (Gen. 12:16; 13:2; 26:12-13; 31:17-18), even though Jacob's laboring for Laban (Gen. 29:20; 31:41) represented a more indirect path to wealth. Jacob's sons, including Joseph (Gen. 37:2), were tenders of flocks before Joseph's path led him to become overseer of Potiphar's household in Egypt (Gen. 39:2). Despite being raised in Pharaoh's house, Moses also became a shepherd when he was exiled in Midian (Exod. 3:1). In none of these stories is work itself characterized in terms of a curse; it appears rather as the way to great prosperity.

The negative perception of work emerges again in the book of Exodus. The people of Israel are in bondage in Egypt, and their slavery is portrayed in terms of oppressive forced labor (Exod. 1:10-14; 2:23; 3:7). When Moses asks Pharaoh's permission for the people to worship God in the wilderness, Pharaoh responds, "Why do you take the people away from their work? Get to your burdens!" (Exod. 5:4). He accuses Moses of seeking to "give them rest from their burdens" (Exod. 5:5), and commands that the Israelites be given even heavier work so "they will pay no heed to lying words" (Exod. 5:9). The Israelite desire to worship is defined in terms of "idleness" (Exod. 5:17).

Against this backdrop of "work as oppression," the commandment to keep the Sabbath holy by resting from work takes on an even greater pertinence. Six days are set aside for work, but the seventh "is a Sabbath to the Lord your God: in it you shall not do any work, you, or your son, or your daughter, or your manservant or your maidservant, or your cattle, or your sojourner who is within your gates" (Exod. 20:8-10; cf. Deut. 5:12-15). In Exodus, the Sabbath observance is grounded in God's rest after creating the world in six days (Exod. 20:11); in Deuteronomy it is connected to the memory of the great deeds that God did in bringing the people out of servitude in Egypt (Deut. 5:15). In both versions, the Sabbath observance is meant to be a blessing: one day a week everyone, including beasts, gets to stop working. In the idealized legislation of Leviticus, the Sabbath rest is extended even to the land (Lev. 25:1-18), and the future exile of the people is envisioned as a Sabbath for the land (Lev. 26:34-35).

Despite the attention given by Torah to laws governing agriculture (Exod. 21:26–22:12), forbidding the oppression of laborers (Exod. 22:21-24; 23:9; Lev. 19:13-16; Deut. 24:14-22), and making allowance through the *peah* for the sojourners, widows, and children (Lev. 19:9; 23:22; see Ruth 2:3), the remainder of the Old Testament pays remarkably little attention to the basic human activity of work, since the great narratives focus on the exploits of judges and kings. That Gideon threshed wheat in a winepress (Judg. 6:11) or that David was a shepherd (1 Sam. 16:11) is of less moment than the great works that God's Spirit worked through them for the salvation of the people. The "work" of those whom God raised up as champions and rulers throughout Israel's history was not the work of everyday people but the work of warfare and ruling.

Only in the Wisdom literature, with its characteristic attention to the nonheroic dimensions of life, do we find any discussion of ordinary work. In Proverbs, the necessity of work is exemplified at one extreme by the work of wisdom in God's creation (Prov. 8:20-31) and the other by the industriousness and foresightedness of the ant (6:6-10). Apart from the most casual references to aspects of agricultural work (14:4; 16:26; 27:23-27; 28:19), Proverbs contents itself with frequent — almost nagging — pleas to avoid laziness (10:4; 13:4; 15:19; 19:18, 24; 20:4; 22:13; 24:30-34). Only in its final encomium to the good wife, drawn in contrast to the seductive woman of the street (6:1–7:27), does Proverbs linger approvingly over all the activities that constitute the work of the female manager of the household (31:10-31).

In Qoheleth, in turn, the term "toil" stands for all human activities, and the Preacher's attitude is characteristically ambivalent. On one side, all forms of human activity are a form of "vanity" that necessarily passes away: "What do people gain from all the toil at which they toil under the sun?" (Qoh. 1:3). On the other side, humans should seek to find pleasure in these activities: "So I commend enjoyment, for there is nothing better for people under the sun than to eat, and drink, and enjoy themselves; for this will go with them in their toil through the days of life that God gives them under the sun" (Qoh. 8:15; cf. 2:18-24; 3:12; 3:22; 5:18).

The New Testament nowhere associates work with a curse; nor does it celebrate the Sabbath as a rest from work; indeed, one of the charges against Jesus is that he "works" on the Sabbath (Mark 2:23–3:6; John 5:9-18). But neither does the New Testament provide a genuinely positive appreciation for the ordinary round of human work. As everyone knows, the parables of Jesus provide vivid vignettes that involve diverse human occupations: sowing and reaping fields (Matt. 13:1-9, 24-30), feeding swine (Luke 15:15-16), catching fish (Matt. 13:47-50), laboring in vineyards (Matt. 20:1-16; 21:33-43), tending sheep (Matt. 18:12-14), managing households (Matt. 18:23-35; 25:14-30). But the work itself is not made thematic in any of these parables. Similarly, Jesus' disciples are drawn from the ranks of fishermen (Matt. 4:18-22) and tax collectors (Matt. 9:9-13), but their "work" becomes that of discipleship, performing the same tasks for the kingdom that Jesus did (Matt. 10:1-25). The Book of Acts similarly provides a catalogue of occupations in the Mediterranean world: royal ministers (Acts 8:27), seamstresses (9:39), tanners (9:43), military personnel (10:1; 21:31; 27:1), maids (12:13), merchants (16:14), jailers (16:27), magistrates (16:35), police (16:35), tentmakers (18:3), workers in silver (19:24), city clerks (19:35), and sailors (27:30). But as in the parables of Jesus, the body at work is not itself given attention.

Work is notable by its absence in the idealized picture of the first spirit-filled community in Jerusalem (Acts 2:41-47; 4:32–5:11). The believers are of one heart and mind, and they hold all their possessions in common. They do not work to acquire goods, but distribute according to need the proceeds gained from the sale of their property. The note that "there was no needy person among them" (Acts 4:34) serves to fulfill the hope of Deuteronomy that, when the commandments are obeyed, there will be no needy person in Israel (Deut. 15:3-6). The restored Israel that is the first Jerusalem community appears to be living within a Sabbath reality rather than in the world of everyday work. Small wonder that the community quickly falls into need and requires assistance from other churches (Acts 11:27-30; 12:25; cf. Gal. 2:10; 1 Cor. 16:1-4; 2 Cor. 8–9; Rom. 15:22-33).

A more positive image of work in Acts is associated with Paul, who in his discourse to the Ephesian elders declares that he coveted no one's goods; instead, "these hands ministered to my necessities, and to those who were with me. In all things I have shown you that by so toiling one must help the weak, remembering the words of the Lord Jesus, how he said, 'It is more blessed to give than to receive'" (Acts 20:33-35). The picture of Paul working to support himself and others is confirmed by his letters. In 1 Corinthians 4:12 he says that he grows weary from the work of his own hands, and he tells the Thessalonians: "We were not idle when we were with you, and we did not eat anyone's bread without paying for it; but with toil and labor we worked night and day, so that we might not burden any of you" (2 Thess. 3:7-8). Paul here presents himself as a model for their behavior. In his first letter to the Thessalonians he had instructed them "to live quietly, to mind your own affairs, and to work with your hands" (1 Thess. 4:11). But because some in the church were living in idleness and acting as busybodies, he commands them once more to live quietly and earn their own living: "Anyone unwilling to work should not eat" (2 Thess. 3:6-12). Again, in Ephesians 4:28, Paul instructs his readers to give up thieving: "Rather, let them labor and work honestly with their own hands, so as to have something to share with the needy." But Paul also tends to refer to his own apostolic efforts and those of his colleagues as "work" or "toil" (see Rom. 16:6, 12; 1 Cor. 15:10; 16:10; Gal. 4:11; Phil. 2:16; 1 Thess. 5:12; 1 Tim. 4:10; 5:17) that will receive a reward (1 Cor. 3:10-14).

Taken as a whole, Scripture provides abundant testimony to work as a fact of life, but is ambivalent with respect to its worth. From one perspective, work is always preferable to idleness, which is associated with laziness and dissoluteness. But from another perspective, it is — at least in its present form — a curse laid on humans because of Adam's sin, and the gift of Sabbath rest provides a glimpse of what the condition of humans should be. See, for example, the way the Letter to the Hebrews thinks of participation in the divine life as a "Sabbath-rest for the people of God" in which "those who enter God's rest cease from their labors as God did from his" (Heb. 4:9-10). Indeed, neither the portrayals of Jesus nor of the early church provide — with the notable exception of Paul — any sense of the importance of ordinary work. Even for Paul, the significance of working with one's own hands is to free others from burdens and providing for the needs of others. Work is simply a means to that end. What is most fascinating is the lack of real attention paid to the experience of work or how actual human work might disclose something of God's Spirit at work in the world. Only in Proverbs are we given a quick glimpse of how such thinking might proceed, when it speaks of God's personified Wisdom at the creation of the world being "beside him, as a master worker, and I was daily his delight, rejoicing before him always. Rejoicing in his inhabited world, and delighting in the human race" (Prov. 8:20-31).

A more positive appreciation for work is found in medieval Christianity, under the strong influence of Saint Benedict's sixth-century *Rule for Monks (RB)*. In a very real way, work defines the monastic life as a whole. In the prologue to his rule, Benedict summons his readers to "the labor of obedience" by which they can return to God from whom they have strayed "by the sloth of disobedience," and he speaks of the Lord "seeking his workman" among the multitudes. The Rule establishes a fine balance between monastic prayer and other activities, all of which Benedict regards as a form of work. Thus, in discussing the twelfth degree of humility, he says, "Whether he is at the work of God (*opus Dei,* i.e., the common prayer in choir), in the oratory, in the monastery, in the garden, on the road, in the fields, or anywhere else," he should be mindful of the divine judgment (*RB* 7).

And if prayer is a kind of work, so are all the other monastic activities; they are equally of a sacred character. Thus does Benedict say of the Cellarer: "Let him look upon all the utensils of the monastery and its whole property as upon the sacred vessels of the altar" (*RB* 31). Nowhere in the earlier tradition was ordinary work accorded this high status as a form of service to God. Since "idleness is the enemy of the soul," Benedict legislates that the time not spent in choir or in sleep or at meals should be spent either in manual labor or in sacred reading. Both are equally forms of work, but they are "most truly monks when they live by the labor of their hands, like our fathers and the apostles" (*RB* 48).

As medieval society made its slow economic transitions, these basic Benedictine values remained strong, not least because the manorial system was based on agricultural labor, with trades and crafts being closely connected to work on the land. The late-fourteenth-century poem by William Langland called *Piers Ploughman* (1360-1387) declares: "Christ would that man work, the psalter saith in the psalm of *Beati Omnes,* he that feedeth himself with his faithful labor he is blessed by the Book in body and soul."[5] Langland has special concern for "laborers that have no land to live on but their hands,"[6] and he says that "all living laborers that live by their hands and take just wages that they honestly earn, and live in law and love

---

5. William Langland, *Piers Ploughman,* Passus VI, 57.
6. Langland, *Piers Ploughman,* Passus VI, 58.

from their loving hearts, have the same absolution that was sent to Piers."[7] Disparities in wealth based in the corrupt practices both of ecclesiastical and secular figures are acknowledged and criticized in writings such as Langland's *Piers* and Geoffrey Chaucer's *Canterbury Tales* (1387-1400), and they at least partially underlie the Peasants' Revolt of 1381. The attacks on monasticism and hierarchy mounted by Reformers such as John Wycliffe, John Hus, Martin Luther, and John Calvin also involve at least an implicit advocacy for those laborers whose dignity was diminished by the wealth and corruption that fed on their exploitation.

But it was only with the Industrial Revolution (1760-1840), with its disruption of traditional agrarian-based economy, its generation of great wealth based on virtual slave labor in mines and factories, and its creation of a vast urban population of the poor and destitute (depicted so vividly in the novels of Charles Dickens) that the inhumane conditions of work became a consuming topic of concern among economists and philosophers. The special target of those designating themselves as socialists (such as Saint-Simon and Proudhon) or communists (such as Marx and Engels) was the economic system they called "capitalism," which they insisted needed to be eliminated if the dignity of work were to be restored.

In response to these upheavals, Pope Leo XIII issued the encyclical *Rerum Novarum* in 1891, in an effort to alleviate "the misery and wretchedness pressing so unjustly on the majority of the working class." The pope walked a fine line between competing voices. Making use of Thomas Aquinas's teaching of human dignity and rights, the pope affirmed on one side the right to hold private property and to make a profit; on the other side, he asserted the right of workers to form associations (unions) for their mutual support and protection, and demanded of owners that they provide workers with a living wage. By enunciating what has come to be called the "principle of subsidiarity," Leo XIII decisively denied the overarching ambitions of the state to run the economy.

Forty years later, Pope Pius XI issued the encyclical *Quadragesimo Anno* (1931). Much of this letter was devoted to asserting the church's authority to teach on matters of social justice. Like his predecessor, Pius XI sought a middle ground between "individualism" and "collectivism," manifested in turn by savage capitalism and state communism. He repeated much of the substance of Leo XIII's teaching, but expanded the demand of a living wage to that of a "family wage": owners needed to take into

---

7. Langland, *Piers Ploughman*, Passus VII, 61.

account not only what a worker was willing to take, but what the worker's family required to survive. These same principles of Catholic social teaching are reiterated by Pope John XXIII's encyclical *Mater et Magistra* (1961) and Pope John Paul II's *Centesimus Annus* (1991). Noteworthy in the letter of John XXIII is an acknowledgment of a more active role of the state in ensuring greater fairness within the economy. Pope John says that work is not simply for the acquisition of property: "Work, which is the immediate expression of a human personality, must always be rated higher than the possession of external goods, which of their nature are merely instrumental."

As important as these papal teachings are — and they are among the most positive contributions of the Catholic tradition to the contemporary world — they do not really bring us any closer to appreciating human work in terms of the revelatory body. Indeed, the all-too-rapid and superficial account concerning work as found in moral and religious texts suggests that ordinary human work has not been approached in this way. The refusal to work because of laziness? Yes. The conditions of work as unfair or oppressive? Yes. But the ways in which work itself might provide intimations of the human and divine spirit, or suppress the movement of the human and divine spirit, have not really been considered. And this is precisely the task to which an inductive theology should commit itself. Otherwise, the activities that occupy the greatest amount of time and effort of the greatest number of people in the world will remain theologically mute.

Approaching Work Inductively

Our approach to the subject of work is inductive when we begin with our own personal experiences of work and reflect on the quality of those experiences — what distinguished them, what linked them, how they exhausted our body and compressed our spirit, or how they elevated our spirit and renewed our body. We all have a rather remarkable repertoire of activities that we can identify as work to which we have given ourselves over the course of our lives, and these activities are a rich source for thought. All of us are also able to observe others at their work, and, even better, to listen to the narratives of labor that others can speak. Observation can tell us only so much; narratives of what specific kinds of work have meant to those doing them allow us to enter more fully into their experience. Finally, we can make use of reports about work that reach us through a variety of written sources such as memoirs, journals, and novels, which focus not on statistical analyses or economic analysis but on the human experience of work itself. With regard to all these sources, we place ourselves in the posture of learners, seeking not to impose categories on lived experience but instead learning to derive categories from the repeated patterns of human embodiedness.

My personal catalogue of work experience begins with hearing stories about, and also witnessing, my grandfather as manager and cook for logging camps in the forests of northern Wisconsin, as well as stories of my uncles and aunts working in that same rural and small-town area as farmers, as dealers and repairers of automobiles, as managers of lumber yards, as soldiers and insurance agents. I grew up hearing about my dad managing a service station and selling insurance as he sought to support a growing family. I watched my widowed mother work as an insurance agent and town clerk and as an amazingly efficient manager of a household with six children. I observed my siblings working long hours as homemaker, small business manager, forestry agent, computer specialist, and clinical psychologist. My early childhood was — as I noted in my chapter on the "body at play" — blessedly free from the absolute necessity to work, but even as a young boy I knew what it was to cut grass and firewood and tend chickens. As an adolescent, I worked for months at a time cleaning house and caring for children. As a monk, I performed with others the "work of God" in choir and labored as a young scholar, but also did the forms of manual labor required by the community: mopping the monastery floors and cleaning the monastic latrines, nursing two older monks in the months of their final illness, mucking the cow stables, driving heavy equipment and transporting heavy construction materials, waiting on tables for visitors, working in the monastic kitchen, washing dishes for the community, decorating the church for festivals, and most of all, performing every variety of mulching, cutting, chopping, raking, and weeding connected with the upkeep of the monastic property.

For the past forty years, I have been a professor, a trade that some may not regard as serious work — what "working man" gets summers off and a sabbatical every seven years? — but that involves, as is known by those who have tried to do it well, a variety of demanding tasks: preparing and conducting classes, grading exams and papers, advising and counseling students, directing dissertations, and serving in a variety of administrative roles. And on top of those tasks, researching and writing articles and books and reviews, writing and delivering papers at conferences and lectures at universities and churches. Although all of these tasks are rightly considered "liberal" rather than "menial," they are nevertheless fully embodied because they demand optimal mental alertness and engagement, and, like other serious work, they take a toll on the bodies of those who perform them over the course of many years. Professors stop teaching, not because they no longer love students or the life of the mind, but because their bodies can no longer endure the labor of grading student papers. Scholars cease writing, not because their minds have failed, but because the sheer energy required to compose — even on the computer — can no longer be summoned.

The work of the professoriate is also arduous in this respect: like other "vocations" — think of law and medicine and ministry — its demands are not neatly demarcated. They spill over, so that the professor is not able to think in terms of a "job" and "free time," precisely because doing competent, much less brilliant, scholarship demands mental attention even when all the other demands of life (family, household, finances, church, friends) are pressing. Therefore, the stereotype of the "absent-minded professor" does bear truth, not because the scholar is fuzzy-headed, but because he is "a million miles away" solving a mental problem, when everyone around him is fully present at a family dinner or a trip to the beach.

The hard-working professor, like the dedicated lawyer and doctor and the devoted minister, is quite capable of distinguishing her "work" from her "life," but constantly struggles with the competing demands made by each. In contrast to the shoe salesman or machinist, for whom hours of work and hours of pay line up neatly, and for whom the job can make no demands apart from those hours of pay, the demands of the professoriate go far beyond the computation of pay for hours. The demands arise from the covenantal rather than contractual character of the profession: she devotes time to students not according to the hours for which she is paid to advise and counsel, but according to the students' needs; she writes not because she will be paid for an article or book (she often is not) but because she has a sense of intellectual urgency concerning the solving of some intellectual puzzle or other.

What I have learned over a long lifetime of work, thinking about my own labors and reflecting on the stories told me by others, is, first of all, how varied are the activities that can be classified as work — ranging from stoop labor in mines and fields to the construction of cathedrals of stone or thought — and how difficult it is to know what is actually involved in such activities unless we are given access through our own experience or the narratives of others. Work that to outsiders might appear as primitive or even brutish (running a hardscrabble farm or digging for coal miles beneath the surface of the earth) turns out to have unexpected complexities and mental demands, and work that to outsiders appears to be easy and comfortable (being a teacher or a psychologist) turns out to have unexpected difficulty and stress. As a dimension of human embodiedness, work is much more complex, various, and opaque than the realm of play, which is always discrete, ruled, and temporary. I conclude that I know something about the kinds of work I have done, but that I remain ignorant of the kinds of work done by others.

The second thing I have learned is how diverse and unpredictable are the ways that humans relate to their work. Some people derive great satisfaction from their work, while others find their work only an irritant. These responses, oddly, do not line up with what we might think of as the intrinsic importance or interest of the work. One hewer of wood draws joy from well-struck strokes of the ax and the symmetry of the stacks of firewood, while another wants only to get in out of the winter chill. One maid mops the floor with attentiveness to every corner, while another swishes the mop in the center of the floor and then leans on it idly. The difference is not, I think, simply a matter of character. The diligent maid might be totally unreliable in other aspects of her life, while the uninterested one may be a pillar of probity. The difference is more elusive. I have known successful and highly rewarded professionals who grumble constantly about their work and long for the day of their retirement, while other professionals who have experienced little external recognition or reward love what they are doing and dread the day they will have to retire. And there seems to be no absolute correlation between these responses to work and the actual experience of retirement when it comes: one finds release from a career (even if not longed for) to be an opening to other activities and experiences, while another (even the one who constantly griped about his work) finds himself lost and adrift — without a place in the world. What work means to us has many more dimensions than those of financial reward or honor.

In short, although human work may seem to fall rather obviously into the realm of the problematic, it turns out, as with other forms of embodiedness, to participate equally in the realm of the mysterious. The tasks of work are individually a matter of problem-solving by means of applied intelligence and physical effort: clear this space, construct that building, contract for this trade. But what work means to those working is less clearly accessible. For many, it remains opaque even with regard to their own lives. No aspect of work is more elusive than that which touches on the subject I am pursuing in this book, namely, the ways our bodily experience can disclose or obscure the transcendence of the human spirit and the activity of God's Holy Spirit in the world.

Work and the Alienation of Spirit

Some things are clear enough. All the social protests of the nineteenth and twentieth centuries — protests that are continued in forms of liberation theology — agreed that certain kinds of work or work under certain conditions diminishes the human spirit, even to the extent that the very humanity of the worker is put in peril. I am much more comfortable talking about "under certain conditions" rather than "certain kinds of work," because of the point I made earlier in this chapter about the astonishing range of activities that humans freely undertake in this world and the manifold ways in which they respond to those activities. Hence I am unwilling to cede that slaughtering animals or scraping septic tanks or any of the other tasks depicted in the television program *Dirty Jobs* intrinsically alienate or diminish the human spirit. Indeed, that TV program itself demonstrated what inexplicable pleasure some humans can take in doing work that the majority of us would find repugnant. But it is clear to me that "certain conditions" can in fact serve to make of work an alienation of the human spirit and in turn obscure the work of God's Holy Spirit.

The Conditions of Constraint

I have suggested that work always involves some form of necessity: we work because there is something that needs to be done. But there is a great difference between responding to a necessity inherent in the task — the cows must be milked if they are not to be in pain and grow sick — and having the necessity imposed by the will of another. The most obvious example of work as alienating the spirit, then, is work carried out under conditions of servitude. The slave works because the master demands his labor; he works at this task because this is the task the master orders; he works not for payment but to avoid punishment, and perhaps even death. Even if not technically "owned" by a master, the slave is in reality treated as a piece of property rather than as a person. In the eyes of the owner, slaves are ideally instrumental and interchangeable: they can be moved from one task to another, or removed altogether, without any consideration for anything beyond the master's whim. If work is ideally, in John XXIII's words, "an immediate expression of a human personality," the denial of the personhood of a slave profoundly affects the character of the slave's work. It is not properly "his" or "her" work, but the work of the master, for which the slave has served as one instrument among others.

In the ancient world, slaves rather than technology performed all the most dangerous and dirty jobs, enabling the sort of leisure for the nobility that was the basis of classical culture. Slaves could win or be granted their freedom in a number of ways, but while they were in servitude, they were not persons: they were the property of the master, as available for abuse of every kind as an animal or implement, and just as easily discarded. The institution of slavery in the nineteenth-century United States imposed such a dehumanizing on a single group, defined by color and place of origin. Enforced through systems of control that included the separation of families, deprivation of education, sexual exploitation, physical beating, and public execution, the American system of slavery made the many labors carried out by African Americans not an expression of their personality but the expression of their master's will. They could not take pride in their work because it was not, in the elaborate fiction of slaveholding, their work.

The condition of African-American slaves in the brutal fields of the deep South perfectly realized the prophetic words of the Letter of James: "Behold, the wages of the laborers who mowed your fields, which you kept back by fraud, cry out; and the cries of the harvesters have reached the ears of the Lord of Hosts" (James 5:4). What is most remarkable about this example of work constrained by slavery is that it not only gave rise to a great Civil War, which led eventually to the emancipation of the slaves and their labor, but also stimulated the amazingly powerful songs of anguish and longing that are called Negro spirituals, stunning witness to the miraculous capacity of the human spirit to transform even the most demeaning of circumstances into art — and into prayer.

Between 1934 and 1945, in Germany and Poland, "labor camps" were established by the Third Reich for the enslavement and eventual extermination of Jews and others defined by Nazi ideology as deviant and subhuman. In these camps, the technology of slavery was perfected, with all the techniques of humiliation and control exercised with passionless precision: laborers were separated from loved ones, imprisoned in brutal conditions, kept in a state of semi-starvation, subject to medical experiments, forced to perform tasks in service to the Nazi war effort, liable to be singled out for physical abuse or public execution for the slightest hint of anything but total subjugation of their bodies and spirits. Their clothes, their eyeglasses, and the fillings in their teeth, were all claimed as property by the regime, and in the end, they were shot and left in mass graves or were gassed and burned in crematoria. The sign at the entrance to the camp at Auschwitz-Birkenau, which read *Arbeit macht frei* ("Work makes you free"), provided the proper commentary for this evil parody, which used the rubric of work as a means to alienate the human spirit from the body.

The beginning of the twenty-first century has seen, in turn, the flourishing of another form of human slavery, namely, the international trafficking in "sex-workers." Something that has always been an element in slavery, the sexual vulnerability of those held captive, is made the exclusive point of the servitude in the sex trade. Young girls are sold by or stolen from their parents in impoverished countries and are shipped against their will (even if it is under false promises) to cities and countries far from their homes, for the precise purpose of laboring in the sex trade. Once more we see the classic techniques: separation from home and family and their structures of support, making them completely dependent on their keepers; deprivation of sleep and long hours of repetitive labor; the use of drugs to create further dependence and alienation from what they are forced to do.

What makes this contemporary form of slave labor so appalling is not simply the age and gender of those so enslaved — many of them are literally children — but the fact that they are forced to engage (over and over in numbing sequence around the clock) in the most intimate of acts with complete strangers for the benefit of their owners. The sexual act, which should represent the joining of body and spirit in mutual love, is here reduced to the crudest form of physical commodity, the sale of which does not even profit the worker but only serves to degrade her. It is difficult to find a more pernicious form of slave labor, or one that more systemically works to alienate the human spirit and obscure the spirit of the Living God.

Sometimes, though, work is constrained, not by the direct will of a master, but by economic conditions as such. Here again, the element of necessity, which is intrinsic to work, is not demanded by this or that task to be performed, but by the sheer necessity of surviving, when the conditions of existence threaten survival itself. Leo XIII spoke of the "misery and wretchedness pressing so unjustly on the majority of the working class." And it is certainly the case that those who labor at the edge of penury or who live at the level of bare subsistence — especially within urban technological societies — experience work within a cycle of despair, a never-ending and hopeless grind that diminishes their spirit. The components of such misery are well known, and they form the basis for all the muckraking and reformist literature of recent centuries. Although not technically a slave, the worker is a "wage-slave," who is unable to change or better his circumstances because he is caught in a web of grim necessity: too long hours for too little pay; too many children and too little education; too many debts and too few resources. The laborer is dependent on a wage to live, but the wage is never enough to live freely or with dignity.

Such workers find themselves and their families prey to both physical and psychological illnesses, which tend to grow greater because the workers — and in present-day circumstances this often includes all adults in a family — cannot afford to leave work to attend to such problems. The fatigue and depression induced by constant labor that sees no real gain or reward has the effect of alienating the spirit in at least two ways. One response is apathy, simply shutting down, cultivating a complete lack of affect, becoming as close as possible to an automaton, slogging through days and moving from one form of necessity to another with as little consciousness as possible. Another response is to live within a constant state of anxiety caused by the gap between what needs to be done and the lack of resources to do what needs to be done. I know my child needs a doctor's appointment; I know that the gas will be shut off this afternoon for nonpayment; I know that my husband has not had a decent meal in weeks, I know that the left front tire on my car will blow at any time — and knowing all this, I still cannot leave my post at this job that does not pay me enough to meet any one of those needs. Missing work to attend to life can easily result in losing that job, and with the job, a paycheck, and with a paycheck, the rent, and with the rent, shelter for my family. It is not in the least bit surprising that workers caught in such helpless circumstances also find themselves prey to any number of addictions — the lottery, drink, drugs, and, as Marx saw, religion itself — that offer at least temporary relief but have the effect of perpetuating the vicious cycle of entrapment.

The Conditions of Prosperity

Work can also conspire to alienate the human spirit even when workers are free to choose their tasks (i.e., they are not subject to the will of a master) and their resources are more than sufficient for life (i.e., they are not impoverished). The first way this can happen is when, through a kind of self-enslavement or addiction, work is treated as something absolute rather than relative. Instead of working in order to live, one lives in order to work. The need to work is not located in the nature of the task to be performed or even in the reward that might follow from performing the task; rather, the need is located within the worker, who feels empty when not engaged in the chosen form of labor. The current jargon calls this "workaholism," viewing it as a sickness, an addiction analogous to alcoholism. Biblical language identifies it as a form of idolatry, in which something meant to be relative is made the center around which everything else revolves.

The symptoms are easily identified. If it were possible, work would take up all of one's time, not because of external imposition but because of internal compulsion. Life becomes organized around the activity of work, with time spent in work regarded as worthwhile and time away from work regarded as "wasted." Everything else in life is made subordinate to the activity of work: spouse, children, friends, and especially play. Leisure time is actually feared and avoided ("I spent my time on the beach staying in touch with the office"). As a result, great areas of human existence are closed off: beauty, art, piety, love, and just plain fun. The spirit is narrowed to a self-chosen focus, and it willingly embraces its servitude.

This syndrome is often found often among those who work in the professions — medicine, law, teaching, ministry — because, as I observed above, these vocations have a tendency to overspill their boundaries and rapaciously consume more and more of life. Especially when professionals see themselves as serving an ever-expanding group of students, patients, clients, and congregants, they can convince themselves of their indispensability, and can then define themselves totally by their work: I am what I do. But the syndrome also appears in the realms of business, science and technology, and the arts, demonstrating that it is not simply the kind of activity that is responsible for workaholism but something within a person that leads him to isolate himself from every human activity but one, and thus restrict the range of her spirit to the narrow functionality of work. The surest sign of the addictive or idolatrous character of workaholism is that it is, without outside intervention, almost impossible to turn it off, even when the personal needs and desires of others go unattended or even when the physical and mental health of the worker herself is threatened.

Another way that work can be connected to the alienation of spirit among the prosperous is by becoming the instrument of envy. Hesiod was the first of many Greeks to note how envy creates conflict among workers; his line "potter envies potter" became proverbial in classical antiquity. Work is supremely the human activity that can yield concrete rewards to the worker, and in some economic environments, greater and more effective work — or the vagaries of the marketplace — can lead to the acquisition and accumulation of profits, which in turn can provide the one who works with a range of comforts and services not available to others. There is nothing problematic in any of this; indeed, it is a natural consequence of the convergence of talent, energy, effort, and good fortune. One farmer's soil is simply better than a neighbor's soil; with equivalent effort and skill, it will yield better crops than will the farm next door, and bring greater prosperity to the farmer. One novelist may have the same talent and expend the same effort as another, but her choice of subject makes her novel only a critics' choice, while the other's theme catches the popular fancy and her book becomes a bestseller that not only earns millions but generates movie deals. In the world of the marketplace, life truly is not fair — if by fair we mean that equal effort should always yield equal reward.

Nor is there anything problematic in seeking to improve the conditions of life for oneself and one's family through hard work, in the hope that such a commitment of talent and effort will produce a safer and more comfortable existence for those one loves. Indeed, as I will note below, such commitment to work seems to be an important, if not essential, element in human dignity. But the disease of the soul called envy corrupts such dedication by making an absolute equation between being and having. The logic of envy sees the world, not as one constantly gifted and renewed by God's creative presence, but as a closed system in which there are only a finite number of possessions available; and it views humans as though in a life-or-death struggle for these possessions. Having more means being more. Greater wealth means greater worth. This logic leads not simply to cutthroat competition but, as the ancients clearly perceived, to conflict, social upheaval, murder, and war (see James 4:1-3). Like workaholism, this distortion also reveals itself in a compulsive approach to work, with this difference, that it is not the working itself that is ultimate, but the rewards that work brings. By earning more, I can claim to *be* more than my neighbor.

Sadly, this distortion of the human spirit is widely pervasive in contemporary First World societies, given legitimacy as the "ethos of success," with success meaning the accumulation of status through the accumulation of goods (of whatever sort). In these contexts, it is not enough to do well;

one must do best. From the small child being pushed by parents to become a world-class athlete through endless camps and training, to the new law associate learning how gaining partnership means losing one's life, to the scholar who writes endless grant proposals because his sense of self derives from fellowships earned, work is distorted precisely through an exclusive focus on the external reward and recognition that work can bring.

Work and the Elevation of Spirit

I have argued here that work locates us in the realm of the necessary. In the simplest terms, humans are required to work if they are to survive. The earth has been given by God to humans as a garden to keep and to tend, but the fruits of that garden do not bestow themselves without tilling and tending. Even gathering and hunting demand labor, if plants are to be gathered and animals to be killed. Even the most casual and temporary shelter demands the cutting and bending of branches. Even the most rudimentary of clothes requires the cutting and fitting and fastening of hide or cloth. The greater the complexity of human society, the more complex and constant are the forms of work that are necessary.

To work, then, means to be a "grownup" in the human family, to be someone who participates in the common task of enabling the human family to survive and possibly even thrive. We rightly perceive play to be, above all, the activity of children, who are in most circumstances free from the necessities of work, except in the form of play that mimics adult roles. For adults, by contrast, play is an escape into the freedom that is enjoyed naturally by children and into the construction of imaginative worlds such as children construct in their play. Whereas for children, play can be everyday life, for those who are grown-up members of the human family and responsible for the family's survival, play must be an alternative to everyday life, whether through recreation or ritual, a form of renewal that enables the world of hard necessity to be faced once more.

The ability and willingness to take on the world of necessity represented by work is, indeed, a major component in human dignity. Taking away the opportunity to work can therefore have devastating consequences for the human sense of dignity and worth. Enforced idleness — because of losing a job or because of forced retirement — can engender a sense of helplessness and uselessness and dependency that represent, from the adult perspective, the negative aspects of childhood. To be deprived of the opportunity to work is often experienced as a kind of infantilization. Likewise, adults who refuse to engage the world of necessity represented by work, who choose idleness and dependence on the work of others, are rightly perceived as having refused to accept full grown-up responsibility within the human family. Fairly or unfairly, they are perceived more as children than as adults; their claim to dignity is dramatically reduced.

A fascinating contemporary example of this set of evaluations is the English royal family. Although enjoying astonishing privilege and wealth that is a result of no effort on the part of the Windsors, the monarchy has thrived since the time of Queen Mary — and above all in the reign of Queen Elizabeth II — precisely because it has cultivated an ethic of very public work in behalf of the British population. The dignity of the monarchy is closely connected to this public posture of service to the populace. The members of the royal family who have abandoned that role of duty, most notably the Duke of Windsor, who abdicated in favor of a personal relationship, are perceived to lack dignity altogether. They are childish.

Of special interest to an inductive theology seeking to discern the work of the divine spirit in and through the embodied human spirit, however, is the way in which work, at its best, enables humans to participate in, and even extend, God's own creative work in the world. I say "at its best" because I have already described some of the ways in which work can suppress or alienate what is best in the human spirit, either because the conditions of work are dehumanizing or because humans distort work through their spiritual sickness. Such distortions are frequent enough to lead us to think of work in negative rather than in positive terms, to see it as suppressing rather than elevating the human spirit. But we often also catch glimpses of the way work can engage and elevate the spirit.

In my own experience of work and my observations of the work of others, I have found that kind of spiritual engagement first in forms of work that were in close touch with God's own ongoing creation. All those forms of work that require of humans close attention to the movements and impulses of worldly bodies other than their own can fit into this category: the farmer whose attentiveness I sketched earlier in this chapter, but equally the sailor on the open sea, the hunter for game and the fisherman, and all those whose livelihood depends on an ability to respond in body and spirit to the movements of God's creation as it emerges. Such work is a kind of dance with creation, requiring and rewarding the closest attention and applied intelligence.

Add to these forms of work all the sciences that seek to understand —

and all the technologies that seek to channel — the creative energies in the world that God brings into being at every moment. In such forms of work we can understand the meaning of the biblical conviction that humans are created in the image of God, for they require of humans an intelligence and will that responds to what has been set in motion by the intelligence and will of God. In these cases, the dignity of work is not merely a matter of engaging the necessary as an adult member of the human family; it is also a matter of participating spiritually in creation as it is coming-into-being.

Giving even greater dignity to the work of humans is its capacity to extend God's own creation. This labor is most direct and obvious in the labor of giving birth to and raising children. Although conceiving children may often be a matter of biological chance or even accident, and sexual pleasure is by no means always "purposeful," the actual birthing of a child is a well-designated form of labor that the mother performs, and the actual raising of children is, for both parents, a continuous and demanding work that extends from infancy to adulthood (and sometimes beyond). Child-rearing exemplifies so much of what we mean by work. It is undertaken in response to necessity — the children cannot raise themselves — and demands an adult taking-of-responsibility. It is well known that parents do not make children, but that children make parents. Child-rearing engages our time, our energy, and our best practical intelligence. It is also full of risk because the results of the labor dedicated to the rearing of children are not predictable. It is a human work that extends God's own work in the world through bringing into being new bodies (in our image) through whose spirit God's spirit can also be expressed.

The extension of God's creation, or perhaps, more precisely, a kind of co-creation, is found also in all those forms of human work in which the visions shaped by the imagination find physical realization. The designation *homo faber* ("man the maker") has been appropriate for humans since the beginning. With great delight the Bible names the first inventors of cities (Gen. 4:17), musical instruments (4:21), and tools of bronze and iron (4:22), as well as those who first dwelt in tents and owned cattle (4:20), or first tilled the soil and planted vineyards (9:20). How rich in invention the human species has been, and continues to be, as new things come into being at an increasingly rapid rate around us. And in all the inventions of engineering and architecture, of electronic and medical technology, of rocketry and weaponry, of art and literature, of music and drama, that spill from the human imagination and find physical realization, we can discern the implicit presence of God's creative Spirit, for God continually creates us with the capacity to create in our image just as God creates us in God's own image.

Precisely because work belongs to the realm of the everyday — is what we do "all the time" in ordinary life — it can paradoxically receive the least real attention from us in terms of discerning the implicit presence of God's spirit in our embodied experience. And because work can also obscure the presence of God's Holy Spirit so frequently, just as it distorts the human spirit through inhumane conditions or through forms of spiritual alienation, the negative aspects of our most common embodied activity can easily be given all the emphasis. But even the few observations here about the ways in which work can elevate the human spirit and disclose the activity of God's spirit can serve as invitations to more adequately interrogate the positive theological implications of the body at work.

CHAPTER EIGHT

The Exceptional Body

Settling on the appropriate title for the present chapter has not been easy. I discarded the options of the "unusual body" and the "irregular body," as well as the "abnormal body," because each of these designations contains both the idea that there is a default notion of body with which most of us work all the time — a fact that I gladly acknowledge — and the connotation that this default notion is a genuine norm or rule to which all bodies should in fact conform, that failure to conform is a deficiency, and even that such a deficiency needs to be "fixed" — a connotation that I emphatically reject. So I settled on the "exceptional body," an expression that allows me to recognize the fact that, while all human bodies are different from each other along a long continuum, some human bodies are, through some excess in difference, capable of surprising and causing us wonder.

The argument I try to develop here is at the heart of an inductive approach to theology, for it examines some of the gaps between our use of words and the ways in which God's creation presses upon us. As I have said from the start, we are required to use language, and the words we use provide us some real access to the world we experience. Our actual bodily experience of the world, however, can never adequately be captured by words. We are nevertheless always tempted to allow the words we use to stand in place of the actual experience. Philosophers and theologians and others whose way of being in the world is based on the manipulation of language are especially subject to such temptation. Linguists and dabblers in language are thus always especially in need of the reminder that naming anything both captures something of what it names and misses much of what it names, that nouns as concepts are necessarily abstractions, and when they are removed from contact with the messy flow and flux of embodied existence, distort as much as they define, perhaps even distort *by* defining.[1]

We can gladly agree, for example, that the binary distinction between "night" and "day" is both true and useful: we are happy to associate dark with one and light with the other. But at the same time we know that the terms "dawn" and "dusk" represent the grey areas between those two decisive periods, and do so only approximately; the many gradations between full light and absolute dark simply cannot be captured — by definition. The clock's twenty-four-hour measure, moreover, rarely corresponds exactly to the times of light and darkness. The "land of the midnight sun" is matched by the day of perpetual darkness. The abstractions are not utterly false, but they are surely inadequate to capture our actual experience of time. We do not want to banish the nouns by which we name day and night, but we do want to recognize that the words do not fully represent the reality.

Likewise, the phrase "human body" serves usefully, if roughly, to distinguish the human from other bodies in the world. The definition "upright biped with opposable thumbs" serves the same function. We are not, in ordinary circumstances, going to mistake an elephant or whale or giraffe or coyote for a human being, though in some circumstances we might mistake a gorilla or a monkey for a human being. We use standard criteria (not unreasonably) to identify a body as human, from the size of skull to the arrangement of limbs to the absence of scales and fur. We are not silly when we think of humans as ambulatory on two legs and capable of grasping objects and of using language for communication. We do not err when we note that some human bodies are biologically capable of bearing offspring and others are not. We do not distort reality when we say that human offspring gestate for nine months and are born helpless and with no survival skills.

Even these few and reasonable generalizations, however, have exceptions. Some human skulls are not standard in size, some human bodies are born without limbs, some humans have something very much like fur while others are covered with scales. Some human bodies have never been ambulatory, can grasp nothing, are mute from birth. Indeed, one of the things that most strikes us when we simply observe human bodies — trying

1. My discussion in this chapter is deeply influenced by Gabriel Marcel, whose whole philosophical project could be called "an obstinate and untiring battle against the spirit of abstraction," which he defines in this way: "As soon as we accord any category, isolated from all other categories, an arbitrary primacy, we are victims of the spirit of abstraction." See Marcel, *Man against Mass Society,* trans. G. S. Fraser (Chicago: Henry Regnery, 1962), pp. 1, 155-56.

to suspend our judgments concerning what is normal or what is usual — is the tremendous variety of appearance even within the frame of our default expectations.

Consider the many sizes in which adult humans are found, ranging in height from the doll-size Tom Thumb to the giant-size Andre the Giant, ranging in weight from wispy to wide-load. Human bodies have amazingly diverse proportions: some are pear-shaped and others angular; some are round and some are square. The strength, speed, and agility of human bodies are likewise diverse: some bodies can lift great weights, while others can barely lift themselves upright; some can run with blinding speed and for great distances, while others can only hobble a few feet; some adults can dance and spin and perform athletically, while others lack the coordination to perform the simplest chores.

Think as well of the many colors and shades of color the human body wears: black, tan, beige, grey, yellow, rose. And all these colors take on different shades and intensities over parts of the bodies of individuals, and appear in different shades and intensities from one individual body to another. Seldom are bodies "rose" or "salmon" or "black" or "brown" in exactly the same degree and consistency. I hold my seventy-one-year-old arm in front of my eyes, and I see patches of deep red, orange, yellow, grey, brown, blue (veins), and white (dry flakes from eczema). What applies to skin color applies also to the colors and textures of hair: red, orange, black, brown, yellow, grey, white; and silky, bushy, kinky, curly, straight. Sometimes hair is absent altogether from the head, or the face, or the torso or limbs. Mentioning the face reminds us of the astonishing variety found among foreheads and jaws, lips, noses, and eyes, and above all, ears. Supposedly, ears are as distinctive as fingerprints.[2]

I have been speaking of "appearances," but we obviously experience bodies through other senses than sight. Nevertheless, the same variety applies. Human bodies emit different odors, and these differences in odor are even different, so far as we can tell, from the sense of smell in different people. The sounds that human bodies make are as various as the size and appearance of bodies: human voices are not in the least uniform, but differ in pitch and timbre and volume. Notoriously, the sense of touch is both objective (this body is hard, that one soft — this one hot, that one cold) and wildly subjective: this body (to my touch) is tender, yielding, pliant, complaisant, eager, or stiff, resistant, and hostile.

2. See http://yalescientific.org/2011/05/ears.

The reason for this semi-Rabelaisian recital of particulars is to remind us that we constantly experience and observe just this rich variety when we encounter actual human bodies. We do not engage other bodies in general, but as particular combinations of all these and many other qualities. The reminder is important, because while the use of some nouns is useful because the terms point to particular aspects of the body — height, weight, shape of nose, color of eyes — the use of other, more abstract nouns and generalizing adjectives can actually serve to obscure the variety of embodied existence through categorization. Thus, when I speak of myself as "short" and "fat," I place myself in physical classifications that have comparison and valuation built into them.

At 5 feet 6 inches I must be "short" with respect to some norm for adult males, for I am certainly "tall" with respect to an eight-year-old boy — and even some adult women. At 220 pounds, I must be "fat" with respect to some ideal ratio of weight-to-height for adult males who are not Sumo wrestlers or bartenders. Such classifications require comparison and bear with them an assumed set of valuations. And these valuations are culturally conditioned — that is, they represent abstract representations of ideal bodies for a specific group of people. In the contemporary First World, it is certainly better to be thin than fat, tall than short. But how thin? Contrary to the fixed conviction of the late Duchess of Windsor, we have come to agree that it is possible to be "too thin": the skeletal look is a social embarrassment. And how tall? Outside of professional sports, especially basketball, anyone over 6 feet 5 inches tends to find his (or her) size equally to be a social liability. It is more to the point to say here that the use of such designations serves to distort the perception of the embodied other by defining the other via an abstract classification, and drawing disproportionate attention to that embodied feature rather than a thousand others that also belong to that body.

The designators "short" and "fat" at least have a connection with specific aspects of specific human bodies. Even more problematic are the abstract categories that locate specific human bodies irrevocably within broad binary classifications. I have in mind here especially the categories of gender (male/female), of race (black/white), of ethno-religion (Jew/Gentile), and ability (able-bodied/disabled). Each classification has some basis in physical traits but each also carries powerful nuances drawn from social construction.[3] It is a biological fact, for example, that some humans

---

3. See, e.g., J. Lorber and S. Farrell, eds., *The Social Construction of Gender* (Boston:

have the capacity to conceive and bear children, while others lack this capacity. In strictly sexual terms, the nouns "woman" and "man" nicely distinguish biological roles. But the terms "male" and "female" are used in a more abstract way to delineate sets of contrasting social expectations and roles: gender is as much or more about such social expectations and roles as it is about biological function. But we know from our lived experience that the actual ways in which men and women inhabit their sexual bodies, much less express their designated social roles, are infinitely varied.

The abstraction "race" is similar. There is some biological (genetic) basis for identifying human bodies according to categories that share certain physical characteristics that others do not: the color and shape of eyes, the color of the skin, the length and shape of limbs, the texture of hair, susceptibility to certain diseases and not others, and so forth. There is also some scientific basis for placing humans within groups with shared familial, linguistic, cultural, and historical links. Noting such groupings of characteristics among sets of bodies is scientifically legitimate and even helpful. But the broad generalizations are simply that: close observation of individual bodies indicates that many — and sometimes all — of the "typical" characteristics that are thought to define a group are absent. This does not mean that such people should be classified in a different group; it simply means that abstractions only roughly cover the messy reality of human embodiedness. But racial categories have also been used ideologically, to attach certain spiritual characteristics — positive or negative — to one group or another, and then to assert the superiority of one group over another on the basis of such supposed physical and mental characteristics. At this point, the abstraction has not only moved away from contact with — or close observation of — specific bodies, it claims to provide a privileged way of perceiving specific bodies with no need for contact or close observation.

Even more problematic is the binary distinction between "able-bodied" and "disabled." I have already noted that bodies differ from each other along a long continuum in their ability to do certain things or to perform certain tasks. Some of these differences are trivial. It does not matter much that I cannot dunk a basketball the way LeBron James can, or sing an aria the way Luciano Pavarotti could, or prepare a soufflé as well

---

Sage Publications, 1990); K. E. Rosenblum and T.-M. C. Travis, eds., *The Meaning of Difference: American Constructions of Race, Sex and Gender, Social Class, Sexual Orientation, and Disability*, 6th ed. (New York: McGraw-Hill, 2011).

as Julia Child could. It doesn't even count for much if I can walk no more than two miles without tiring, or can no longer memorize twelve-digit numerical sequences as I once could, or cannot balance myself on one leg without tipping. No one cares anymore — least of all me. These are all desirable abilities, but they are optional. No real loss comes to the one who lacks them.

But it matters a great deal to me if I cannot see at all, for my livelihood depends on my being able to read, and even struggling with diminished sight aided (miraculously) by spectacles places me at a disadvantage to those who can see at long distances and can read fine print. It matters a lot that my hearing is diminished and distorted through tinnitus and the inability to distinguish sounds, for I find myself isolated in some social exchanges. I experience shame when I have outbreaks of eczema that leave my arms and legs raw with open sores, which reveal to the world the inner stress I am living under.

I can only imagine the effects of an absolute loss of hearing, a complete loss of sight, a total inability to speak, an unrepaired harelip, a scar or birthmark that calls attention to itself. I can only speculate about the terror and sense of desperation that accompanies those whose body and mind fail to connect consistently or accurately with the world, and find themselves caught in a variety of mental conditions that locate them in a world that seems to be distinct from the one inhabited by others. I can only observe the ways in which loved ones struggle with the loss of a mobility they once took for granted, and grieve the absence of simple pleasures that their bodies once allowed but do so no more, or do not fully remember who they once were or even are now.

I have listed all of these "disabilities" in terms of our ordinary, everyday experience of failing to realize expectations and goals. I fully acknowledge that others experience a still more radical gap between what they would hope to do and can do, either through the circumstances of their birth or through injury or illness. The inadequate body, the damaged body, the handicapped body, the failing mind — these are all part of common human experience, though in dramatically different degrees. There is legitimacy to using the term "disabled" when referring to specific human bodies and specific activities, just as there is a limited legitimacy to language about gender and race. But the abstraction "disabled" becomes problematic to the degree that it is used in a totalizing fashion to define humans, and even more when it is used ideologically to exclude some humans from as full a participation in society as might be possible to them.

The Mixed Witness of Scripture

The human tendency to allow abstract concepts or categories to govern the perception of specific bodies as they come into existence at every moment through the power of God's spirit is reinforced by the Old Testament, and only partially (if importantly) mitigated by the New Testament. Humans are created in God's image, Genesis declares: "Male and female he created them" (Gen. 1:26-27). This gender distinction is rigidly applied throughout the law, prophets, and writings. Not only is "woman" distinct from man, but she is subordinate both by nature (Gen. 2:21-24) and as a result of sin (Gen. 3:16). The two aspects of gender differentiation are spelled out especially in the law codes of Israel. First, the genders must remain distinct and unconfused: males should not have sex with males (Lev. 18:22; 20:13), just as both men and women should not have sex with animals (Lev. 18:23; 20:15-16). Women should not wear men's clothes, and men should not wear women's clothes; these things are abhorrent to the Lord (Deut. 22:5). Second, males are privileged. Only males can become priests, and priests are held to an even higher sexual standard than that of nonpriests: they may not marry a prostitute or a divorced woman (Lev. 21:7); they must marry a virgin of their own kin (21:14). The pollution caused by male sexual emission, in turn, is of less seriousness than the uncleanness caused by female birth or menstruation (cf. Lev. 12:2-5; 15:19-30; Deut. 23:10).[4]

These gender differentiations combine in Israel's law with an insistence on ethnic differentiation. It is because Israel is a "particular people," chosen and privileged by God, that it is to avoid the kinds of sexual confusions practiced by other nations: "Do not defile yourselves in any of these ways, for by all these practices the nations I am casting out before you have defiled themselves. Thus the land became defiled; and I punished it for its iniquity and the land vomited out its inhabitants. . . . You shall be holy, for I the Lord your God am holy" (Lev. 18:24-25; 19:2). The holiness of Israel is understood precisely in terms of its "difference" from all other peoples.

The way this difference is expressed is by maintaining the distinction between genders and the distinction between what is clean and unclean. "Thus you shall keep the people of Israel separate from their uncleanness, so that they do not die in their uncleanness by defiling my tabernacle that

---

4. See P. L. Day, ed., *Gender and Difference in Ancient Israel* (Minneapolis: Augsburg, 2000); D. N. Fewell and D. M. Gunn, *Gender, Power and Promise: The Subject of the Bible's First Story* (Nashville: Abingdon, 1992).

is in their midst" (Lev. 15:31). And again: "I am the Lord your God; I have separated you from the people. You shall therefore make a distinction between the unclean and the clean; you shall not bring abomination upon yourselves by animal or by bird or with anything with which the earth teems, which I have set apart for you to hold unclean. You shall be holy to me, for I am the Lord, and I have separated you from other peoples to be mine" (Lev. 20:24-26; see Deut. 14:3-8; 18:9-14).[5]

The forms of uncleanness that temporarily separate Israelites themselves from participation in the assembly and the cult are linked in turn to forms of bodily affliction that have the same effect. See, for example, the long set of proscriptions concerning the lesions on the body that are defined as leprosy and require diagnosis, separation from the people, and slow reintegration into the common activities (Lev. 13:1–14:54). Those with this affliction (probably forms of eczema) were required to stay outside the camp, to wear torn clothes and disheveled hair, to cover their upper lip, and to cry out to passersby, "Unclean, unclean" (Lev. 13:45). Other bodily disabilities marked Israelites as excluded from participation: males whose testicles had been crushed or whose penis had been cut off, or a male who was a bastard child, were to be excluded from the assembly of the people (Deut. 23:1-2) in the same way an Ammonite or Moabite was to be excluded (Deut. 23:3). The males who performed as priests were, logically enough, required to be physically intact; no one with a blemish could approach to offer sacrifice (Lev. 21:16-23), and no priest with a broken foot could approach (Lev. 21:19). The interconnections between the categories of gender, ethnicity, and disability are shown perfectly in the legal requirement that an animal offered for sacrifice had to be a "male without blemish"; the priests were not allowed to accept a sacrificial animal from foreigners because that animal might have a hidden blemish (Lev. 22:21-25).

The New Testament considerably weakens the binary code of the Levitical law, especially with respect to disability, but does not escape categorization according to gender and ethnicity altogether. The Gospels' portrait of Jesus is striking for the way it shows him responding to persons not according to category but as they appear to him, and according to the help they seek. The Gospel of Luke in particular shows Jesus as welcoming

5. See M. Douglas, *Purity and Danger: An Analysis of Pollution and Taboo,* Routledge Classics (London: Taylor, 2002); J. W. Watts, *Ritual and Rhetoric in Leviticus: From Sacrifice to Scripture* (Cambridge, UK: Cambridge University Press, 2007).

into fellowship all those whom society marginalized: women, children, sinners, the poor, and above all, those whose mental and physical afflictions were experienced as the "bondage of Satan" (Luke 13:16). The "good news" from God that Jesus proclaimed (Luke 4:16-18; 6:20-24) reversed the standards ordinarily applied by humans and replaced them with God's vision for the world, a vision of a world in which the captives would be freed and the poor would be blessed. Luke's Gospel shows Jesus embodying and enacting this message through his ministry of inclusion and of healing. Jesus tells the messengers sent by John: "Go and tell John what you have seen and heard: the blind receive their sight, the lame walk, the lepers are cleansed, the deaf hear, the dead are raised, the poor have the good news brought to them" (Luke 7:22).

Jesus' catalogue shows an appropriate use of abstractions: some people are lame and others are not, some people are blind while others have sight. But these abstractions do not become categories that define persons as such, much less categories that define acceptance or exclusion. Rather, the list suggests a recitation that could be indefinitely extended to include all those persons who need to hear the good news of God's acceptance of them. And the actual Gospel stories that display Jesus as healer show him as responding to individuals as individuals, not as representing categories. It is *this* demoniac who sits beside Jesus in his right mind (Luke 8:35), *this* child who should be welcomed (Luke 9:48), *this* woman who is made to stand straight (Luke 13:12), *this* leper who returned to thank Jesus for his healing (Luke 17:15). These stories also show that the goal of healing individuals from mental and physical affliction is their return to their community. Those states and conditions that humans used as excuses for closing off others from participation, Jesus ignores or overcomes in his invitation to participate in God's banquet (Luke 14:15-24).

Jesus' table fellowship with those on the margins of society — the poor, the sinners, the tax-collectors, women and children — takes place within the framework of the great distinction between Jew and Gentile. Luke's Gospel gives hints that the good news of salvation is for "all flesh" (Luke 3:6), and that Jesus will be a light of revelation for the Gentiles (Luke 2:32); but only in Luke's second volume, the Acts of the Apostles, are we shown how God's Holy Spirit leads the early church, not without difficulty and conflict, to extend table fellowship and full participation in God's people to Gentiles (Acts 10–15). With the decision to admit Gentiles without demanding observance of the law of Moses, and with the recognition that "we will be saved through the grace of the Lord Jesus just as they will" (Acts 15:11), Christianity broke fundamentally and decisively with the Levitical code that defined holiness in terms of distinctions between Jews and Gentiles, clean and unclean.[6]

For the most part, the apostle Paul staunchly advocates the Jesus movement's decision concerning the binary distinctions established by the Levitical code. With considerable justice, Jesus is regarded as champion of Gentile acceptance into God's people without any requirement of circumcision or the keeping of the law. In his Letter to the Galatians, Paul fights the battle for Gentile inclusion in explicit terms: "In Christ Jesus neither circumcision nor uncircumcision counts for anything; the only thing that counts is faith working through love" (Gal. 5:6). By extension, this means that Paul also rejected the entire purity classification system. "Nothing is unclean in itself . . . the kingdom of God is not food and drink," he says in Romans 14:14-17; and in Titus 1:15: "To the pure all things are pure, but to the corrupt and unbelieving nothing is pure." Moral dispositions rather than physical classifications are the basis for distinctions among humans.[7]

There is absolutely no indication in Paul's letters, or in any other of earliest Christianity's epistolary literature, that any kind of physical mark or affliction should have any stigmatizing effect. Indeed, Paul's own mentions of physical difference all refer to himself. He considers himself an *ektrōma* in comparison to the other apostles: not one "untimely born," as translations often have it, but a "monster," an aborted fetus (1 Cor. 15:8); he has a "thorn," or "stake," in his flesh (2 Cor. 12:7); his "weakness" when first visiting the Galatians made him fear that they would reject him, and he is elated that they received him "as an angel from God, as Christ Jesus" (Gal. 4:12-14), he bears the *stigmata* of Jesus on his body (Gal. 6:17), and he is in "labor pains" until Christ is formed in them (Gal. 4:19). However, though physical illnesses and deaths of members can be troublesome to the health of the community (1 Thess. 4:13; 1 Cor. 11:30), there is nowhere any suggestion that these compromise the holiness of the church.

In several of his letters, Paul — probably depending on a baptismal formulation preceding him — uses the classic binary distinctions of gender, ethnicity, and social status, precisely in order to relativize them. His

---

6. For the Jesus movement in Luke's Gospel and Acts, see L. T. Johnson, *Prophetic Jesus, Prophetic Church: The Challenge of Luke-Acts for Contemporary Christians* (Grand Rapids: Eerdmans, 2011).

7. On Paul's defense of Gentile inclusion, see L. T. Johnson, "Ritual Imprinting and the Politics of Perfection," in *Religious Experience in Earliest Christianity: A Missing Dimension in New Testament Study* (Minneapolis: Augsburg, 1998), pp. 69-103.

fullest statement is in Galatians 3:27-28: "As many of you as were baptized into Christ have clothed yourselves with Christ. There is no longer Jew or Greek, there is no longer slave or free, there is no longer male and female; for all of you are one in Christ Jesus" (see also 1 Cor. 12:13; Col. 3:10-11). Those distinctions that in "the world" — and in the Law — were used to differentiate humans according to category and assert the privilege of one over another, are now, in the church, to become differences that provide the opportunity for the mutual exchange of gifts. Paul's image of the community as the "Body of Christ" envisions differences in just this way: they are gifts given by the same God, same Lord, and same spirit, for the mutual upbuilding of the body in love (1 Cor. 12:1–13:13).[8]

It is undoubtedly with respect to the binary distinction between male and female, however, that Paul in practice falls most short of the utopian ideal suggested by Galatians 3:28. First, Paul perpetuates the Levitical code in seeing same-sex love as a freely chosen vice that is "against nature" and incompatible with the righteousness of God (Rom. 1:26-27; 1 Cor. 6:9-10; 1 Tim. 1:10). Second, though Paul respects the sexual reciprocity of the genders within marriage (1 Cor. 7:1-7) and respects the Spirit-derived work of specific women in the mission (Rom. 16:1-3, 7; 1 Cor. 16:19; Phil. 4:2), when it comes to their activity within the household-based assembly at worship, he places male leadership above female leadership (1 Cor. 11:3-16; 14:33-36; 1 Tim. 2:11-15), and he requires the submission of women to men within the household (Rom. 7:2-3; Col. 3:18; Eph. 5:22-33; Titus 2:5).[9]

Because of the powerful human tendency to use abstract classifications in ways that obscure the many more meaningful ways in which bodies differ from each other, the Bible's mixed witness demands of theologians a choice. They must make a decision concerning the Old Testament's reinforcement of abstract distinctions concerning gender, ethnicity, and disability. Should they have any normative force at all, or should they be read as, at best, an ancient people's effort to secure a distinct identity through the use of binary oppositions? I maintain that, for Christian theologians today, the entire Levitical system must be read descriptively (it tells us something about antiquity) and not prescriptively: these distinctions should

---

8. See W. A. Meeks, "The Image of the Androgyne: Some Uses of a Symbol in Earliest Christianity," in *In Search of the Early Christians: Selected Essays,* ed. A. R. Hilton and H. G. Snyder (New Haven: Yale University Press, 2002).

9. See the discussion in L. T. Johnson, *The First and Second Letters to Timothy: A New Translation with Introduction and Commentary,* Anchor Bible series 35A (New Haven: Yale University Press, 2001), pp. 203-11.

not have binding force as we seek to discern what God is up to in actual human bodies in the present. But theologians must also make a decision with respect to the New Testament. Should the residual elements of the binary abstractions found in the Gospels and Paul be taken as seriously as a guide to our own thinking as do the elements that explode the ancient dichotomies and push us toward a perception of bodies that is not rigidly governed by them? Here, too, I maintain that we should shape our perceptions according to the example of Jesus displayed in the gospel, where the good news is embodied and enacted by a ministry of inclusion and fellowship without respect to bodily difference, and on the basis of Paul's best insights into the new creation brought into being by the exaltation of Jesus as Lord — so that in Christ there is neither Jew nor Greek, slave nor free, male and female, but all are one in Christ.

What might it mean, then, for us to view the many and diverse forms and expressions of human bodies, not through the rigid categories that, in the effort to provide clear distinctions, end up distorting our perceptions of what God is actually doing, what God is trying to show us about ourselves and indeed about God, through the many ways in which God's spirit finds embodiment? In the sections that follow I will try to work myself more deeply into the gap between abstraction and lived human experience in order to suggest ways in which an inductive approach to theology might discover how the true demand posed by differences is not to classify in order to control but to contemplate in order to wonder and to give praise.

Sexual Difference

It is with respect to the sexual body that the clash between abstract language and actual lived experience has become more visible and pressing in recent years. Many of us were born into a world in which the biblical statement "male and female he made them" could be taken both as self-evidently true at the descriptive level and as a normative measure for actual sexual practice. For the majority of humans at any given time, in fact, the distinction of humanity into two genders is as satisfactory and useful as the contrast between night and day. But I have already suggested earlier in this chapter that, while "night" and "day" are good naming words, they are scarcely adequate for identifying all the shades and degrees of light and darkness of actual experience. The clock may say that it is AM, but both the sky and my bones insist that it is still PM. In just the same manner, designations of sexual difference can be useful in a rough and ready fashion. But the terms male and female also have limitations: they don't by any means cover all the variety of human sexual experience and expression. And when the terms are imposed absolutely or normatively, they can also become tyrannical: they can suppress and distort sexual experience and expression that may escape the neat frame of the abstraction but are nevertheless fully human and, I would argue, possible pointers to what God is up to in the world.

Heterosexuality/Homosexuality

The very awkwardness of these two nouns suggests their abstract character. Both "homosexuality" and "heterosexuality" are, in fact, ideological constructions whose main function is to establish a binary distinction between categories of humans. It is absolutely true to experience to speak of the practice of sex between man and man, and woman and woman, just as it is appropriate to speak of the practice of sex between a man and a woman. And if pressed to state this conveniently, to speak of same-sex love, or other-sex love, is not inappropriate. I can even, without distortion, speak of homosexual acts and heterosexual acts. But I allow language to distort reality when I construct a rigid category called "heterosexuality" or "homosexuality" that supposedly describes or defines a mindset, a "lifestyle," an "orientation," a moral character, or a way of being in the world over and above those specific acts with specific partners. This holds as true for the abstraction "heterosexual" as it does for the abstraction "homosexual": both serve to distort the human experience of sexuality.[10]

First, each term is simply inadequate and inaccurate, missing much of actual human sexual practice. Apart from the fact that the partners involved are either anatomically alike or different, for example, it is impossible to distinguish homosexual and heterosexual practices. Men and women in the privacy of their bedroom can and do engage (according to taste and consent) in all the same sexual acts that gay and lesbian couples (to use these terms) practice when they are alone together. Nor are patterns of

10. See, e.g., M. D. Jordan, *The Invention of Sodomy in Christian Theology,* Worlds of Desire: The Chicago Series on Sexuality, Gender and Culture (Chicago: University of Chicago Press, 1997); S. O. Murphy, *Homosexualities,* Worlds of Desire: The Chicago Series on Sexuality, Gender and Culture (Chicago: University of Chicago Press, 2002); J. N. Katz, *The Invention of Heterosexuality* (Chicago: University of Chicago Press, 2007).

pursuit and seduction, submission and dominance, seriousness and humor, playfulness and anger, notably different among those who are located in one category or another. Nor do these categories accurately place actual humans in terms of the *ways* in which they express their sexual bodies apart from actual sexual acts: the passive and the aggressive, the stoical and the hysterical, the flirtatious and the stand-offish, the public displayer and the protector of privacy — these are all found equally distributed in both of the supposedly descriptive categories.

In truth, nothing distinguishes homosexual and heterosexual humans except the desire and choice to engage sexually with anatomically similar or anatomically dissimilar persons. But even that concession goes too far, because it ignores the substantial numbers of humans — both in the past and in the present — who can call themselves "bisexual" because their desire for and/or choice of partners can go in either direction.[11] Sometimes bisexual activity is culturally situated. In ancient Greece and Rome, for example, male bisexuality flourished and was culturally supported in diverse ways. What is most important to note is that men of the highest moral probity and the most serious commitment to marriage and family also engaged in sex with other men.[12] In today's world, bisexuality — at least in the so-called First World — tends to be found most prevalently (or obviously) among all-male or all-female institutions, where sexual access to persons of the opposite sex is limited or absent. Thus prisons, the military, and some religious organizations have a higher than usual incidence of same-sex practice among those who intuitively and ideologically would claim to be "heterosexual."

Second, the term "homosexuality" has not ordinarily been used simply in a neutral, descriptive sense. Although less offensive than the long list of pejoratives that have been applied to those who engage in same-sex practices — "sodomites, catamites, perverts, deviants, queers" — the term is used not only to classify a set of sexual practices but, negatively, to label a part of the human population. In the binary opposition, the heterosexual is assumed to be normal, regular, usual, and "according to nature"; in contrast, the homosexual is necessarily defined as abnormal, irregular, unusual, and unnatural. In effect, the contrast functions in precisely the same

11. See M. S. Weinberg et al., *Dual Attraction: Understanding Bisexuality* (New York: Oxford University Press, 1995).

12. See E. Cantarella, *Bisexuality in the Ancient World*, trans. C. O. Cuilleanain (New Haven: Yale University Press, 2002).

ways that the binary opposition between the "clean" and the "unclean" functioned in the Levitical code: the person who engages in same-sex love is stigmatized, identified as one whose presence and participation are a threat to the holiness of the community. Nothing more need be said about such a person; he or she falls outside the community's concern and care. In contrast, the one identified as "heterosexual," who may in many more ways defy the standards and principles of the community in other areas of life, is assumed to be safe, and his or her presence and participation in the life of the community are unquestioned.

The categories of *heterosexual* and *homosexual* are clearly of very limited usefulness, and are potentially destructive. The same can be said of the politically more acceptable terms, such as "gay" and "lesbian" and "bi" and "straight." They do the same discriminatory work in the opposite direction, so that "straight" functions as a category that defines rather than simply describes. Although it is not possible — given our need to use abstract nouns to organize our experience — it would be far better if we avoided all these categories of persons and focused instead on the multiform ways in which actual human bodies reveal themselves as sexual. It would be a great advance if we could acknowledge the evidence presented to us by thousands of human stories and regard those who are drawn by desire to persons of the same sex, not as indulging in a freely chosen vice "against nature" out of a rebellious disposition, but rather as following the nature that God has placed in them. Such a disposition would enable us to contemplate all the mysterious ways in which the human spirit finds embodied expression, discovering that the spirit is not totally governed or controlled by physical configuration, but appears in surprising forms. In the contemplation of the diverse embodied expressions of the human spirit, in turn, we can discern something more of how variously God is at work in the world, and give God glory.[13]

Such openness to a diversity of sexual expression does not in the least suggest the abandoning of moral standards with regard to human sexuality; it only means that moral standards are applied evenly and without prejudice. If, for example, we rightly condemn the practice of gay or lesbian sex that is promiscuous, predatory, violent, abusive, or obsessive, so do we also condemn the practice of straight sex that is promiscuous, preda-

13. See L. T. Johnson, "Debate and Discernment: Scripture and the Spirit," in the issue "Disputed Questions: Homosexuality," *Commonweal* 121 (1994): 11-13; Johnson, "Homosexuality and the Church: Scripture and Experience," *Commonweal* 134 (2007): 14-17.

tory, violent, abusive, or obsessive. If holiness in sex is incompatible with bathhouses and pornography in same-sex practice, so is holiness incompatible with pornography and massage parlors in other-sex practice. The same fairness can be applied on the positive side. If we rightly insist that those who partner in straight sex seek to be faithful in covenant, display fruitfulness, and seek to be chaste in their sexual relationships, so we can ask of those who partner in gay or lesbian sex that they seek to remain in covenant faithfully, that their relationship enhances life for others, and that they are chaste in their sexual relations. Moral standards are not abandoned, but they are properly focused on real dispositions and practices rather than on abstract categories.[14]

Intersexuality

One of the inadequacies of the binary opposition between heterosexual and homosexual, we have found, is that it does not cover all the variety of ways humans embody themselves sexually. Transvestites, for example, have a powerful yearning to clothe themselves and adopt the manner of a gender not ostensibly their own. This urge and its enactment (private or public) do not align precisely with the gay/straight or lesbian/straight distinction, although transvestism can also express itself in acts of same-sex intercourse. Some transvestites who desire to clothe themselves and mimic the manner of the other sex, however, remain otherwise conventional in their actual practice of sex.

Transvestism may represent a mild form of gender displacement (or misplacement), the sense that one really belongs in another gender than the one apparently dictated by the arrangement of one's sexual organs. A more dramatic form of such displacement is found among people who are utterly convinced, often from a remarkably early age, that although anatomically men, they are really women, or although anatomically women, they are really men. With the medical technology made available in recent years, some with this conviction — sometimes called "transsexual" or "transgendered" — have undertaken to change their gender anatomically, hormonally, and behaviorally, while others "fix" their condition to some degree of satisfaction without resort to actual surgical intervention.

14. See L. T. Johnson, "Sexuality and the Holiness of the Church," http://Covnetpres .org/2004/11/sexuality.

Transgendered persons have the profound psychological experience of being embodied in the wrong way: they are convinced that their present sexual configuration is a distortion of who they were meant to be, their real identity. Transvestites and transsexuals reveal the gap between the complex experience of sexuality among some humans and the simple-minded and thoughtless application of the biblical proposition "male and female he created them" — as though it were both obvious and absolute.[15]

A still greater challenge is put to the binary opposition of male/female by the phenomenon called intersexuality.[16] Here is not a matter of subjective experience, as with the transsexual; here is the biologically verifiable situation of 1 to 2 percent of human bodies. In my own city of Atlanta, with a population of some six million, that would mean more than 60,000 people. The term "intersex" is used to refer to one of several variations of biological anomaly that manifests itself, either at birth or after, with respect to gender placement. Some humans are born with complete sets of both male and female reproductive organs (classic hermaphroditism); others are born with one set or the other partially developed; others are born with genetic indicators of gender inconsonant with their sexual organs; others have the usual set of organs of one gender or another but display hormones that are more characteristic of the other gender. These anomalies can appear in various combinations and in degrees of lesser or greater severity.

The most obvious condition was identified by nineteenth-century medicine as "hermaphroditism," and, beginning in the 1960s, the complexity of manifestations was gathered under the term "intersex." The United Nations High Commissioner provides this definition:

> An intersex person is born with sexual anatomy, reproductive organs, and/or chromosomal patterns that do not fit the typical definition of male-female. This may be apparent at birth or become so later in life. An intersex person may identify as male or female or neither. Intersex status is not about sexual orientation or gender identity; intersex people experience the same range of sexual orientations and gender identities as non-intersex people.[17]

15. See D. Valentine, *Imagining Transgender: An Ethnography of a Category* (Durham: Duke University Press, 2007).

16. For a superb depiction, see J. Eugenides, *Middlesex: A Novel* (New York: Picador, 2007); I am particularly indebted to Margaret Farley, *Just Love: A Framework for Christian Sexual Ethics* (London: Bloomsbury Academic, 2008).

17. For the citation, see http://en.wikipedia.org/wiki/Intersex.

In short, intersexuality is not a matter of choice or a matter of subjective feelings or desires; it is a matter of coming into the world with a sexual body that simply does not correspond to the biblical disjunction between male and female.

The tyranny of the binary distinction is revealed, however, by the response to the intersexed by doctors and parents. In some societies, it appears, the intersexed were regarded with special awe, and often served in shamanistic roles; they were, in short, regarded as different precisely as a gift from the gods to humanity. But until the recent establishment of legal rights for the intersexed, the approach in First World societies was to regard intersex as something that needed fixing, precisely because the child presented an indeterminate sexual status. Therefore, parents and physicians frequently altered the sex organs of such children surgically. They administered regimens of hormonal treatment to encourage greater physical and emotional conformity to one standard gender or the other. And they would enter into a process of socialization to ensure that the child was raised as a standard little boy or standard little girl. Such surgical, chemical, and ideological manipulation may have been undertaken out of fear or concern, but it not only involved physical mutilation and psychological trauma but often led to the situation in which the intersexed adult realized that he or she was, once again, trapped in an identity that was not his or her own. Most shocking here is the fact that intersexuality is not something that requires fixing, but is rather the way in which God brings a small percentage of humans into the world. As the Council of Europe declared in 1952, in its resolution on children's right to physical integrity: "[T]his is a naturally occurring variation in humans, not a medical condition."[18]

An inductive approach to theology must begin by perceiving and honoring the great diversity in bodies, not least as they manifest themselves sexually. Rather than imposing the abstract classifications of male and female in a wooden and even oppressive way — demanding of humans that they conform to an abstraction that is, even descriptively, of only limited value — this approach asks first what we can learn about ourselves and what we can learn about God's creative inventiveness from the diversity of ways humans can inhabit sexual bodies.

18. See http://en.wikipedia.org/wiki/Intersex.

Ability and Disability

Theological reflection about differences in human ability should begin with a sense of wonder and thanksgiving for the miracle of the sheer existence of an embodied spirit such as we are. When we consider the odds against ever becoming a functioning adult in the world, the term miracle is not excessive: the difficult mating of this sperm and this ovum to begin the process of gestation; surviving the dangers of pregnancy; being born with all limbs and fingers and organs — all of this makes up a wonder to be celebrated rather than an automatic process to be taken for granted. Then, to have all five senses working, to be able to walk and to speak, beyond speaking being able to reason, and, to top it all off, to participate in the process of God's creation through raising children and generating other forms of fruitful endeavor — none of these can be assumed. None of these is simply "normal" in the sense of being utterly predictable. Becoming a functioning adult human is a process fraught with peril: so many things can go wrong, so many limbs can remain undeveloped, so many brain circuits can remain unconnected, and so many senses and sensibilities can remain inactive. Then, that there should appear among us such prodigies of thought and invention as Mozart and Einstein, and such prodigies of spiritual insight as Jesus and Siddhartha — or that appearing among us are humans such as Helen Keller, who lacked both sight and hearing but, through careful tutelage, was able to employ her operative senses of smell and touch and taste to break through to human communication at a high level.[19] These remarkable fellow humans cause us to have an even greater sense of appreciation for what Teilhard de Chardin called "the phenomenon of Man."

My use of the term "functioning adult" may obscure the truth that part of the variety of human embodiedness is a tremendous diversity with respect to ability. Precisely what it means to be "functional" always depends on the specific action or task to be undertaken, and is always relative to others who undertake the same action or task. Each of us has more or less ability to do certain things, and each of us lack the capacity to do some things altogether. I have made this point sufficiently, I think, in the first section of the chapter. How, then, should we think theologically about the category "disabled"?

---

19. See D. Herrmann, *Helen Keller: A Life* (Chicago: University of Chicago Press, 1999).

The Disabled Body

When, for example, is it legitimate to use the term "disabled" or "disability," given the range of human abilities and lack of abilities across all areas of life? It is, I think, both legitimate and important to name specific disabilities, whether physical, emotional, or mental, when the unknown or unnamed presence of that disability can bring damage either to the one with the disability or to the community that person is a member of — or seeks to be. Such naming should, when possible, be initiated by the person with the perceived disability: "I cannot walk up those stairs, and thus cannot reach the restroom." "I am dyslexic and cannot read the assigned material in the allotted time." "I have Tourette's Syndrome and may disrupt the worship service without intending to." "I am blind and cannot read these ballots and so cannot cast my vote."

The issue in such cases is not whether one can sing an aria like Anna Netrebko or hit a baseball like Derek Jeter, for these are optional activities dependent on exceptional talent. You can't do those things, and I can't, and the vast majority of humans on the planet cannot. Rather, the issue is exclusion from activities that are required for participation in society (reaching a bathroom, taking part in worship) and for making legitimate contributions to society (advancing in education, having a vote). In all these areas it is the joint responsibility of the affected individuals and of the affected communities to identify the specific disability and to seek ways to enable as full a participation in the life of the community as generous effort and technology will allow. Such naming and responding are ways in which societies today legitimately respond to specific disabilities.

Such reciprocal naming and responding, which lead to the possibility of greater participation by all members in the activities of a community, are the exact opposite of the kind of societal "naming" that excludes first of all by removing the person with a specific disability from the process of naming, and then excludes further by stigmatizing individuals by identifying them simply with their disability — and without any nuance. They are "the blind" or "the crippled" or "the schizophrenic" or "the retarded" or "the epileptic." A single facet or aspect of a person is thus made the defining element in the eyes of society, and society's problem becomes "what to do about them." Does society exclude them from participation — for "their own good" or for the "protection" of others? Does society seek to include them in its actions, thus demanding special consideration and care to make such participation possible?

By being so named by society alone, however, the disabled are reduced to being objects to be dealt with rather than subjects who are themselves free moral agents. The process of categorization distorts the reality of the specific existence of those so categorized, and prevents others from accurately perceiving in them — as in all others — the complex combinations of ability and lack of ability that is the common human heritage. The designation "disabled" in this societal projection functions analogously to the designation "homosexual": it enables those who are fearful of difference to distance themselves from it and at the same time avoid the necessity of perceiving what is alike as well as what is unlike in the other.

In effect, such abstract designations also serve as did the ancient distinctions between the clean and unclean: to protect those who suppose themselves to be "able" from the fearful contagion of those who are "disabled." Unfortunately, the process of stigmatization can also be internalized, so that an individual with a disability can likewise define herself in terms of this aspect of her existence, and either acquiesce in that identity and live as a victim, or fight the designation and the society that imposed it. But in either case, sadly, she lives a life defined and governed by some aspect of her embodied being that may not in the least be the most important or interesting thing about her. As with the other abstractions discussed in this chapter, the real damage is done when categories replace contact with lived human experience either in the self or in the other.

An honest appraisal is necessary: there is no question that dramatic differences in ability create stress and require of society vigorous problem-solving. The problems presented by visible physical disabilities are difficult but actually easier to address: we can build ramps and provide mobility to those who are immobile; we can provide signers for the deaf and guides for the blind. The difficulties presented by invisible disabilities are more complex and less easy to solve: the challenges to full participation caused by chronic illness and fatigue, or the disruptive and debilitating potential of emotional and mental illness. But once a community is willing to acknowledge and respond to such dramatic differences as they become known, they are problems that are, with good will and great effort, potentially and at least partially solvable. A community that resists such openness and effort, however, falls short of the ethical standard demanded of a good society, and it certainly betrays in a fundamental fashion the good news of God's rule as announced and enacted by Jesus.

For an inductive approach to theology, however, the infinite range of human abilities and disabilities poses another kind of challenge, not that of solving problems of access and participation, but that of embracing and learning from the manifestations of God's Spirit via the ways in which the human spirit shines through even the most dramatic forms of physical, emotional, and mental disability.

As in other cases, the trick here is to turn the perspective, so that we approach human diversity not with the question "What's wrong here?" but with the question "What does God want us to learn here?" The turn means that we engage our embodiedness not as a problem but as a mystery. The differences between us become opportunities to discern the diversity of God's work in the world. The openness to mystery starts with reflection on our own embodiedness, and the ways in which we both have and do not have abilities commensurate with our desires. It extends to the hospitality we show to the diversity of abilities and disabilities revealed to us by others in our lives with them. Out of such reflection we can grow to a much greater appreciation for what the human spirit can accomplish. We all wonder at a Helen Keller or a Stephen Hawking, people whose spirit has shown through and triumphed within the most severe of physical limitations. But we also wonder at the ways in which the human spirit manages to reveal itself even through the tortured inner lives of those who are caught in profoundly inhibiting emotional and mental tangles.

And if we push this line of reflection even further, we can come to a deeper appreciation of how God's own Spirit works through the limitations of embodiedness. Nancy Eiesland captures one dimension of this truth in her pioneering work *The Disabled God*. She argues that, via the incarnation, God experienced a self-limitation to a single human body with specific (and limited) human capacities, and through that self-limitation — or in traditional Pauline terms, *kenosis* — God's Spirit was made powerfully available to all other humans.[20] What is true of the embodiedness of God's Word through the incarnation is analogously true of creation itself. Body can never fully or adequately express spirit, so that even in bringing the world into being at every moment, God chooses to work within the limits of material reality that is always and everywhere "disabled" with respect to fully disclosing the creator.

20. N. Eiesland, *The Disabled God: Toward a Liberatory Theology of Disability* (Nashville: Abingdon, 1994).

The Body Beautiful

There is another way in which human bodies can be exceptional and be the subject of more than ordinary attention. Some human bodies are bigger, stronger, more symmetrical, more agile, shinier, more radiant, and healthier than the bodies of other humans. Notions of beauty differ from culture to culture, to be sure. At one time, robustness is desired in women, and at another time, lissomeness; at one time, baldness is regarded as an affliction for men, and at another time baldness is taken to be a sign of wisdom.[21] In one part of the world this skin tone, this shape of eye, this shape of nose and mouth, this type of physique, is considered superior; in another part of the world, a different set of appearances sets the standard of beauty.

Within this diversity, however, there are two constants: the first is that every culture has a standard by which it can declare that such and such a body has a pleasing appearance; the second is that, despite the variations at the superficial level, certain physical characteristics — the ones I have listed — are always preferred to their opposites. The large and strong body is more impressive than the small and weak one; the radiantly healthy body is always preferred to one that is manifestly injured or sickly; the athletic body is privileged over the awkward body. Although the privilege accorded the beautiful and powerful body is extraordinary in the contemporary First World, it has abundant precedent in antiquity and throughout history. Think of the attention given to the size and handsomeness of Saul (1 Sam. 9:2) and the "ruddiness" and athletic prowess of King David (1 Sam. 16:12; 17:42), history's first truly "charismatic" leaders. Think also of the ways in which ancient athletes and great beauties in ancient Greece were regarded as close to divine.[22]

The social dynamics for the body that is exceptional through beauty or power is in some ways the opposite of those applying to the unclean and the disabled. If the unclean and disabled are excluded from participation in the life of the people, the beautiful and the powerful are welcomed everywhere: they have access to everything, even to governing power. Like the very wealthy, humans marked by what their society regards as great beauty are automatically considered to be socially acceptable. Indeed,

21. See A. J. Malherbe, "A Physical Description of Paul," in *Paul and the Popular Philosophers* (Minneapolis: Augsburg, 1989).

22. As in Aphrodisias, *Chaereas and Callirhoe* 1.1.16; 1.14.1; 3.2.15-17; Xenophon, *The Ephesians* 1.12.1; Heliodorus, *The Ethiopians* 1.2.1; Ovid, *Metamorphoses* 1.390-779; 2.466-95.

groups feel honored to have them present. Politicians and actors and professional athletes together form an A-list of societal status from which virtually all ordinary people are excluded. The President of the United States honors champion athletes in the Oval Office; actors and musicians vie to mingle with equally beautiful politicians and athletes at venues such as the Super Bowl, the Academy Awards, and other presentations for excellence in theater, musical composition, television programming, and so forth.

In this discussion I focus more on physical beauty than on athletic prowess, though what applies to one in large measure applies to the other as well. And my examples are drawn from our society's obsession with the beauty of the female body. The cult of female beauty is pervasive in First World countries and is a key component in the marketing campaigns that sustain economies based in nonessential goods. Contemporary media exacerbate the natural tendency to privilege physical beauty and power by focusing obsessive attention on the bodies — faces above all, but increasingly naked bodies as well — of accomplished actors and athletes, but even of those "celebrities" who have nothing other to recommend them but the arrangement of their facial and other bodily features. Indeed, the media improve the beauty of those they celebrate: the "stars" that adorn magazine covers and fashion spreads are airbrushed and photo-shopped to a physical perfection they do not themselves possess.

The downside of such obsessive attention to a set of physical attributes is clear. Those considered by society to be beautiful can become as defined and trapped by the category of *beauty* as those with manifest physical weaknesses become defined and trapped by the label of *disabled*. Because their extraordinary social access and privilege is based on fragile physical properties, beautiful people tend to be viewed by others, and also begin to view themselves, in terms of those attributes. And since the possession of the special properties constituting beauty is always threatened by injury, sickness, and age, those who internalize society's assessment of them in terms of these properties expend huge amounts of time and effort and money to enhance and sustain that fragile and fickle arrangement of bone and muscle and skin that makes them seem beautiful to others — but very often not to themselves.

Clothes, jewelry, and makeup are critical to the upkeep and maintenance of physical appearance, as are the ministrations of hairdressers and manicurists. Staying at exactly the weight that is demanded by society's current notion of what is beautiful can require endless diets and exercise under the supervision of physical trainers. Staving off the ravages of age may require the services of plastic surgeons. All of this effort is dictated by an arbitrary standard of acceptance and an accidental arrangement of features. A human life that is thus organized around the maintenance of physical beauty is as narrow and restricted as one organized around a physical disability.

The damage is not only — or most importantly — done to those elect ones whose faces and physiques are celebrated by the media. The greater damage is done to those consumers of the media's message that the standard of body they have selected is the ideal to which all other bodies should aspire, even though — given the effects of photo-shopping and airbrushing, not to mention cosmetics — the bodies they portray through the media have no actual physical existence. The goal of advertisers is plain enough: they want women to buy the beauty products and exercise and diet programs that might enable them to approach this ideal (in the sense of unreal) standard of beauty. And the desire to emulate the great beauties that are displayed everywhere an ordinary woman looks, leads precisely to great expenditures along predictable paths.

But the unspoken message underlying all the media presentations of the beautiful bodies is even more destructive: it implies that failure to meet the artificially constructed standard of beauty — the standard that makes all these celebrities accepted and honored and celebrated — will lead to rejection and loneliness. Thus is lack of beauty a form of stigma. Especially among young women, this powerful subtext to the pervasive placarding of the beautiful body generates all the appalling consequences of dysmorphia: young women — and, increasingly, girls — view their own bodies as ugly. They either torture themselves into new shapes by way of bulimia or anorexia or the practice of body-sculpting through plastic surgery in a futile effort to meet the media-imposed standard; or, in rebellion against the imposition of this stereotyped ideal, they seek to transform their bodies with piercings and tattoos.[23]

The sense of despair suggested by such desperate measures has some basis. Bodies that do not fit the standard definition of beauty are in fact ostracized within our society. The morbidly obese and the physically disfigured and the irredeemably ugly (by the current measure) are treated as though they posed as much a threat to the company of the fit and beautiful as the "uncleanness" of lepers threatened the holiness of Israel. At an ex-

23. See K. A. Phillips, *The Broken Mirror: Understanding and Treating Body Dysmorphic Disorder,* rev. and enlarged ed. (New York: Oxford University Press, 2005).

treme, abortion and sterilization have been practiced by individuals and states in the quest to produce through eugenics only those children who are acceptable according to contemporary standards of health and beauty.[24]

The distortions here, as in the cases discussed earlier in this chapter, result from a failure to pay attention to and appreciate the diversity in bodily appearance, and the imposition of an abstract concept of beauty that seeks to categorize and define humans. As in the cases of gender and disability, the use of abstract concepts with regard to beauty works its damage in two directions: first, by placing bodies in one category or another, it closes off an appreciation for all the manifestations of embodied spirit among individuals: by being so defined, they are also delimited. Second, the category serves to function in a discriminatory way to exclude or diminish those who do not fit within it.

The appearance of beauty among bodies is one of the glories of God's creation, and the appreciation for beauty is one of the capacities distinctive to humans. The perception of beauty fuels passion and desire, and the love of beauty funds the creative impulse that finds expression in art and music and literature. The hunger for beauty is a component in the mysterious human attraction to play and to worship. An inductive approach to theology would be deeply inconsistent if it were to reject an appreciation for the beautiful — in human bodies as much as in the rest of creation. Such a rejection would simply replace one abstraction with another. Instead, an inductive approach would rejoice in the many ways God's creative spirit reveals itself in a way that is pleasing to human senses and inspiring to the human spirit. Above all, such an inductive approach would utterly resist the idolatrous impulse to establish and impose one norm for the beautiful. It would appreciate how beauty truly is in the eye of the beholder, and it would turn its contemplation to how the mystery of God's creation is deepened and enriched by such an appreciation.

24. See the prescient essay by G. K. Chesterton, *Eugenics and Other Evils: An Argument against the Scientifically Organized State* (New York: Dodd Mead, 1927).

CHAPTER NINE

The Aging Body

The human body begins aging from the time of its conception, but we rarely become aware of its aging until many years have passed and the signs of mortality appear in unmistakable fashion. Aging, indeed, is the gentlest signature of mortality. Bodies die at all stages of life and in many abrupt and often violent ways. To have been born, to have lived a full life, to have survived to the point of being able to say, "I am old," is indeed to have been singularly blessed. At the same time, the recognition that one has in fact aged, that one's demise is now probably not to be by accident or war but by the slow diminishment of one's physical and mental capacities, brings with it terror of its own. Whereas in youth the awareness of mortality can be suppressed or denied through sheer exuberance and energy, in old age the shadow of mortality is unavoidable. Life choices now seem more portentous than ever before, yet the basis for making such choices — simple predictability — is out of our control as never before. As our years diminish, so do our options, and the greatest courage is required to exist simply and gracefully in conditions that are often complex and awkward.

The effort to live and think faithfully to the end of their days is made more difficult for Christians, who find themselves caught within two kinds of cognitive dissonance. The first is the massive societal denial of aging, which is in effect a denial of death, at the very moment that ever-increasing numbers of the population in First World countries are elderly by any measure.[1] The premise in the United States today, if we are to judge by the pro-

---

1. For an unflinching analysis of the individual and societal mechanisms for such denial, see E. Becker, *The Denial of Death* (New York: Free Press, 1973).

paganda advanced by the mass media, is that the ideal state of humanity is to be young and strong and beautiful, and the ideal goal of humanity is to remain young and strong and beautiful forever. To acquiesce in aging, that is, to refuse exercising and every other mode of perpetuating a youthful appearance, amounts to a social offense, a letting down of the side. In an earlier chapter I described the ways in which the "exceptional body" could be categorized and marginalized by society: as the unclean were excluded from ancient Israel, so are the disabled and the unattractive excluded from contemporary acceptance. The same discrimination is practiced toward the bodies of the elderly that move more slowly, that require more assistance, that fall in public. They are an embarrassment precisely because they visibly challenge the premise that we all remain young forever. Better that they be sequestered by themselves than that they be allowed to interrupt or impede our own rapid movement through life.[2] The acceptable elderly are those whose appearance and energy belie their chronology. Those who visibly and even painfully age, in contrast, are a reproach. It is tempting for elderly Christians to fit themselves within this ideology of death-denial both with respect to their own practices and with respect to their attitudes toward others who are aged.

For believers, the second form of cognitive dissonance is caused by the tension between the bodily experience of diminishment — the pull of mortality is ever more obvious — and the Christian hope for a "life everlasting" in the form of a bodily resurrection. The confession that God will raise to new life a "spiritual body" that enables believers to "be with Jesus" forever has never been easy to comprehend, even though the centrality of this conviction to the Good News is clear (1 Cor. 15:1-8). Paul's complex discussion of the resurrection in 1 Corinthians 15 makes clear that, even from the beginning, the notion of transcending mortality through the means and in the manner of the Christ who now as Lord shares the presence and power of God escaped easy understanding. The passage of centuries since the birth of Christianity has made the hope more difficult to sustain, so many have been those slain by death and so few and subtle the evidence for their continued or exalted existence. But for those who live in the shadow of their own mortality and who physically sense the approach of what seems an absolute end to their existence, maintaining a vivid expectation of a

---

2. Note how the brochures for "retirement communities" emphasize the range of activities that members can engage in rather than the nursing facilities that provide care before death.

future life can seem even to themselves to be a desperate illusion sustained only to enable the survival of increasingly shortened days.

The Experience of Aging

With this topic above all, theology must begin with experience, for if one has not yet experienced aging in one's own body, then it can truly be said that one does not know what one is talking about. Yet in this as in so many other aspects of embodied existence, the human experience of aging is far from uniform. We age at different rates, under very different circumstances, and with distinct characteristics. Relatively good health, relatively strong relationships, and above all, relatively greater wealth, make a huge difference in the experience of aging. Moreover, aging is common — but by no means universal. It is not simply that some people — like my remarkable aunt Odile, who died at 105 without ever having had a day of sickness — actually do remain "young" until they die. Many more never get the chance to age, such as those who die in infancy or who are stricken with fatal diseases as children, or those who are killed in battle or by disease while still young. My father, for example, died at thirty-six, my mother at forty-five, a friend from my youth in his thirties.

Those energetic octogenarian ladies who do yoga classes at the country club in between cruises with their husbands simply live in a different world than the sixty-year-old women whose lifelong poverty and grinding work have had as their accompaniment bad medical care, bad diet, abusive relationships, and a total abstinence from yoga or cruises. Molly has had knee replacement surgery and, slender and fit at seventy-five, still plays tennis; Marge has never heard of knee replacement surgery, could never afford the hypothetical insurance that would enable it, and at sixty grows obese in the wheelchair she has occupied since the difficult birth of her eighth child. Sam has an athletic body that has lost a step or two, but at ninety-three he is still as mentally sharp as he ever was, and continues to work productively, earning as much as he ever did, and enjoying his grandchildren and great-grandchildren. Saul is only sixty-five, but he has suffered from Alzheimer's disease since the age of fifty-eight, when his growing dementia forced him from work and plunged his family into economic distress and a chronic anxiety from which Saul himself is shielded only because he is no longer aware of his circumstances or even of his family.

The experience of aging, then, is as various as the many embodied spirits in whom aging happens. It is crucial to respect and to learn from this great variety. There are, nevertheless, certain aspects of aging that are broadly shared, and it is appropriate to begin this reflection with some attention to those common traits. As in other chapters, I speak not as a disinterested observer but as a participant, not with the methodology of social science but with simple attention to the ache in my own bones and to the other personal reminders that death is not only inevitable but far nearer than I could ever have imagined when I was young.

Full disclosure: at the age of seventy-one I am still able to do all of life's essential chores, and even some that are not essential, such as my teaching and my writing. I am, therefore, profoundly blessed. My age slows me but has not yet stopped me. I am still able to take long walks, read novels, watch movies, play with the dog, drive the car — even for long distances — and lecture in distant places. Most of all, I am still able to care for my eighty-one-year-old wife in her diminished condition. But still, when I assess my life year by year, or decade by decade, I am aware of a process that gradually picked up speed and continues to accelerate, promising even greater changes than the ones I have yet experienced. The changes involve my body itself, my mental abilities, and my emotions, in a complex tangle of cause and effect.

Looking back, I can't remember before the age of forty that I was ever conscious of my body — apart from a sporadically nervous stomach and myopia — as anything other than a totally reliable friend that I could call on to do whatever I desired. I did heavy manual labor without suffering more than slight aches, studied for long hours with no lag in concentration or energy, played a variety of sports with exhilaration and little fatigue, ate and drank at will, and enjoyed normal and predictable forms of sexual expression. In my thirties, I could still join a game of volleyball with no warmup, leaping and lunging with abandon; I could pick up a basketball, football, or baseball and propel them with speed and accuracy. In my forties I could still do all these things, but with this difference: I was slower, got tired a little faster, and needed to work more diligently to maintain physical fitness. I could no longer realistically think of myself as athletic. I could think a better game of tennis than when I was younger, but I could no longer get to the ball to return it.

Still, during my forties, I could still expend prodigious effort with relatively little cost: I did about sixty miles of aerobic exercise a week, could start writing books and articles and reviews at 7:00 AM, teach a full schedule, and grade papers late into the night. I could jump off chairs, climb ladders, run up and down three flights of stairs without ever looking down or using a railing. My students delighted in my annual demonstration of leaping straight up onto the surface of a desk from a flat-footed stance on the floor. But I began to find myself more susceptible to backache, to occasional attacks of pleurisy and other infections, some of which seemed connected to times of fatigue at the end of semesters.

In most ways, my fifth decade was a period of great satisfaction, as it is for many. We know how to live life and do our work, and we take great pleasure in the freedom such power gives us. We are, finally, mature. In this same decade, however, the signs of physical slowing also grow stronger. Even trifocal lenses were insufficient for me to see the fine print in Greek texts. Weight came on more quickly and was harder to lose. I found that I could not throw a football or baseball effectively. I could not move around the tennis court as I had, and I found less delight in swimming. Writing caused tendonitis; grading papers gave me headaches. But for me, the decade of my sixties, especially the last half, was the most revealing in terms of physical change. All at once, it seems, the warranty elapses, and everything starts to fall apart. It is, of course, not "all at once," but just another stage in a long process. But now I am alert to my weaknesses more than I am to my strengths.

My body now seems to me less a reliable friend than an unpredictable and sometimes resentful companion. My eyes are worse, my hearing is bad — I will be fitted with hearing aids shortly — and arthritis stabs me with pain despite my taking a time-released anti-inflammatory. I have hypertension. My weight insists on staying. My prostate is enlarged and my libido is shrunk. I am dyspeptic. All my teeth are capped. My hair is white and thinning. To compensate for the loss of hair on the head, my ears and nose produce lush if untended foliage. My skin, which had always been smooth and supple, is now not only splotchy in color but is the host for skin tags, psoriasis (legs), and eczema (arms). My lower back is in very bad shape. I now need to walk an hour every day, and faithfully do back exercises, simply to remain mobile. If a baseball or football comes my way, I don't even think about picking up the ball and throwing it; the thought of the consequent pain in my shoulder is sufficient to prevent any such fantasy. Indeed, I cannot really remember my muscular and athletic body. I do not climb ladders. I do not step easily off a chair. I watch where I place my feet when I descend stairs. Wow, how did *this* happen? And remember, I am among the singularly blessed! Unlike so many men of my age, I have not had to deal with the long-term effects of addictions or war wounds or industrial accidents; I have not suffered from the ravages of diabetes or COPD or cancer. In this sense, my aging process is absolutely normal. But I still don't like it.

How do I experience aging mentally? Here there is certainly both good news and bad news. The good news is real. Because I am a scholar and a lifelong voracious reader, I find that my mind is much more fully furnished than when I was young. I have learned a lot, and have remembered a lot of what I learned. In this sense, my mental efficiency is greater in certain respects because I can move more quickly among the multiple databases stored in my brain. Little of what I encounter in my field of study holds any surprise: I can recognize in the presentation of any novel theory the echoes of all its previous iterations. Consequently, my scholarly judgment is quicker and more secure than it was when I was younger. I am better able to distinguish between the authentic and the counterfeit.

My age and seniority in the guild also enables me to have relatively less passion and prejudice in my intellectual judgments. I am less caught up in academic competition, partly because I recognize its fatuity and partly because I am secure in my position. Long experience has also made me a better mentor for the intellectual labor of others: having written many books and directed many dissertations, I am able to guide others more surely than I ever could have done when I first began my scholarly life. I hope that the good news I find in my scholarly life applies also to other aspects of life. I know how to do things that matter and can distinguish better between what matters and what doesn't. I have the wisdom to know I must learn from others and thus have grown in my appreciation for the knowledge and skill of others.

There is also bad news concerning my mind. Although my knowledge base is large, and I find myself able to learn new things, I find that I now have less sheer intellectual curiosity and energy than I once had. My ability to simply absorb data is less. I would not even think now about trying to learn a new language, for example, when once such a task seemed, if not easy, then certainly possible. I am able to imagine articles and books when in the shower, but am less able to actually compose books and articles. It is here that I find the link to the loss of physical energy to be most obvious and telling. And although I am still able to remember fairly remarkable amounts of material from the libraries I have read, I experience the frustrating inability to remember, without special prompting, the specific names and dates and places that once were always available.

Like others of my age, this memory loss is most evident, not in the sphere of work, but in everyday activities. I have become the caricature of the "absent-minded professor," who cannot find his keys, who forgets why he drove to the pharmacy, who can't locate his parked car, who can't remember the name of the person to whom he has just been introduced, who needs to adhere to a rigid ritual to take his medications when he should. As far as I can tell, I am far from any state of senile dementia or Alzheimer's, but I am aware that mentally I am on a continuum with those so afflicted.

The emotional entailments of aging are perhaps the most complex and difficult to disentangle. As I enter the final stage of my life, I am more and more aware of the finality of that life, and I have mixed feelings concerning both the life I have, in fact, lived and those that I might have but did not live. I regret more the things I had wanted to do but could not because of my own life choices — such as travel the world and develop my talent for singing. Because my spouse is a decade older than me and diminished in some marked ways, I know precisely what this next stage will require of me, and that realization arouses a number of emotions: fear and anxiety concerning my ability to meet those challenges in light of my own lessened energy and strength; depression at the prospect of having more struggle than fun to face in the years to come; grief at the slow loss of one so dearly loved and compassion for her brave struggle to remain herself; fear concerning my own slow slide into the same or a similar loss of self. At the same time, I experience an even sharper joy in the simple beauties and pleasures of everyday life: a smile or laugh from my wife is as good as a trip to France; a call from my daughters is an emotional oasis; conversation with a friend is solace; seeing my sweet and talented grandchildren is both amusement and hope; the dignity and simplicity of the church's prayer is deep comfort.

More and more, I have been struck by the truth that the world leaves us before we leave the world. I am increasingly aware of how strange the world appears to me. The world in which I grew up no longer exists apart from my memory of it. The longer I live, the more my world is populated by strangers. My parents, my teachers, my colleagues, have disappeared all around me, and with their departure, my sense of sharing the same coherent universe also vanishes. The world that emerges around me every day, moreover, seems to belong completely to others. And I find that I do not much understand the language, the music, the art, or the values of the emergent world. To the degree that I do understand them, I find that I do not much like them. How crotchety does *that* sound? Yet it is what I am experiencing.[3]

My reaction to this awareness is multiform. From one side, it helps me see that my life and my life's work have made and will make very little difference to the larger world. Passing into history really means passing. As I contemplate my retirement from teaching next year, I realize that an event of great significance to me will matter very little to the institution. With Aquinas, moreover, I am able to say of all that I have written, "It is so much straw" — not with a sense of despair but with a realistic sense of appreciation for the transient character of all human effort. From another side, I am more ready to leave a world that seems increasingly alien to me. I suspect that this sense of alienation — in the proper sense of the word — is perhaps part of the way God prepares us to leave the world with less regret. It is no longer our world anyway.

Like others who have been blessed with the gift of time, I seek the wisdom that can guide and support me, and others like me, in the last days of life, however many they may be. Above all, I long for a sense that living for this long has real and specific value. Is a life better for having been extended? Is age simply a delay of the inevitable, or does it have a meaning all its own that we who age are invited to discover? As a theologian, in particular, I seek to learn what wisdom I am able to receive from Scripture and the tradition. But as in some of the other aspects of embodiedness that I have considered, I find that the witness of Scripture and tradition is complex, inconsistent, and less than fully satisfying.

Scripture on Aging

The witness of the Old Testament on aging is more mixed than we might expect. Certainly, the dominant note is struck by the Deuteronomic principle: those who keep the commandments will "live long" on the land (Deut. 30:20), while those who do not keep God's precepts will "perish quickly" (28:20). That a long life is a blessing connected with righteousness is repeated especially in the Wisdom writings (see Ps. 21:4; 37:28; 61:6; 128:6; Prov. 3:2; 4:10; 9:11; 11:28; 14:27; 19:20; 24:19-20; Sir. 1:12, 20; 2:3;

---

3. It is a recent and humbling realization — humbling because it should have been obvious but was not — that the loneliness of extreme age is a matter not only of what is now gone but also what is now present. Old age is a diaspora.

3:6; 7:27). The same literature constantly reinforces the point that wickedness leads to a premature end to life (Ps. 37:2, 9, 20, 28; 73:19-20; Prov. 10:27; 12:28; 14:27; 19:20; 21:7; 24:19-20). Proverbs states the ideal neatly: "Gray hair is a crown of glory; it is gained in a righteous life" (16:31), and "the glory of youths is their strength, but the beauty of the aged is their gray hair" (20:29).

The same conviction is communicated narratively through the exaggerated longevity ascribed to the descendants of Adam (see especially the *toledoth* in Genesis 5 and 11). The patriarchs also lived to an extended age and remained vigorous to the end: Abraham lived to "a good old age" and died at 175 (Gen. 25:7); at 108, Isaac died as an "old man of ripe age" (Gen. 35:29). Moses represented the ideal in its fullness: he "was a hundred and twenty years old when he died; his eye was not dim, nor his natural forces abated" (Deut. 34:7). The lawgiver himself demonstrated how righteousness led to a good old age. Moses could agree with the psalmist who declares, "I have been young and am now old; yet I have not seen the righteous forsaken" (Ps. 37:25; see also Ps. 71:17-18), and that even in old age, one's "youth is renewed like the eagle's" (Ps. 103:5).

Other texts are more cautious about asserting the connection between righteousness and longevity, between longevity and happiness. Some assert the plain fact that both righteous and unrighteous die young (Ps. 49:10-12), that the righteous one in particular can experience years cut short (Ps. 102:23-24), that, in any case, all human life is transitory (Ps. 90:3-6; 103:14-16; Sir. 18:9) and not necessarily pleasant: "The years of our life are threescore and ten, or if by reason of strength fourscore, yet their span is but toil and trouble: they are soon gone and we fly away" (Ps. 90:10). Some narrative texts suggest, indeed, that advanced age brings weakness in judgment and ability. The Bible explicitly connects the priest Eli's helplessness in the face of his corrupt sons to his advanced age (1 Sam. 2:22): his eyes are dim, and he cannot see what they are doing (1 Sam. 3:2; 4:15). When he was told of the death of his sons and the capture of the ark of the covenant, "Eli fell over backward from his seat by the side of the gate; and his neck was broken and he died, for he was an old man" (1 Sam. 4:18). Similarly, Samuel, who was anointed by Eli when he was still a youth, lacked power and judgment when he himself became elderly: he appointed his sons as judges, but they proved to be unjust (1 Sam. 8:1-3). The people tell him that it is because "you are old" that they pressure him to appoint a king for Israel as other nations have done (1 Sam. 8:4-5). The aged King David finds himself chilled and requires the ministrations of a young maid to warm his bones (1 Kings 1:1-4); more tellingly, he is now susceptible to the maneuverings of palace plotters (1 Kings 1:5-53).

Even the Wisdom compositions that maintain the Deuteronomic principle recognize that the experience of aging itself is ambiguous. Ideally, age should lead to wisdom. The younger man is urged: "Do not disregard the discourse of the aged, for they themselves learned from their fathers; because from them you will gain understanding and learn how to give an answer in time of need" (Sir. 8:9). Again, "what an attractive thing is judgment in gray-haired men and for the aged to possess good counsel. How attractive is wisdom in the aged and understanding and counsel in honorable men. Rich experience is the crown of the aged, and their boast is the fear of the Lord" (Sir. 25:3-6; see 32:3; 39:11). The young man is thus to "stand in the assembly of the elders. Who is wise? Cleave to him" (Sir. 6:34). The proper attitude of the younger to the elderly is respect (Prov. 23:22; Wis. 2:10).

But age does not always lead to wisdom. The Wisdom of Solomon notes that the old age of the wicked is without honor (Wis. 3:17). Sirach observes that the elderly may be held in contempt because they lack understanding (Sir. 3:12-16; 8:6), and the writer himself despises an "adulterous old man who lacks sense" (Sir 25:2). Still, empathy toward the elderly is advised; Sirach tells his reader, "Do not despise a man when he is old, for some of us are growing old" (Sir. 8:6). And in a poignant rendering of the command to honor father and mother, he declares, "O Son, help your father in his old age; do not grieve him as long as he lives; even if he is lacking in understanding, show forbearance; in all your strength do not despise him. For kindness to a father will not be forgotten, and against your sins it will be credited to you; in the day of your affliction, it will be remembered in your favor. . . . [W]hoever forsakes his father is like a blasphemer, and whoever angers his mother is cursed by the Lord" (Sir. 3:12-16).

Two Wisdom compositions challenge the assumption that age is a blessing. For the Wisdom of Solomon, which grapples with the problem of the virtuous man dying young because of enemies (Wis. 2:10-20), virtue and understanding count for more than mere longevity: "For old age is not honored for length of time, nor measured by number of years; but understanding is gray hair for men, and a blameless life is ripe old age" (Wis. 4:7-9). Since this is the case, a youth gifted with wisdom is more blessed than a foolish old man: "The youth that is quickly perfected will condemn the prolonged old age of the unrighteous man" (Wis. 4:16).

Qoheleth even more decisively cuts the Deuteronomic cord: he ob-

serves that righteous people die young and wicked people live to an old age
(Qoh. 7:15; 8:12). Wisdom is not the exclusive prerogative of age: "Better
a poor and wise youth than an old and foolish king who will no longer
take advice" (Qoh. 4:13). For Qoheleth, true wisdom consists in taking
appropriate pleasure in one's work and relationships (Qoh. 2:24; 3:12-13;
5:18; 8:15; 9:7, 9). Therefore, "if a man begets a hundred children and lives
many years, so that the days of his years are many, but he does not enjoy
life's good things, and also has no burial, I say that an untimely birth is better off than he . . . even though he should live a thousand years twice told,
yet enjoy no good — do not all go to the same place?" (Qoh. 6:3-6). The
problem with extended age, though, is precisely that it makes such pleasure and delight more difficult: "If a man lives many years, let him rejoice
in them all; but let him remember that the days of darkness will be many"
(Qoh. 11:8). And Qoheleth poignantly points to such days of darkness in
his metaphorical evocation of old age:

> Remember also your creator in the days of youth before the
>   evil days come,
> And the years draw nigh, when you will say, "I have no pleasure
>   in them";
> Before the sun and the light and the moon and the stars are darkened
> And the clouds return after the rain;
> In the day when the keepers of the house tremble, and the
>   strong men are bent,
> And the grinders cease because they are few,
> And those who look through the windows are dimmed,
> And the doors on the street are shut; when the sound of the
>   grinding is low,
> And one rises up at the sound of a bird, and all the daughters of song
> Are brought low; they are afraid also of what is high, and terrors
>   are in the way;
> The almond tree blossoms, the grasshopper drags itself along
> And desire fails; because man goes to his eternal home, and the
> Mourners go about in the streets;
> Before the silver cord is snapped, or the golden bowl is broken,
> Or the pitcher is broken at the fountain, or the wheel broken
> At the cistern, and the dust returns to the earth as it was,
> And the spirit returns to the God who gave it. Vanity of vanities,
> Says the Preacher; all is vanity. (Qoh. 12:1-8)

The spirit returns to the God who gave it — at the end of his work. Qoheleth provides a partial response to the problem he posed earlier in his reflection, namely, why a longing for eternity persists in a creature manifestly mortal like all other creatures: "I have seen the business that God has given to everyone to be busy with. He has made everything suitable to its time; moreover he has put a sense of past and future into their minds, yet they cannot find out what God has done from the beginning to the end" (Qoh. 3:10-11). It is the spirit that will return to God, which longs to know God's work from beginning to end. Qoheleth recommends taking pleasure in what life offers (3:12-13). But if at the end no pleasure is possible, then the return of the spirit to God truly seems empty, a vanity of vanities.

In sum, the Old Testament understands old age to be a blessing, but scarcely an unequivocal one, since experience shows that wicked people enjoy as much longevity as the virtuous. Old age itself brings with it weakness and sometimes foolishness rather than wisdom. It is a stage of life that should command respect and honor, but it often invites ridicule and contempt. What is most striking in the Old Testament's collection of observations about age is the paucity of actual wisdom concerning how to age appropriately in the Lord. In terms of exhortation to the elderly themselves, there is only the Preacher's advice to enjoy life while you can, and Sirach's admonition not to interrupt the music when speaking at a banquet (Sir. 32:3).

If the Old Testament is ambivalent about aging, the New Testament almost ignores it altogether. In the Gospels, the contrast to the eager attention paid to children is striking: nowhere are "the old" included among the poor and lowly who are the special recipients of the good news (see, e.g., Luke 7:22). Remarkably, there are not even any elderly characters in the Gospel narratives, apart from the parents of John the Baptist (Luke 1:18, 36), the prophets Simeon (by implication) and Anna (Luke 2:25, 36-37); for the sake of inclusiveness, one could possibly add the lame man at the gate in Jerusalem (Acts 4:22) and the father of Publius (Acts 28:8). The epistolary literature of the New Testament is similarly inattentive to the elderly. The most noteworthy exception is Paul's First Letter to Timothy, where Paul enjoins respect for older men on his delegate (5:1), and where he gives particular attention to the care of widows — especially those who are aged — by their relatives and the church (5:3-16). Otherwise, we can safely say that the aged are simply not "seen" by the writers of Christianity's earliest compositions.

The reasons for such lack of attention to aging are fairly obvious. Perhaps the least important, though not entirely insignificant, is sociological. The Christian movement began as a new sect within Judaism but within a matter of decades included as many (or more) Gentiles among its members as Jews. It gained members at first through conversion of individuals and households, which meant that its members had broken with their prior allegiances in order to join the messianic cult. As a diaspora phenomenon that lacked deep local and ethnic traditions, the Christian association was, in the Mediterranean world, a "new thing" that encompassed both Jews and Gentiles. Given this sociological instability, appealing to ancestral traditions and the elderly, who would be the transmitter of those traditions, would not be a natural reflex.[4]

Although assessing the exact character and extent of early Christian eschatological expectation is difficult, there is no question that the conviction that the ordinary order of the world had been disrupted through Christ, and would be even more decisively disrupted in the future, also had a profoundly destabilizing effect. If the end of all things could happen soon, attention to the process of aging would seem irrelevant. When Paul tells the Corinthians that "the form of this world is passing away," he invites them to an eschatological detachment from ordinary life — and nothing is more ordinary than aging. The sense of living in the end-time was also connected to the eschatological gift of the Holy Spirit (Acts 2:5-28), which was the source of wisdom within the community without respect to age or social position (1 Cor. 1:18–2:16). If "the mind of Christ" is available through the immediate gift of the Holy Spirit rather than through the slow accumulation of years, one of the key reasons for showing respect to age in the Old Testament has been eliminated.

Without question, however, the decisive difference was made by the death and resurrection of Jesus Christ. His death did not come at the end of a long life and by natural means. He was violently put to death at an early age by way of execution on a cross. The manner of his death should, according to the Deuteronomic principle, prove that he was an unrighteous man and a false messiah: "Cursed be everyone who hangs upon a tree" (Deut. 21:23). But the believers' experience of Jesus as supremely God's "righteous one" (Luke 23:47; Acts 3:14; Rom. 1:17) challenged the

---

4. See L. T. Johnson, "Proselytism and Witness in Earliest Christianity: A Study in Origins," in *Sharing the Book: Religious Perspectives on the Rights and Wrongs of Proselytism*, ed. J. Witte Jr. and R. C. Martin, Religion and Human Rights series no. 4 (Maryknoll, NY: Orbis, 1999), pp. 145-57, 376-84.

Deuteronomic equation. The resurrection of Jesus was understood, not as a resuscitation in which mortality was deferred, but an exaltation to new life in which mortality was transcended. Jesus was "at the right hand of God," sharing in the full presence and power of God as "Lord" (Acts 2:24-36; Heb. 1:3). As "Life-Giving Spirit" (1 Cor. 15:45), then, the exalted Lord became the source of the Holy Spirit to others (Acts 2:33), so that the possession of the Holy Spirit and the confession of Jesus as Lord were inextricably linked (1 Cor. 12:3). The sign of God's blessing is thus no longer physical longevity, physical descendants, or possession of the material land, but is now the possession of the Holy Spirit, who brings "eternal life" (Acts 2:37-39; Gal. 3:1-29; Rom. 5:1-21). Indeed, the New Testament characteristically sets in opposition the kind of "life" *(bios)* that is available through human capacity and the eternal "life" *(zōē)* that can come only through the power of God.[5]

Therefore, the writings of the New Testament are suffused with the language of newness, not in the sense of novelty (the newest thing) but in the sense of profound renewal and regeneration. They were not only joined in a new covenant with God (1 Cor. 11:25; 2 Cor. 3:7-18; Heb. 9:15); because they shared in a "new life" that came from God (Rom. 6:4; Eph. 4:24), they participated in a "new humanity" (Eph. 2:15; Col. 3:10), and were part of a "new creation" (Gal. 6:15; 2 Cor. 5:17) by which God was making "all things new" (Rev. 21:5). Paul exults: "If anyone is in Christ, there is a new creation . . . behold all things are new!" (2 Cor. 5:17). Inevitably, this sense of utter newness through the power of God involved a contrast to what was not "new" in the same way. Therefore, the past and what was "old" was characterized also by weakness, inadequacy, and imperfection: "The old things have passed away" (2 Cor. 5:17); the "old covenant" needed replacement by the promised "new [and better] covenant" (Heb. 8:6-12; Jer. 31:31-34), which renders the old one "obsolete" (Heb. 8:13).

Thus, in two decisive ways the New Testament relativizes the significance of human aging. It not only provides no christological exemplar for aging — because Jesus died young and violently — it replaces the value of human longevity with an "eternal life" that comes by gift from God. The impact can be seen in the church's calendar of saints: the vast majority of those recognized as bearers of Christ's image are martyrs and virgins, whose heroic life and death testifies to the reality of the resurrection rather

---

5. See L. T. Johnson, *Living Jesus: Learning the Heart of the Gospel* (San Francisco: HarperSanFrancisco, 1998).

than to the virtues of an ordinary — if lengthily extended — human existence. If the Old Testament seems to provide a highly muted and nuanced appreciation for the value of aging, the New Testament appears — at least by implication — to deny it any significance at all.

Scripture as a whole, then, does not in any obvious way provide much insight into the mystery of human aging. The New Testament appears to nullify its significance, and the Old Testament offers little sense of how living a long life might actually be a blessing rather than a burden. Does the moral tradition of the West provide any better guidance?

Philosophical Aging

An exact contemporary of Jesus was the Roman statesman and philosopher Lucius Annaeus Seneca (4 BCE–65 CE). He lived a turbulent life that included great material prosperity and political influence within the empire, as well as exile and death by suicide. Although a fervent follower of Stoicism, Seneca was fond of Epicurus, and Seneca's *Moral Epistles,* written to his friend Lucilius, make frequent references to Epicurean convictions. In these letters Seneca turned frequently to the topic of old age and death (he was himself about sixty-seven years old when he wrote them).

Seneca does not develop any overall teaching with regard to aging, but he repeats and develops a number of discrete observations. It is important to keep death before one's eyes, he says, for it can come at any time, either in youth or in age (4.4; 24.21); "there is no fixed count of our years" (26.8); "everywhere he is near at hand" (49.11). Because life is so short, every moment should be given to substantial rather than trivial things (49.5). Retirement from active affairs enables contemplation of wisdom (68.10-14; 76). And philosophy helps diminish the terror of death: "We should strip the mask, not only from men, but from things, and restore to each thing its own aspect. . . . Death either annihilates us or strips us bare. If we are then released, there remains the better part, after the burden has been withdrawn; if we are annihilated, nothing remains: good and bad alike are removed" (24.14, 19). Death, then, should be despised (82.16). Old age is full of pleasures if one knows how to use them (12.5). Age brings the diminishing of appetites (12.6) — a good thing, especially if it leaves the mind clear (26.2-4). Every day should be lived to its fullest (12.10). Suicide — "slipping the cable" — is always an available out if circumstances become too onerous (12.11; 24.9-11; 26.4). With regard to suicide, the moral issue is not "whether," but "when and in what circumstances" (70.28; 77.20), for the supreme value for the Stoic Seneca is to retain control over one's own existence.

A hundred years before Seneca, Marcus Tullius Cicero (106-43 BCE) sought to provide a philosophical defense of aging. In his *De Senectute* ("On Old Age"), written about sixty years before the birth of Christ and in his own sixty-second year, the Roman statesman and philosopher writes to his friend Atticus to lighten "the common burden of old age," convinced that philosophy "enables the man who is obedient to her precepts to pass every season of life without worry" (2). Cicero uses the form of the dialogue, but puts the greatest amount of exposition in the mouth of the historical figure Marcus Cato (Cato the Elder), who responds to his friends' wonder "that he bears his age so well" (3). Cato declares that he is wise because "I follow Nature as the best of guides and obey her as a god" (5).

Nature has determined distinct seasons of "life's race-course," each of which must be run in turn, each with its own quality, and each with its own rewards: the weakness of childhood, the impetuousness of youth, the seriousness of middle life, the maturity of old age (33). Unhappiness in old age is not the fault of that stage of existence; it is due to a deficiency in character (7, 65). The best way to live out one's old age is thus with virtue — and with the memory of a virtuous life (9).

The bulk of Cicero's composition is devoted to refuting four major complaints about old age: the fact that it removes one from active pursuits; the bodily weakness attached to it; the loss of physical pleasure; and the fact that in old age we are closer to death (15). His response to the first point is simple denial: age enables one to direct the activities of others from a position of authority: "It is not by muscle, speed, or physical dexterity that great things are achieved, but by reflection, force of character, and judgment; in these qualities old age is usually not only not poorer, but is even richer" (17). He insists that mental capacities are not diminished, unless through disuse: the elderly remember what they are interested in (22) and are fully capable of learning new things (26). As for physical strength, it, too, can remain vigorous in old age as many examples demonstrate, although some loss of strength is to be expected: "And yet, even that very loss of strength is more often chargeable to the dissipations of youth than to any fault of old age; for an intemperate and indulgent youth delivers to old age a body all worn out" (30).

The third objection to old age is that it means the loss of pleasure. As far as physical pleasures are concerned, Cicero's Cato agrees with Seneca:

it is actually a good thing that the passions are weakened by age (39-44); remember the Greco-Roman moralists' deep antagonism toward the passionate body (see chap. 6 above). But he insists that other pleasures are available to the elderly. When he was young, he was more interested at banquets in the food and drink, whereas now he is more engaged by the conversation (46). Old age also provides the time for study and learning that youth did not (49). The "delights" of agriculture are more appealing to a man of advanced age (51); most pleasurable is the exercise of influence over others: "Surely old age, when crowned with public honors, enjoys an influence which is of more account than all the sensual pleasures of youth" (61).

Despite these lively rejoinders, it is clear that even the (fictional) elderly Cato regards age as a threat that must be resisted. His words of warning sound remarkably modern:

> But it is our duty, my young friends, to resist old age; to compensate for its defects by a watchful care; to fight against it as we would fight against a disease; to adopt a regimen of health; to practice moderate exercise; and to take just enough of food and drink to restore our strength and not to overburden it. . . . Much greater care is due to the mind and soul; for they too, like lamps, grow dim with time . . . so that senile debility, usually called "dotage" [*deliratio*] is a characteristic, not of all old men, but only those who are weak in mind and will. (36)

As with Seneca, old age is here regarded as deserving respect only when independence is maintained: "For old age is honored only on the condition that it defends itself, maintains its rights, is subservient to no one, and to the last breath rules over its own domain" (38).

Cicero's response to the final complaint about age is in some ways the most interesting. Aging brings a greater awareness of death, it is true. But this awareness should have been there all along: "Is there anyone so foolish, even though he is young, as to feel absolutely sure that he will be alive when evening comes?" (67). Everything human is transitory (69): "But this should be thought on from our youth up, so that we may be indifferent to death, and without this thought, no one can be in a tranquil state of mind. For it is certain that we must die, and, for aught we know, this very day" (74). And the death of the elderly does not have the tragic dimension of the death of the young: "With the young, death comes as a result of force, while to the old, it is the result of ripeness" (71).

As for the fear of death, Cicero has Cato agree with Seneca that it should be despised: "For clearly death is negligible, if it utterly annihilates the soul, or even desirable, if it conducts the soul to some place where it can live forever" (66). Cicero has Cato himself subscribe to the conviction that the soul is immortal by nature and will enjoy a future life: "The soul is celestial, brought down from its most exalted home and buried, as it were, in earth, a place uncongenial to its divine and eternal nature. I believe that the immortal gods implanted souls in human bodies so as to have beings who would care for the earth and who, while contemplating the celestial order, would imitate it in the moderation and consistency of their lives" (77). This conviction enables the hope that the soul will in the future join the ranks of those whose lives were ennobled by virtue: "O Glorious day, when I shall set out to join the assembled hosts of souls divine and leave this world of strife and sin!" (84). Armed with these convictions, Cato declares that "old age sits lightly upon me . . . and not only is not burdensome, but is even happy" (85).

The reflections of Seneca and Cicero are easy to dismiss, not least because they were composed by the ancient equivalents of the octogenarian women doing yoga at the country club. Seneca and Cicero occupied the highest rank in society, had tremendous wealth, and enjoyed the benefits of physical comfort and intellectual stimulation. They wrote, moreover, at a time of their own life when genuine physical and mental decline had not yet occurred. They could still maintain the illusion that complete self-control was within their grasp — though each man died violently and not entirely by choice within a few years of their writing these works! When they had soreness in the muscles, slaves were available to anoint and massage their limbs. Cicero's rapturous account of agriculture as a pleasure for the elderly is most revealing; he speaks from the perspective of the "gentleman farmer" who supervises and observes the labor of others, not from the perspective of an old man still working in the field.

Nevertheless, Cicero's *De Senectute* represents a high point in ancient philosophical thinking about old age, and philosophy did not subsequently add much to his contribution. Medieval Christian philosophers, who operated within the framework of Aristotle and Augustine, gave equally short shrift to childhood and aging, saving their best thoughts for the age of maturity *(iuventus)*, which they identified as corresponding to the age of Christ's ministry. In contrast with this perfect human state, the conditions of youth and age alike were seen in terms of deficiency. Youth does not yet possess physical, mental, and spiritual maturity, and old age is a long process of losing it. Thus, for Thomas Aquinas, the elderly are to be held in reverence not because of the condition of their body, but because of their wisdom — even though such wisdom is available even to the young through God's gift. The elderly have some advantage over the very young because their passions are quieted and they can enjoy spiritual more than material pleasures. But Thomas is convinced, reflecting the tradition before him, that the age of the body in the resurrection will be the same as Christ's when he died and was raised from the dead, namely, the perfect human condition of *iuventus*.[6]

Learning from Age Inductively

To a very considerable extent, the voices I have assembled from Scripture and from philosophy have spoken about aging as an ideal or an affliction affecting someone else. Discussions have been "disembodied" in the sense that they have addressed aging as a topic about human experience but have not reflected from within that human experience. Most of the interpretations of aging have come from people who were not yet at that stage of life. Only seldom has the voice of first-person experience appeared, as with the psalmist who declares, "I have been young and am now old; yet I have not seen the righteous forsaken" (Ps. 37:25), or with the philosopher Seneca, who notes how the collapsing buildings, gnarled trees, and suddenly toothless slaves on his estate make him aware of how swiftly he also has reached a stage of decrepitude.[7]

But as I suggested at the beginning of this chapter, with aging above all, if you have not yourself entered the embodied experience, then you don't know what you're talking about. The first step, then, is procedural. In order to do theology inductively in this case, we must make the shift from speaking about aging as a general stage of life to bearing witness from within the personal experience of aging. To discover the nature and meaning of aging, we must pay attention to and learn from the voices of the elderly. Certainly those who are aging can teach and learn from each other concerning the significance of their experience; but it is of even greater importance that

6. See P. L. Reynolds, "Thomas Aquinas and the Paradigms of Childhood," in *The Vocation of the Child,* ed. P. M. Brennan, Religion, Marriage, and Family series (Grand Rapids: Eerdmans, 2008), pp. 154-88.

7. Seneca, *Moral Epistles* 12.1-5.

witness concerning the experience of aging be made available to those approaching that stage of life — from whatever distance.

But the challenges facing such a commitment are noteworthy. To begin with, many who are experiencing aging find that speaking about the experience is difficult, in some cases because the powers of speech have been affected — perhaps even eliminated — by the process of aging itself, in some cases because the experience is too complex and difficult to be captured by any kind of verbalization. Many reach old age with little sense of how to think of their lives in terms of a narrative, much less a narrative about God's work in their life, and even less as a narrative that might prove exemplary to others. And even if such speech were possible to the elderly, is there anyone interested in hearing? One of the painful aspects of aging, especially in our society, is isolation from that very company of others who look to the elderly as a source of wisdom. When the elderly are segregated into communities consisting only of the old, whatever wisdom the elderly might have to share with those younger than they are lacks expression because of the lack of an audience. I may have a powerful story to tell, but if there is no one interested in hearing it and perhaps learning from it, I will die with the story still locked within me — of use to no one. I have lived a long life, but the story of that life remains untold, and the witness that my life might have been teaches no one.

Here, above all, an inductive approach to theology demands collaborative effort for the witness of embodied experience to reach expression. On one side it demands of those at any stage of aging the willingness to disclose their experience to others, whether through statements, stories, or only the mute testimony of the body itself. We must ask of the aging that they tell their stories of faith as best they can, that they make available to those around them what they have learned through their many years and what they continue to learn through the changes in their body and spirit. Now, as never before, they must speak or even simply point to the truth with transparency and complete candor. They can do this even when words fail them, in the confidence that God's spirit can continue to speak even through their mute bodies.

On the other side, it requires of those in attendance on the elderly — such as family, friends, caregivers — that they seek eagerly and persistently for whatever witness the elderly can express. The care of the old must encompass more than ministrations to the body — indeed, must include an openness to the spirit that seeks expression through the body. Such openness requires not only ears to hear what is said but also eyes to observe what is said by the body outside of speech, and touch to feel what the body signals that cannot be expressed in words. Unless there are some who truly want to hear the story that can be told by the aged, their story will not be told, and we will miss the chance of discovering what God is up to among our brothers and sisters who move before us in pilgrimage to God.

I want to emphasize that such collaborative effort is more than a matter of showing compassion toward the elderly, or of showing them hospitality, or of inviting them to participate more fully in the human community by giving them a voice; it is a matter of seeking to discover God's work and purpose in every aspect of God's creation, at every stage of human existence. The effort is properly theological.[8]

What are some of the things that we might expect to learn among and from the aged? We may hope to learn first of all what it means to grow old "in the Lord." There is no other source from which we can learn this most critical truth than the testimony (spoken or mute) of the aged themselves. Neither the New Testament nor the tradition provides a christological model for aging: our savior died young and violently. As with our sexual lives and our parenting, we must discern through the guidance of the Holy Spirit how "the mind of Christ" (1 Cor. 2:16) might be translated into situations that Christ's own human mind never considered. In both those cases, we may be led and strengthened by the Spirit, but we are also provided examples of holy sexual lives and of holy parenting from others. But the case of aging is much more challenging, for it is not simply an activity or practice; it is a human condition that extends for decades and brings us to places where none of us individually have been before.

If we are to learn what it means to be a disciple in old age, how to grow old "in the Lord," we must learn it from those who have been aged disciples before us.[9] We can learn what elements of the Creed seem more important than ever and which ones seem less meaningful, what aspects of ecclesial life now appear significant and which now seem an utter waste of time or effort. We can learn with and from them the challenges to living faith that the condition of aging brings with it, and what aspects of faith are now more meaningful. From them we may learn new dimensions of faith, not as a single dramatic existential decision but as a series of decisions

8. Although it very much involves hospitality in the profound sense elaborated by H. J. M. Nouwen in *Reaching Out: Three Movements of the Spiritual Life* (New York: Image, 1986), pp. 63-110.

9. See the method of listening to the stories of elderly women in K. Scheib, *Challenging Invisibility: Practices of Care with Older Women* (St. Louis: Chalice Press, 2004).

made over the course of decades, not only as belief or trust or obedience, but as a form of loyalty that must be renewed day after day in the face of diminishing prospects. From them we may learn what words and deeds of Jesus speak most clearly and directly to their hearts: perhaps not "leave all and follow me," but "in patient endurance you shall save your souls" (Luke 5:27; 21:19); perhaps less "you will be fishers of men" than "today you will be with me in paradise" (Luke 5:10; 23:43). From them, above all, we may learn the true significance — and cost — of accepting Jesus' demand of "taking up the cross daily" and following him (Luke 9:23).

A second truth to which the aging in particular can bear witness is that human worth and dignity do not depend on independence from others but rather on a deep and mutual interdependence. That humans are dependent creatures — contingent and in no way necessary — should be immediately obvious, but much of our activity and a great deal of our society collude in the delusion that we are independent and self-sufficient. Furthermore, society advances the assumption that human worth and dignity is based on such independence. But the state of childhood and the state of aging alike challenge that assumption.

Children need to be nourished and disciplined and taught, and they are blessed if they have parents who carry out those tasks gladly and well. Otherwise, children must depend on the generosity of others for their essential physical, mental, and emotional needs. Likewise, those in an advanced stage of aging need physical and emotional attention. At a certain point, like children, they also need to be fed, clothed, bathed, and cleaned. They are dependent on those willing to perform these tasks for them. They are blessed if they have children who are able and willing to now act as parents to their own parents gladly and well. But if they do not have children capable of performing these tasks, the aged must depend on others to provide their essential physical, mental, and emotional needs.

Apart from a relatively short period of adulthood, then, human life at either end is manifestly one of need and dependence. Growth from childhood and survival until death are possible only because others support us. But because the aged have already passed through the earlier childhood stage of dependence and the stage of (supposedly) adult independence, they are uniquely able to witness to the truth that, in fact, every stage of life involves dependence on others. Adults also require assistance and support in virtually every aspect of their existence. No one is truly and fully "independent" of others. Only a narrow focus on their work and their earnings and on their "societal contribution" and on their "carrying their own weight" enables them temporarily to avoid recognizing the fact that they are as fully — if not as visibly — dependent on others as are children and the elderly. What the aged have the opportunity to teach through the language of their bodies, and what others among us have the chance to learn, is the art of accepting such dependence gracefully and gratefully.

The process of aging is inevitably a process of losing our apparent independence. It is true that when we drove a car, we were never really independent of those who maintained and fueled and guarded the car and built and maintained the roads — or the care and attention of other drivers on the road! But losing the ability to drive a car means a profound and personal loss of self-determination. The same inevitably applies to other forms of movement outside and then within the house, from control over meals and medications to hygiene and even bodily functions. Each such loss brings a corresponding dependence on another. How difficult this is! How daunting it is to maintain a sense of self, of personal integrity, when our power over speech and our memory of even basic functions disappears. What a gift is given to others when those whose lives extend to this ultimate point of dependence can manifest, through the motions of their arms, through the light in their eyes, through the touch of their hands, the sweetness of self-relinquishment, the handing over of willfulness, and the embrace of the gift that is given by another — moment by moment. Participating in the interdependence that is necessarily a component of aging enables all involved, those cared for and those caregiving, to learn more profoundly the meaning of Paul's instruction to the Galatians: "Bear one another's burdens, and in this way you will fulfill the law of Christ" (Gal. 6:2).

A third truth to which the aging in particular are privileged to bear witness through their bodies is the truth of the resurrection. In his discussion of the resurrection in 1 Corinthians, Paul declares confidently: "Just as we have borne the image of the man of dust, so we will also bear the image of the man of heaven" in the resurrection (1 Cor. 15:49). He assures the Thessalonians that, whether dead or alive at the last day, "we will be with the Lord forever" (1 Thess. 4:17). His own longing for such fellowship with the risen Christ is poignant. He tells the Philippians, "My desire is to depart and be with Christ, for that is far better" (Phil. 1:23), and he shares that desire with the Corinthians in words that should have special resonance with those whose bodies are aging:

So we do not lose heart. Although our outer nature is wasting away, our inner nature is being renewed day by day. For this slight momentary affliction is preparing us for an eternal weight of glory beyond all measure, because we look not at what can be seen but at what cannot be seen; for what can be seen is temporary, but what cannot be seen is eternal. For we know that if the earthly tent we live in is destroyed, we have a building from God, a house not made with hands, eternal in the heavens. For in this tent we groan, longing to be clothed with our heavenly dwelling — if indeed, when we have taken it off, we shall not be found naked. For while we are still in this tent, we groan under our burden, because we wish not to be unclothed but to be further clothed, so that what is mortal may be swallowed up by life. He who has prepared us for this very thing is God, who has given us the Spirit as a guarantee. (2 Cor. 4:16–5:5)

The real question that only the aging can answer is what these texts now mean to them in light of their own physical and mental fragility, when the "wasting away" of their outer nature is most obvious, and when the "groan" that accompanies the burden of mortality in its final stages is most painful. Throughout this book I have argued that the human spirit transcends the body and gives expression to God's Holy Spirit in the world, through play and work, through passion and pain. What appears to the observer of the aged is that the spirit seems weakened, played out, diminished, gone into retreat within the shell of mortality. But is "what is seen" in this case true? Or is the Spirit that God has given as a pledge of the resurrection — that which is "unseen" to outsiders — a present reality to the aged?

If so, in what way is it experienced? What is the shape of the hope that sustains the aging, that enables them "not to lose heart" even as they lose so much else? Is it, with Cicero and much of the ancient Greco-Roman world, a hope of immortality that involves only the soul, or is it, with the unanimous witness of the New Testament, a hope for the resurrection of the full human person to a share in the life of God in the condition that Paul called a "spiritual body" (*sōma pneumatikon*, 1 Cor. 15:44). The conviction that the body has a future beyond aging and death is difficult for believers of all ages. Is it more or less difficult for believers who live more intimately with their own mortality, whose experience of the body's disintegration and (for some) the soul's disorientation is more immediate?

Do believers who have reached the time of the near-end through the obvious diminishment of their bodies and the apparent diminishment of their spirit say to themselves that the hope for resurrection has been a great illusion, or do they find their spirit strengthened by the realization that they are now finally in the position to know the mystery toward which their faith has for so many years pointed them? Do they, perhaps, remember that Paul himself argued that the resurrection of Jesus was analogous to God's creating out of nothing (Rom. 4:16-25), and that the signs of age and death only gave occasion for the display of God's mighty power? Do they draw close to themselves, for comfort and strength, the words Paul spoke about Abraham's faith?

> For this reason it depends on faith . . . in the presence of the God in whom he believed, who gives life to the dead and calls into existence things that do not exist. Hoping against hope, he believed that he would become "the father of many nations," according to what was said, "so numerous shall your descendants be." He did not weaken in faith when he considered his own body, which was already as good as dead (for he was about a hundred years old) or when he considered the barrenness of Sarah's womb. No distrust made him waver concerning the promise of God, but he grew strong in his faith as he gave glory to God, being fully convinced that God was able to do what he had promised.

We do not know — our theology is not informed — unless we help enable the aging to express what they experience in body and spirit as they approach the end of their mortal lives, unless we take seriously the witness borne by them in body and spirit, a witness all the more valuable because it is given by those whose faith is being tested by the last and most difficult trial.

Epilogue

Quickly, and without much fuss, I want to summarize here at the end what I consider to be the major points of this book and to indicate what I think are some implications for both the practice and the teaching of theology.

Of the greatest importance, and grounding everything else, is my conviction that God continues to create the world at every moment, and by so creating, continues to reveal Godself in what is coming-into-being. If this understanding of the Living God — an understanding I think underpinning everything said in Scripture — is not correct, then everything I have said in this book is false.

If God acted only in the past, and those actions are adequately reported by Scripture, then the Bible can indeed be said to "contain" revelation, and nothing more needs doing apart from the systematic exposition of propositions based on the biblical accounts. The major problem with this is that it posits a God who is no longer active — in effect, a dead god. But if God is, in fact, active in the work of creation, the work that underlies all of God's "activity" in the world, then authentic faith — and, by extension, authentic theology — must consistently fix its attention on what God is up to here and now.

I have argued from a variety of angles that the human body is the preeminent place of God's continuing revelation in the world, and that theology must pay close attention to what is happening in actual human experience, which is always in some way somatic. Scripture itself, I have shown, declares that, not itself, but the human body is the place where God's word particularly is expressed and where God's work is done. But I have also argued that, without being formed by Scripture, theologians are not able to perceive the movement of the Spirit in human bodies as expressing the word and work of God. Scripture participates in revelation first by providing the lens for perceiving human experience, and second by being given new meaning and pertinence through engagement with God's living work.

One of the surprising discoveries for me in the course of this study has been how little Scripture actually speaks, or speaks helpfully, to the subjects I have chosen for analysis. This lack is all the more telling because my topics are far from recondite. They are the obvious topics to consider if one wants to talk about real human experience: play, work, pain, pleasure, and aging. As I have shown, Scripture has virtually nothing on play, and little of real use on work. On the passions, Scripture certainly needs correction — or, if you prefer, amplification. Its witness is mixed if not radically inconsistent on the subjects of the exceptional body and the aging body; and though Scripture speaks often about suffering, it does so exclusively within the framework of sin and salvation, which falls far short of addressing the actual human experience of pain.

The most difficult part of my argument was dealing with the intersections between body and spirit. I fully acknowledge my failure to provide perfect clarity in that section of the book. I am not, however, convinced that perfect clarity is either possible or even desirable. The reason why we need to pay close attention to the body is so that we can learn the movements of God's spirit. But we need to recognize that, precisely because we are not juggling concepts but observing life, we cannot easily distinguish where body ends and spirit begins, or even more, where the human embodied spirit also expresses the Holy Spirit of God.

No less complex has been the analysis of the several somatic states. When we seriously consider the body at work or at play; when we think with the passionate or aging body; when we ponder the exceptional body — in all these reflections we quickly discover that it is by no means easy either to see clearly or to speak precisely when engaged with real human experience. By no means have the lessons always been positive: we have seen that the body can obscure the work of God as well as reveal it. Nor have I tried to derive a set of standard conclusions for each analysis. Inviting the reader into a process of reflection has been my main goal, not providing a set of firm propositions.

Because of the inherent ambiguity built into the effort to discern spirit in body, I have emphasized that theology must be inductive rather than deductive and an art rather than a science. It must be inductive because the work of the Living God continues to be disclosed in the world. The data of revelation keeps pouring in, if we have eyes with which to see. To act as though God no longer acted in and through human bodies is to deny in the most fundamental way the entire import of Scripture itself.

It must be an art because discernment is essentially learned through practice rather than through theory. No more than a therapist can effectively practice counseling from a textbook on psychology, without countless hours of listening to patients, can a theologian effectively practice theology from a textbook of systematics, without countless hours of observing human behavior in light of God's word. In both cases, appropriate response to a living subject constitutes the art, not the application of abstract concepts. And in both cases, the therapist and the theologian essentially *learn* their subject from such engagement with living bodies.

The therapist and the theologian, to be sure, both need solid and even systematic learning in their respective disciplines if they are to responsibly practice their art. The therapist must have a coherent framework concerning the human personality and character, and a guide to psychological pathologies. The theologian must know Scripture and the tradition, and must have a creedal framework within which to think about human behavior. But these are only propaedeutic to the learning of therapy and theology as living arts, which learning occurs above all in direct engagement with human bodies.

I have argued in other places that Christian theology should be less an academic than an ecclesial activity, and that the best medium for theological thinking is open and ongoing conversation for the edification of the church rather than the publication of books written for other scholars.[1] This is, to be sure, a utopian vision, given the present academic captivity of the church. But perhaps if students in schools of theology whose learning is directed to the service of the church learned theology as an inductive art, and practiced theology within their ministry as an ecclesial activity, theology within the academy might also be reinvigorated by contact with the powerful work of the Living God in human lives.

---

1. See L. T. Johnson and W. S. Kurz, *The Future of Catholic Biblical Scholarship: A Constructive Conversation* (Grand Rapids: Eerdmans, 2002); L. T. Johnson, *Scripture and Discernment: Decision Making in the Church* (Nashville: Abingdon, 1996); L. T. Johnson, "Does a Theology of the Synoptic Gospels Make Sense?" in *The Nature of New Testament Theology: Essays in Honor of Robert Morgan,* ed. C. Rowland and C. Tuckett (Oxford: Blackwell, 2006), pp. 93-108.

Index of Subjects

Adam and Eve, 108, 112. *See also* Creation
Aging, 206; characteristics of, 207-13; denial of, 206-7; dependence during, 227-28; philosophical view of, 220-24; sign of blessing, 214, 216, 222
Anhedonia, 142, 144. *See also* Pleasure
Anti-Semitism, 34, 49. *See also* Holocaust
Apatheia, 132, 152-53. *See also* Passions
Aquinas. *See* Thomas Aquinas
Aristotle, 10, 136, 140, 159, 223. *See also* Philosophy, ancient
Asceticism, 142-43
Attention: to aging, 215, 218, 224-26; to body, 24, 28, 65, 82; to desire, 151; to passions, 137, 139, 144; to pleasure, 140, 146; to spirit, 2, 67-68, 74-75, 233; to work, 158, 177
Autarkeia, 143-44. *See also* Passions

Bisexuality, 193. *See also* Sexuality
Body: ambiguity of, 4, 5, 11, 18, 35, 65, 84, 117, 129, 169, 208, 232; beauty of, 202-4; of Christ, 11, 44, 57, 62, 77-78, 100, 128-29, 190; diminishment of, 227, 229; diverse forms of, 181-85, 188-89, 191, 197, 205; expression of spirit, 6, 65, 82, 84-85, 105, 191, 201, 230, 232; individual, 79, 94; language of, 51-52, 56, 61, 83, 156, 228; phenomenology of, 23-24, 27, 29; sexual, 28-30, 31, 61, 82, 191, 197; social (collective), 62, 79, 81, 183; spiritual body, 207, 229

Canonization process, 8-9, 38-40
Children, 52, 58, 81, 88-89, 93, 103, 112, 116, 119, 124-25, 138, 149, 158, 167, 172-73, 176-78, 198, 217, 227-28. *See also* Play
Cicero, 221. *See also* Philosophy, ancient
Commodification, 72, 81, 106, 172
Compassion, 126-27. *See also* Suffering
Contraception, 21, 32-33. *See also* Sexuality
Coveting, 134-36, 146-49, 162. *See also* Envy
Creation, 1-2, 7, 18, 34, 39, 46, 53-57, 59, 64-65, 74, 113, 115, 119, 128, 131, 161, 177-78, 180, 198, 205, 226, 231; account of, 26, 36; in Genesis 1–3, 108, 112. *See also* New creation
Creeds, 2-5, 18, 36, 226, 23

Desire, 146, 154-55; objects of, 147-48; sexual, 149, 151; and union, 149-51, 153. *See also* Passions
Deuteronomic principle, 109, 111-14, 213, 215, 218. *See also* Suffering: sin and
Dieting/abstinence from food, 141-43
Disability, 184-85, 198-201; definition of, 199-200; stigmatization of, 200
Discernment, 1-2, 5, 7, 15, 17-18, 34, 46, 66, 75, 139, 144, 233. *See also* Theology: as inductive art
Dualism, 65, 130-32, 134-35, 137, 139, 142, 149
Dysmorphia, 142, 204

Eiesland, Nancy, 125, 201
Embodied existence, 22-24, 55, 66, 78, 127, 168-69, 177, 201, 208, 224-25, 232. *See also* Body
Enlightenment, 69-71, 79
Envy, 133-36, 174-75
Epictetus, 124, 140, 153. *See also* Philosophy, ancient
Epicurus, 67, 132, 140, 220. *See also* Philosophy, ancient
Eros, 132, 149-52
Eternal life, 113, 207, 219
Experience (general), 12, 24, 40, 46-47
Experience, interpretation of, 4, 14, 16-18, 38, 41, 45-48; religious, 13, 41, 42-44, 68; scripture and, 17, 34, 37, 39, 41-42

Faith, openness to God's activity, 18, 48, 119, 155, 231
First World, 115, 138, 175, 183, 193, 197, 202-3, 206

Gentiles, 43, 45-48, 58, 135, 188-89, 218
God: always creating, 18, 46-47, 53, 177-78, 180, 226, 231; Living, viii, 1, 3, 5, 7, 12, 14-15, 18, 34-36, 42, 45-46, 48, 77, 151, 154, 156, 172, 231-33; passions of, 133, 151

Heresy, 8-9, 57, 131; Docetism, 57; Gnosticism, 4, 8-9, 65, 130-31, 149; Manichaeism, 6, 131; Marcionism, 8, 130, 135; Montanism, 8-9
Hermaphroditism, 196. *See also* Sexuality
Heterosexuality, 85, 192-95. *See also* Sexuality
Holocaust, 49, 84, 171. *See also* Anti-Semitism
Holy Spirit, 10, 25, 44, 47-48, 53, 63, 69, 85, 105, 128
Homosexuality, 27, 192-94, 200. *See also* Sexuality
Huizinga, Johan, 19, 86n2, 90-92, 157. *See also* Play
Humanae Vitae, 22, 28, 31, 34

Idolatry, 1-3, 5, 12, 17, 35, 38, 45, 74, 174, 205

Image of God, 29, 46, 54-55, 97, 106, 128, 130, 178. *See also* Body; Creation
Immortality, 62, 229
Incarnation, 53, 56-57, 59, 77, 127, 151, 201. *See also* Body
Inspiration, 39, 50, 68. *See also* Canonization process; Revelation: body as arena of
Intersexuality, 27, 195-97. *See also* Sexuality

Jesus: death of, 36, 43, 78, 113, 127, 154, 218-20; life-giving Spirit, 37, 44, 62, 69, 74, 77, 100, 219; resurrection of, 18, 36, 60, 69, 218-19
John Paul II, 21-37, 59, 144, 149, 166

Language, 1-3, 180-81
Leo XIII, 165, 172
Levitical code, 189, 190, 194
Literature and poetry, 10, 19, 24, 96, 165, 167
Liturgy, ix, 98-100, 105-6. *See also* Play

Male and female, 27, 54, 186, 190-92, 196-97. *See also* Creation
Marcel, Gabriel, ix, 20, 28, 66, 80n13, 115n3, 181n1. *See also* Mystery
Materialism, 6, 67, 71-72. *See also* Secularization
Mind of Christ, 44, 50, 218, 226
Modernity, 67, 70, 72, 75, 79, 115. *See also* Enlightenment
Monasticism, 10, 164-65, 167
Mortality, 206-7, 219, 229
Mystery, 18, 23-24, 28, 66, 72, 78, 80, 115n3, 124, 151-52, 169, 194, 201, 205, 220, 230
Mysticism, 11, 77, 131, 152

New creation, 18, 37, 39, 47, 62, 191, 219. *See also* Creation

Passions, 55, 65, 130-39, 147, 152-55, 222, 224, 232; in Greek philosophy, 131-33, 139-40, 222. *See also* Desire; Pleasure
Paul IV, 21-22, 31-32, 34. *See also* Humanae Vitae
Philo of Alexandria, 42, 133, 148

Philosophy, ancient, 42, 130, 135, 149, 220-21, 223-24

Plato, 65, 68, 131-33, 136, 148, 159

Play, ix, 86-87, 104-6, 146, 156, 158; art and, 95-96; characteristics of, 87-90, 92-93; definition of, 90; liturgy and, 97-100; rules of, 90-94; sports and, 100-104. *See also* Huizinga, Johan

Pleasure, 29, 134, 136, 139-46. *See also* Passions

Race, 16, 183-85

Reformation, 11, 36

Resurrection, 37, 62, 78, 82, 207, 219, 224, 228-30. *See also* New creation

Revelation: body as arena of, ix, 1, 2, 3, 7, 18, 35, 38, 40, 47, 51, 53-57, 59, 64-66, 112-13, 155, 194, 201, 205, 224, 231; mediated through experience, 7, 40, 45, 85, 104, 155, 177-78, 194, 224, 231, 233; scripture as witness and participant in, 8, 38, 45, 64, 231-32

Sabbath, 160-63

Schleiermacher, Friedrich, 12-13

Science, 32, 34, 71-73, 75, 78, 174, 177-78. *See also* Secularization; Technology

Scripture: on aging, 213-20; complexity of, 36-37; on desire, 146-49; on different bodies, 186-91; diversity of, 36, 40; experience and, 7, 17, 43-45, 47-50; on pain/suffering, 108-14; on passions, 132-35; on play, 86; reinterpretation of, 47-50, 64, 134; on spirit, 68-75; symbolic world of, 18, 36, 42, 45-47, 75; on work, 160-64

Secularization, 71-72, 74-75, 81. *See also* Enlightenment; Modernity

Seneca, 140, 220-24. *See also* Philosophy, ancient

Sexual immorality, 26, 59-60. *See also* Sexuality

Sexuality, 12, 18, 21-28, 30, 32, 35, 144, 192, 194-97; ideological construction of, 192-93; moral standards, 194-95; reproduction, 28, 30, 32, 144

Slaves/slavery, 49-50, 159, 171-73, 223-24. *See also* Work

Socrates, 131, 136. *See also* Philosophy, ancient

Soul, 67-70, 73, 130-32, 140, 223, 229

Spirit: alienation of, 170, 173-74; definition of, 75-76; diminishment of, 121-24, 170, 174-75, 229; embodiment of, 55, 66, 69, 77, 126, 231; enlargement of, 124-25, 177, 179

Stoicism, 132, 134, 140, 220. *See also* Philosophy, ancient

Suffering, 30, 107; characteristics of, 121; Christians and, 113-15; cosmos and, 113; definition of, 116-18; Jesus and, 113-14; moral valence of, 116, 119; positive value of, 114, 119-20, 124; sin and, 108-10, 112, 118-19; vicarious, 110, 113-14. *See also* Jesus: death of; Suffering Servant

Suffering Servant, 110, 113

Technology, 71, 73. *See also* Modernity; Science

Teilhard de Chardin, Pierre, 71, 198

Theology: as academic exercise, 4, 10, 12, 14, 20; as deductive science, vii, 5, 9, 15, 38; as inductive art, viii, 1, 5, 7, 17, 20, 34, 88, 166, 180, 200, 224, 231-33; liberation theology, 15-16

Thomas Aquinas, 140, 224

Transcendence, 76, 93-94, 97-100, 124-25, 150-51, 154, 156, 229

Transformation, 62, 84, 128. *See also* God; New creation

Transgender, 195-96. *See also* Sexuality

Virtue, 130, 132-34, 136, 140, 144, 152, 154, 221

Weigel, George, 22, 23, 31, 34

Work: of apostles, 163; as curse, 160, 164; definition of, 156-58; diversity of, 166-68; as idol, 174-75; necessity of, 170, 176; as physical labor, 159-60; positive value of, 164, 176-78. *See also* Deuteronomic principle; Slaves/slavery; Suffering

Index of Scripture References

OLD TESTAMENT

Genesis

1–3	108, 112
1	27
1:2	54, 68
1:26-27	54, 186
2	26-27, 36
2:7	54, 62, 68
2:15	160
2:21-24	186
2:24	59
3:8-10	51
3:16	109, 186
3:17-18	160
3:19	109
3:22	109
4:2	160
4:6	132
4:17	178
4:20	178
4:21	178
4:22	178
5	214
5:28	160
6:3	68
6:5-8	133
9:6	54
9:20	160, 178
11	214
12:13	160
13:2	160
13:23-24	160
15:12-16	40
16:4-5	132
18:2	51
19:4-9	132
20:7	56
20:30	160
21:20	160
24:9	51
25:7	214
25:27	160
25:29-34	132
26:8	86
26:12-13	160
27:41-45	132
29:20	160
31:17	160
31:30	147
31:41	160
34:7	132
35:29	214
37:2	160
37:4	133
37:5	133
37:8	133
37:11	132
39:2	160
39:7-12	132
45:26	132
48:14	51

Exodus

1:10-14	160
2:23	160
3:1	160
3:7	160
5:4	160
5:5	160
5:9	160
5:17	160
11:8	132
14:21	51
17:11	51
18:11	161
20:8-10	161
20:17	136, 147
21:26–22:12	161
22:21-24	161
23:9	161
24:9-11	40
32:6	86
32:10	133
32:12	133
32:19	132
32:22	132
34:6	133
34:24	147

Leviticus

12:2-5	186
12:19-30	186
13:1–14:54	187
13:4	187

15:31	187	28	20	**1 Kings**	
18:5	109	28:1-6	108	1:1-4	215
18:21	186	28:15-16	108	1:5-54	215
18:22-23	186	28:20	213	11:1-13	109
18:24-25	186	28:27-57	108	11:30-31	52
19:2	186	28:60	108	15:25-30	109
19:9	161	28:63	108	16:15-20	109
19:13-16	161	30:19	109	18:21	68
20:13	186	30:20	213		
20:15-16	186	34:7	214	**2 Kings**	
20:24-26	187			2:9	68
21:7	186	**Joshua**		2:15	68
21:14	186	10:24-25	52	3:1-3	109
21:16-23	187	24:19-28	109	10:28-36	109
22:1-9	187				
22:21-25	187	**Judges**		**Job**	
23:22	161	2:11-15	109	14:1-2	111
25:1-18	161	2:19-23	109	33:4	68
26:34-35	161	3:10	68	40:20	86
		6:2	161	41:5	86
Numbers		6:34	68		
11:4	147	8:33-35	109	**Psalms**	
11:10	133	11:29	68	1	40
11:16-25	68	13:1	109	2	40
11:33	133	13:25	68	3:5-7	41
11:34	147	19:29	52	4:1	41
12:9	133			4:8	41
20:11	51	**Ruth**		6:2	41
27:18	68	2:3	161	6:6	41
				6:8-9	41
Deuteronomy		**1 Samuel**		7:17	41
5:12-15	161	2:22	214	8:1-2	53
5:15	161	3:2	214	8:3	41
5:21	136, 147	4:15	214	9:1	41
7:25	147	4:18	214	9:13	41
12:20	147	8:1-3	214	9:24	147
12:21	86	8:4-5	214	10:1	41
14:3-8	187	10:6	68	10:1-18	110
14:26	147	15:27-28	52	10:17-18	111
15:3-6	162	16:11-16	161	12:1	41
18:6	147	16:13	68	13:1-2	41
18:9-14	187	16:16-17	86	13:6	41
18:15-22	56	20:4	147	16:1-2	41
21:23	47, 218	21:15	86	16:5-6	41
22:5	186	23:15	147	16:8	41
23:1-2	187			16:9	41
23:3	187	**2 Samuel**		17:1-2	41
23:10	186	6:21	86	17:15	41
24:14-22	161	11:2-5	132	18:6-19	41

18:7-15	53	50:10-17	68	103:5	214
18:32-46	41	51:1-5	41	103:14-16	214
18:49-50	41	52:8-9	41	104	40
19	40	54:1-7	41	104:1-35	53
19:1-4	53	55:1-7	41	104:26	86
20:4	147	56:10-11	41	105	40
21:4	213	57:7-14	41	106	40
22:1-18	41	59:16-17	41	106:14	147
22:1-31	110	61:1-2	41	106:29	133
22:19	41	61:6	213	106:32	133
22:22-24	41	62:1-12	41	106:40	133
23:1-4	41	63:1-8	41	107:33-43	53
24	40	65:9-13	53	110	40
25:1-2	41	67:13-20	41	111:1	41
25:16	41	69:1-36	41, 110	113:7-9	53
26:1	41	69:9	41	116:1-19	41
26:9-10	41	69:30-33	41	117:1-2	41
27:1-3	41	71:1-21	41	118:20	147
27:4	41	71:6	41	118:40	147
27:8	41	71:17-18	214	119	40
27:13	41	71:22-24	41	119:20	41
28:1-2	41	73:1-5	111	120:1-7	41
28:6-7	41	73:19-20	214	121–135	40
29:2-11	53	73:23-28	41	121:1-2	41
30	40	73:25-26	111	128:6	213
30:1-3	41	74:12-17	53	130:1-4	41
30:11-12	41	76:3	68	130:5-6	41
31:21-22	41	76:6	68	131:3	41
32:3-4	41	77:3-6	41	137:5-6	41
33:1-3	41	77:16-20	53	138:1-8	41
33:3	86	78	40	138:7	68
33:6-9	53	78:1-31	53	139:1-18	41, 53
34:4	41	78:18	147	140:8	147
37:2	214	78:21	133	142:1-7	41
37:5	224	78:31	133	143:1-12	41
37:9	214	78:49-50	133	143:4	68
37:12	213	78:58-59	133	143:7	68
37:20	214	79:9	133	143:10	68
37:25	214	80:14	133	145:1-21	41
37:28	213-14	84:1-2	41		
37:34	111	88:1-18	41	**Proverbs**	
37:40	110	90:3-6	214	3:2	213
38:1-22	41	90:10	214	4:10	213
39:7-11	41	95	40	5:12-15	133
39:12-13	41	96	40	5:20-23	133
40:1-3	41	100:1-5	41	6:1–7:27	161
43:1-5	41	102:23-24	214	6:6-10	161
45	40	103	40	6:6-11	133
49:10-12	214	103:4	68	6:17	133

6:19	133	27:23-27	161	53:5-6	110
6:25	147	28:19	161	53:6	110
6:30	133	28:25	133	53:8	110
6:32	133	29:22	133	53:9	110
7:1-27	133	29:23	133	53:10	110
8:20-31	161	31:10-30	161	53:11	110
8:30-31	87			53:12	110
9:11	213	**Qohelet (Ecclesiastes)**		58:2	147
10:4	161	1:2	111	58:11	147
10:24	147	1:3	161		
10:27	214	1:8	139	**Jeremiah**	
11:23	147	2:14-15	111	1:4-10	41
11:28	213	2:18-24	162	2:1-6	151
12:12	147	2:24	111, 141, 216	3:6-25	109
12:28	214	3:10-11	217	4:8-31	109
13:4	161	3:12	162	6:9-15	133
14:4	161	3:12-13	141, 216-17	7:1-20	42
14:27	213-14	3:16	111	9:13	42
14:29	133	3:19	111	12:1-4	42
14:30	133	3:22	141, 162	13:1-9	52
15:19	161	4:1-3	111	13:1-11	42
15:27	133	4:13	216	15:10-21	42
16:18	133	5:18	141, 162, 216	16:1-9	42
16:26	161	6:3-6	216	17:14-18	42
16:31	214	6:15	216	18:1-23	42
16:32	133	7:15	111	20:1-18	42
19:15	133	8:8	111	25:15-29	42
19:18	161	8:11	216	32:6-15	52
19:19	133	8:11-13	112		
19:20	213-14	8:15	141, 162, 216	**Ezekiel**	
19:24	161	9:2	112	1:4-3:4	41
20:4	161	9:7	216	4:1-7	42
20:29	214	9:9	216	4:1-5:12	52
21:4	133	11:8	216	5:1-12	42
21:7	213-14	12:1-8	216	6:11	52
21:17	133	12:7	68	8:1-9:11	42
21:26	147	13:9	68	12:1-21	42
22:12	161			12:11	52
23:3	147	**Isaiah**		13:1-23	109
23:20-21	133	1:21-26	109	16:1-63	109, 151
23:22	215	3:1-26	109	16:26	133
24:1	133, 147	6:1-13	41	16:38	133
24:19-20	213-14	8:1-4	42	18	113
24:30	133	8:16-17	42	18:20	110
24:30-34	161	11:8	86	23:1-49	151
26:28	133	38:1-39:8	42	23:25	133
27:1	133	52-53	113	24:15-27	42
27:4	133	52:13-53:12	110	33:32	86
27:20	133	53:3-7	110		

Hosea

1:2	52
1:2–2:23	151
1:2–3:5	41-42
3:3	86
4:15	86
8:1-14	109

Amos

2:1-16	109
3:10-11	109
4:1-13	109
5:18	147
7:14-15	42
8:4-14	109

Obadiah

1:1	42

Micah

1:1	42
3:1-12	109

Nahum

1:1	42

Habakkuk

1:1	42

Zephaniah

1:1	42
1:2-18	109

Haggai

1:1-3	42

Zechariah

1:1	42
1:7	42

Wisdom of Solomon

1:10	133
1:11	133
2:6-8	133
2:10	215
2:10-20	215
3:17	215
4:1	133
4:7-9	215

4:12	133, 147
4:16	215
5:2	147
5:6	133
5:8	133
5:13	133
6:2	147
6:12	147
6:12-22	133
6:17	147
6:20	147
6:23	133
7:22	133
7:22-27	69
8:1	133
8:7	133
14:12	133
14:25-26	133
15:12-13	133
16:3	147
18:30-31	147
19:11	147

Ben Sira

1:12	213
1:20	213
1:23	147
2:3	213
3:6	214
3:12-16	215
6:34	215
6:37	147
7:27	214
8:6	215
8:9	215
18:9	214
25:2	215
25:3-6	215
32:3	215, 217
39:11	215

4 Maccabees

1:22	147
1:25-26	148
1:31-32	147
2:4	147
2:5	147
2:6	148
3:2	148

NEW TESTAMENT

Matthew

1:23	127
4:18-22	162
5:3	69
5:8	25
5:21-22	136
5:28	148
5:32	26
9:2-13	112
9:9-13	162
9:36	126
10:1	69
10:1-25	162
11:17	86
12:28	69
12:43	69
13:1-9	162
13:17	148
13:47-50	162
14:14	126
15:1-20	135
15:32	126
18:12-14	162
18:20	58
18:23-35	162
18:27	126
19:3-9	26
19:5	26
19:9	26
20:1-16	162
20:34	126
21:33-43	162
22:43	69
25:14-30	162
25:45	59
26:41	69
26:49	83
28:19	69
28:20	58

Mark

1:41	52
2:5-11	112
2:23–3:6	162
4:9	148
7:21-23	135
7:33	52

8:1-9	52	17:15	188	8:7	69
8:22-26	52	17:22	148	8:27	162
9:33-37	58	21:19	227	9:39	162
10:13-16	58	22:15	148	9:43	162
10:16	52	23:43	227	10–15	188
10:45	113, 127	23:46	69	10:1	162
14:22	52	23:47	113, 218	10:44-48	47
14:24	113	24:26	113	11:18	48
14:38	69			11:27-30	162
		John		12:13	162
Luke		1:14	53, 56, 127	12:25	162
1:15	69	1:17-18	56	15:11	189
1:18	217	1:18	57	15:12-21	48
1:25	217	1:33	69	16:14	162
1:35	69	2:11	56	16:18	69
1:36	217	2:19-21	53	16:27	162
1:36-37	217	3:6	56	16:35	162
1:41	69	3:6-8	69	18:3	162
1:80	69	3:8	68	19:23	162
2:27	69	3:16	127	20:33	148
2:32	188	5:9-18	162	20:33-35	163
3:6	188	8:44	148	21:11	69
3:22	69	9:1-3	112	21:31	162
4:1	69	9:3	48, 144	27:1	162
4:16-18	188	9:24-41	48	27:30	162
4:33	69	9:34	48	28:8	217
4:40	52	13:20	58		
5:10	227	15:1-25	58	**Romans**	
5:20-24	112	15:26–16:15	58	1:9	69
5:27	227	17:1-26	57	1:17	218
6:18	52	19:30	69	1:18-25	134
6:20-24	188	20:22	69	1:18-32	119
7:14	52			1:24	148
7:16	53	**Acts**		1:26-27	134, 190
7:21	69	2:1-4	68	3:21	59
7:22	188, 217	2:4	69	3:21-26	113
7:32	86	2:5-28	218	4:16-25	230
8:35	188	2:14-21	48	5:5	69, 77
8:55	69	2:17-21	58	5:6	128
9:23	227	2:36	43	5:12-14	113
9:29-36	59	2:41-47	162	5:12-21	37, 113
9:48	188	3:14	113, 218	6:12	148
11:20	53	4:22	217	6:19	78
12:15	136	4:32–5:11	162	7:2-3	190
13:11	69	4:34	162	7:4	78
13:12	188	5:1-42	58	7:7	148
13:13	52	5:3	69	7:7-8	136
13:16	188	7:55	69	7:8	148
14:15-24	188	7:59	69	8:2	69

8:9	69	7:14	61	15:56	113
8:11	69, 78	7:34	69	16:1-4	162
8:14	69	8:1-2	44	16:10	163
8:15-16	77	8:1-13	44	16:19	190
8:16	69	8:11	113		
8:18-21	114	8:12	58	**2 Corinthians**	
8:18-39	128	9:1	44	1:3-7	113, 128
8:28-30	114	10:6	148	1:7	127
10:9	43	10:7	86	1:22	69
12:1	78	10:14-30	78	2:13	69
12:5	78	10:14-33	44	3:1-18	56
13:9	148	10:31–11:1	44	3:12–5:21	113
13:13	134	11:3-16	37, 44, 190	3:17	69
13:14	148	11:17-33	44	3:17-18	63
14:14-17	189	11:30	189	4:10	78
15:22-33	162	12	62, 63	4:16–5:5	229
16:1-3	190	12:1–13:13	190	5:17	37
16:6	163	12:3	43	5:19	128
16:7	190	12:4-11	44	5:21	128
16:12	163	12:8	69	8–9	162
		12:11	69	8:8-21	44
1 Corinthians		12:12-13	44, 62	8:9	128
1:5	44	12:13	190	10:1–11:33	44
1:11-13	44	12:14-26	129	11:1-6	44
1:18-25	43	12:27	57, 78	11:7-11	44
1:18–2:16	218	13:1-13	44	12:1-5	44
2:4	69	14:6-12	68	12:7	189
2:6-16	44	14:7	86	12:9	44
2:11	69	14:18	44	12:12	44
2:12	69	14:18-19	44	13:4	128
2:16	44, 226	14:26-33	44		
3:10-14	163	14:33-36	190	**Galatians**	
3:16	69	15	62, 63	2:10	162
4:12	163	15:1-8	207	3:5	69
6	63	15:3	113	3:6-29	113
6:1-8	44	15:3-4	47	3:13	47
6:9-10	190	15:7	189	3:14	69
6:11	69	15:8	44	3:27-28	190
6:12	61, 78	15:10	163	3:28	50, 190
6:12-20	59, 61, 78	15:21-34	62	4:11	163
6:16	163	15:26	113	4:12-14	189
6:18	24, 59	15:28	113	4:19	189
6:19	69	15:35	62	5:6	189
7	63	15:42-45	62	5:16	148
7:1-4	60	15:44	229	5:17	148
7:1-7	190	15:45	44, 69	5:18	69
7:1-40	44	15:45-49	37	5:19-20	135
7:7	146	15:49	37, 63, 228	5:24	149
7:12-16	78	15:51	78	6:2	228

6:16	37	**1 Timothy**		1:15	149
6:17	78, 189	1:10	190	1:18	55
		2:11-15	190	2:26	65
Ephesians		3:1	148	4:1-2	136
2:3	135, 148	4:1	69	4:1-3	175
3:9	78	4:3-5	142	4:2	148
3:9-10	58	4:10	163	4:2-3	135
4:22	149	5:1	217	4:5	69
4:24	37	5:3-16	217	5:4	171
4:28	163	5:17	163	5:16	55
4:31–5:13	135	5:23	142		
5:3	136	6:8	143	**1 Peter**	
5:22-23	190	6:9	148	1:11	113
		6:17	29, 141	1:14	148
Philippians				2:4	69
1:19	69	**2 Timothy**		2:11	148
1:23	148, 228	3:6	148	2:21	113
2:11	43	4:3	148	2:24	113
2:16	163			3:8	126
3:10	126	**Titus**		3:18	113
4:2	190	1:15	189	4:2	148
		2:5	190	4:4	69
Colossians		2:12	149	4:13	126-27
1:15	57	3:3	135		
1:24	113	3:13	149	**2 Peter**	
2:2	78			1:4	148
2:5	69	**Hebrews**		1:12	148
2:9	57	1:7	69	1:21	69
2:11-12	56	1:14	68	2:10	148
2:29	58	2:4	69	3:3	148
3:5-10	135	2:10-18	114		
3:10	37, 57	2:17-18	57	**1 John**	
3:10-11	190	3:7	69	2:16-17	148
3:18	190	4:9-10	163	3:16-17	135
		4:12	69	4:1	69
1 Thessalonians		4:13	45	4:1-3	57
2:17	148	5:7-9	114		
4:5	135, 148	6:11	148	**Revelation**	
4:8	69	8:1-13	56	1:9	43
4:11	163	9:28	114	2:1–3:22	43
4:13	189	12:3-11	114	3:1	69
4:17	228	12:7	114	4:1	69
5:12	163	13:3	114, 126	5:1-15	43
5:23	69	13:12-13	114	11:11	69
				14:2	86
2 Thessalonians		**James**		16:14	69
3:6-12	163	1:14	135, 149	17:1–18:24	43
3:7-8	163	1:14-15	135		

Index of Other Ancient Sources

Aeclepius
22.26   132n10

Aeschylus
Persians
507   67

Aetius
Placita
1.6   68

Aphrodisias
Chaereas
1.1.16   202n22
1.14.1   202n22
3.2.15-17   202n22

Aristotle
Nichomachean Ethics
1095B   140n26
1176A-B   140n26

Politics
1   159n1
7   159n1

Saint Benedict
The Rule of Saint Benedict
7   164
31   164
48   164

Cicero
Divine Office
1.19.37   67

Duties
1.42   159n3

Pro Roscio
75   159n3

De Senectute
2   221
3   221
5   221
7   221
9   221
15   221
17   221
22   221
26   221
30   221
33   221
36   222
38   222
39-44   222
46   222
49   222
51   222
61   222
65   221
66   223
67   222
69   222

71   222
74   222
77   223
84   223
85   223

Diogenes Laertius
Lives of Eminent Philosophers
10.11   140n21
10.63   67
10.123   140n25
10.131   140n25

Epictetus
Discourses
1.1   132n12
2.16.45   148n31
2.18.8   148n31
3.1.14ff.   67
3.2.1-3   132n12
3.7.20   137n19
3.9.21   148n31
3.23.30   140n23
3.24.37-39   140n23

Epicurus
Sovereign Maxims
5   132n13
7   140n25
10   140n25

14	132n14
18	140n25
20	140n25

Euripides
Hecuba

57	67

Suppliants

532ff.	68

Heliodorus
Ethiopia

1.2.1	202n22

Hesiod
Works and Days

II, 170	159
II, 293-313	159
II, 381-82	159
II, 383-828	159
II, 646	159

Livy
History of Rome

3.14-26	159n2

Ovid
Metamorphoses

1.390-779	202n22
2.466-95	202n22

Philo
Allegorical Interpretation

3.233	133n15

On Husbandry

22-25	133n16, 148n33

On the Contemplative Life

2	148n34
74	148n32

On the Decalogue

60	133n15

On the Migration of Abraham

60	148n34

Preliminary Studies

172	148n34

Sacrifices of Abel and Cain

15-20	134n18

Special Laws

3.4	134n17
4.93-94	148n32

Plato
Cratylus

400C	132n7

Gorgias

493C	132n7

Phaedo

62B-67A-B	132n7
67C-D	68
83B	148n30

Phaedrus

232B	148n30
246C-247C	132n9

Symposium

199C-212C	132n8

Plutarch
Against Colotes 140n22

On the Obsolescence of Oracles

40	68

A Pleasant Life Is Impossible 140n22

Poimandres

26-26	132n11

Seneca
Moral Epistles

4.4	220
8.8	140n24
12.1-5	224n7
12.5	220
12.6	220
12.10	220

21.9	140n24
24.14	220
24.19	220
24.21	220
26.2-4	220
26.8	220
33.2	140n24
49.5	220
49.11	220
68.10-14	220
70.28	221
76	220
77.20	221
82.16	220

Strabo
Geography

9.3.5	68

Talmud
Mishna Sanhedrin

4.5	55

Testament of the Twelve Patriarchs
Testament of Dan

2.2	134

Testament of Gad

3.3	134

Testament of Joseph

7.1-8	143, 148n33

Testament of Reuben

3.5	134

Testament of Simeon

4.8	134

Thomas Aquinas
Summa Theologica

I, 2, 31-39	141n28

Xenophon
Ephesians

1.12.1	202n22